M000290832

Scales of Justice

New Directions in Critical Theory
Amy Allen, General Editor

New Directions in Critical Theory presents outstanding classic and contemporary texts in the tradition of critical social theory, broadly construed. The series aims to renew and advance the program of critical social theory, with a particular focus on theorizing contemporary struggles around gender, race, sexuality, class, and globalization and their complex interconnections.

Scales of Justice

Reimagining Political Space in a Globalizing World

Nancy Fraser

Columbia University Press　　New York

Columbia University Press
Publishers Since 1893
New York   Chichester, West Sussex

Copyright © 2009 Columbia University Press
Paperback edition, 2010
All rights reserved

Library of Congress Cataloging-in-Publication Data
Fraser, Nancy.
   Scales of justice: reimagining political space in a globalizing world/Nancy
Fraser.
      p.   cm.—(New directions in critical theory)
Includes index.
   ISBN   978-0-231-14680-7 (cloth : alk. paper)—
   ISBN   978-0-231-14681-4 (pbk. : alk. paper)—
   ISBN   978-0-231-51962-5 (e-book)
   1. Justice.   2. Distributive justice.   3. Globalization—Moral and
ethical.   I. Title   II. Series
JC578. F6967 2008
320.01'1—dc22   2008018716

Columbia University Press books are printed on permanent and durable
acid-free paper.

This book is printed on paper with recycled content.
Printed in the United States of America

c   10   9   8   7   6   5   4   3   2   1
p   10   9   8   7   6   5   4   3   2   1

for Jenny Mansbridge,
a dear friend of the heart and of the mind

Contents

Acknowledgments

This volume is the fruit of several years of work, both solitary and collaborative. Chapters two and three originated as my 2004 Spinoza Lectures at the University of Amsterdam, where I enjoyed unparalleled hospitality, stimulation, and a congenial atmosphere of aesthetically charged urbanity. The Wissenschaftskolleg zu Berlin provided a tranquil environment for writing chapters four and six and for revising several others, as well as for enjoying the pleasures of new friendships, ravishing music, and discussions with colleagues, especially "The Globalization Girls." Virtually every chapter owes some inspiration to the intense engaged intellectuality I am privileged to breathe everyday at the New School for Social Research, my institutional home for the last twelve years and an oasis of critical, progressive thought in the United States. Every chapter, too, was refined through stimulating discussions at conferences and colloquia and thoughtful readings by colleagues and friends. Thanks especially to Marek Hrubec and the members of the vibrant international network of Critical Theorists that meets every May in Prague; to David Held and his colleagues at the London School of Economics; to Kate Nash, Vikki, Bell and the participants at the Goldsmiths conference on "Scales of Justice"; to Alessandro Ferrara and his colleagues in Rome; to Setha Low, Neil Smith, and the participants at the CUNY conference on "Public Space"; to Juliet Mitchell, Jude Browne, Andrea Maibofer, and the participants at the Cambridge conference on "Gender Equality and Social Change" and the Basel conference on "Gender in Motion"; to Axel Honneth, the Institut für Sozialforschung, and the participants at the Frankfurt conference on Foucault; to Catherine Audard, Alan Montefiore, the Forum for European Philosophy, and the participants at the London conference on Hannah Arendt; to Andy Blunden and Robert Goodin for a memorable Australian sojourn; to Tom Mitchell and the *Critical Inquiry* editorial collective; to Patricia Morey and her colleagues and students at the National University of Cordoba, Argentina; and to Richard J, Bernstein, Amy Allen, Rainer Forst, Nancy Naples, Bert van den Brink, Jane Mansbridge, Daved Peritz, Maria Pia Lara, Dmitri Nikulin, Seyla Benhabib, Manuel Cruz, John Thompson, and Wendy Lochner Thanks, finally, and above all, to Eli Zaretsky, who read every sentence many times with just the right mix of critical skepticism and inspiriting enthusiasm.

Chapter Nine is reproduced with kind permission of SAGE Publications, London, Los Angeles, New Delhi and Singapore, from *Theory, Culture, and Society* 24, "The Politics of Framing: An Interview with Nancy Fraser," by Kate Nash and Vikki Bell (2007): p. 73--86, copyright © Theory, Culture & Society, 2007.

1

Scales of Justice, the Balance and the Map

An Introduction

My title, *Scales of Justice*, evokes two images. The first one is very familiar, almost a cliché: the moral balance in which an impartial judge weighs the relative merits of conflicting claims. Long central to the understanding of justice, this image still inspires struggles for social justice in the present era, notwithstanding widespread skepticism concerning the very idea of an impartial judge. The second image is less familiar: the geographer's metric for representing spatial relationships. Only recently salient in justice theorizing, this image is now informing struggles over globalization, as transnational social movements contest the national frame within which justice conflicts have historically been situated and seek to re-map the bounds of justice on a broader scale.

Each of these images – the *balance* and the *map* – stands for a knot of difficult questions. The balance stands for the problematic of *impartiality*: What, if anything, can guarantee a fair assessment of competing claims? Always thorny, this issue surfaces in every context of power asymmetry, when disadvantaged people cry out for justice, as if addressing an impartial judge, even though they know full well that none exists and that the standards by which they will be judged are stacked against them. But over and above that general dilemma, the problematic of impartiality faces another, more radical challenge in the present era. Thanks to an epochal shift in political culture, today's social-justice movements lack a shared

understanding of the *substance* of justice. Unlike their twentieth-century predecessors, who militated mostly for "redistribution," present-day claimants couch their demands in a variety
of idioms, which are oriented to competing goals. Today, for
example, class-accented appeals for economic redistribution
are routinely pitted against minority-group demands for "recognition," while feminist claims for gender justice often collide
with demands for supposedly traditional forms of religious or
communal justice. The result is a radical heterogeneity of
justice discourse, which poses a major challenge to the idea of
the moral balance: Where is the scale of justice on which such
heterogeneous claims can be impartially weighed?

The image of the map, in contrast, stands for the problematic
of *framing*: What, if anything, should delimit the bounds of
justice? Unlike that of impartiality, which is generally contested
in one form or another, the problematic of the map can lie
dormant for long historical stretches, when a hegemonic frame
is naturalized and taken for granted. This was arguably the case
in the heyday of social democracy when it went without saying
that the unit within which justice applied was the modern
territorial state. In that context, most political antagonists
shared the unspoken assumption that obligations of distributive
justice applied only among fellow citizens. Today, by contrast,
this "Westphalian" framing of justice is in dispute. Currently
resurfacing as a stake of struggle, the frame is now contested,
as human-rights activists and international feminists join
critics of the World Trade Organization in foregrounding
transborder injustices. Today, accordingly, justice claims are
increasingly mapped in competing geographical scales – as,
for example, when claims on behalf of "the global poor" are
pitted against the claims of citizens of bounded polities. This
sort of heterogeneity raises a radical challenge of another kind:
Given the plurality of competing frames for organizing, and
resolving, justice conflicts, how do we know which scale of
justice is truly just?

For both problematics, then, that of the balance and that of
the map, the challenges posed in the present epoch are truly
radical. In both cases, too, the plural form, *scales* of justice,
signals the heightened character of the difficulty. In the case
of the balance, the difficulty stems from the plurality of competing idioms for articulating claims, which threatens to explode

the conventional image of impartiality. Envisioning a conflict of pro and con, that image represents impartial justice as the mutual weighing, on a single apparatus, of two sets of considerations, countervailing but nevertheless commensurable. That representation may have seemed plausible in the Cold War era, when a distinctive understanding of the substance of justice was widely shared. In that period, major political currents converged on a *distributive* conception, which equated social justice with the fair allocation of divisible goods, typically economic in nature. A shared presupposition of first-world social democracy, second-world communism, and third-world developmentalism, that view supplied a measure of commensurability to conflicting demands. Subtending fierce disputes about what should count as a just distribution, the hegemonic distributivist imaginary lent some credibility to the conventional representation of the moral balance. If all parties were arguing about the same thing, then perhaps their claims could be weighed on a single scale.

Today, however, the received image of the balance is stretched to the breaking point. Current conflicts exceed its template of a simple dualism of commensurable alternatives, as present-day claims for justice routinely run up against counterclaims whose underlying ontological assumptions they do not share. For example, movements demanding economic redistribution often clash not only with defenders of the economic status quo, but also with movements seeking recognition of group specificity, on the one hand, and with those seeking new schemes of political representation, on the other. In such cases, the question is not simply, redistribution: pro or con? Nor even, redistribution: how much or how little? Where claimants hold conflicting views of the substance of justice, another question is also at issue: redistribution or recognition or representation? The effect is to raise suspicions that the conventional ideal of impartiality may be incoherent, as what is disputed today is not just conflicting claims but conflicting ontologies, which entail conflicting criteria for assessing claims. What looms, accordingly, is not just the threat of partiality, but the specter of *incommensurability*. Can substantively heterogeneous claims really be fairly weighed on a single balance? And failing that, what remains of the ideal of impartiality?

Under these conditions, the impartiality problematic cannot be conceived in the usual way. Rather, that problematic must be radicalized – so as to confront, and if possible dispel, the threat of incommensurability. Forswearing the conventional interpretation of the balance image, those who would theorize justice in the present era must ask: Given the clash of rival conceptions of the substance of justice, each effectively equipped with its own set of scales, how should we decide which balance to use in a given case? How can we reconstruct the ideal of impartiality to assure that heterogeneous claims can be fairly assessed?

In the case of the second, cartographic, image, the plural form, *scales* of justice, also signals the gravity of present-day difficulties. The trouble here stems from the plurality of conflicting framings of the bounds of justice, which has dena- turalized the Westphalian mapping of political space. Long hegemonic, that metric represented political communities as geographically bounded units, demarcated by sharply drawn borders and arrayed side by side. Associating each such polity with a state of its own, the Westphalian political imaginary invested the state with exclusive, undivided sovereignty over its territory, barring "external interference" in its "internal affairs" and foreclosing deference to any higher, supranational power. In addition, this view enshrined a sharp division between two qualitatively different kinds of political space. Whereas "domes-tic" space was imagined as the pacified civil realm of the social contract, subject to law and obligations of justice, "interna-tional" space was envisioned as a state of nature, a warlike realm of strategic bargaining and *raison d'état*, devoid of any binding duties of justice. In the Westphalian imaginary, accordingly, the subjects of justice could only be fellow members of a territo-rialized citizenry. To be sure, this mapping of political space was never fully realized; international law tamed relations among states to some degree, while Great Power hegemony and modern imperialism belied the notion of an international system of equal sovereign states. Yet this imaginary exercised a powerful sway, inflecting the independence dreams of colo-nized peoples, who mostly yearned for Westphalian states of their own.

Today, however, the Westphalian mapping of political space is losing its hold. Certainly, its posit of exclusive, undivided state sovereignty is no longer plausible, given a ramifying human-rights regime, on the one hand, and spiraling networks of global governance, on the other. Equally questionable is the notion of a sharp division between domestic and international space, given novel forms of "intermestic" politics, practiced by new, trans-territorial non-state actors, including transnational social movements, intergovernmental organizations, and international nongovernmental organizations. Also dubious is the view of territoriality as the sole basis for assigning obligations of justice, given patently trans-territorial problems, such as global warming or genetically modified agriculture, which prompt many to think in terms of functionally defined "communities of risk" that expand the bounds of justice to include everyone potentially affected. No wonder, then, that activists contesting transnational inequities reject the view that justice can only be imagined territorially, as a domestic relation among fellow citizens. Positing postwestphalian views of "who counts," they are subjecting the Westphalian frame to explicit critique.

The upshot is that the framing problematic no longer goes without saying – in theory and practice. Now that the mapping of political space is an object of struggle, those interested in justice today cannot fail to ask: Given the clash of rival views of the bounds of justice, how should we decide whose interests ought to count? Faced with competing framings of social conflicts, how should we determine which mapping of political space is just?

In general, then, both images of *scales of justice* harbor formidable challenges to received understandings in the present era. In the case of the balance, the challenge stems from competing views of the "what" of justice: redistribution or recognition or representation? In the case of the map, the trouble arises from conflicting framings of the "who": territorialized citizenries or global humanity or transnational communities of risk? In the problematic of the balance, then, the central issue is: *What* counts as a bonafide matter of justice? In that of the map, by contrast, the question is: *Who* counts as a bonafide subject of justice?

The present volume aims to respond to both of these challenges. Originally prepared as a stand-alone essay, lecture, or interview, each chapter addresses current conundrums concerning the "what" and the "who." Read together, they propose distinctive analyses of, and answers to, those questions. Addressing the problematic of the balance, I elaborate a *three-dimensional* account of the "what" of justice, encompassing *redistribution, recognition,* and *representation.* Addressing the problematic of the map, I propose a *critical theory of framing* aimed at clarifying the "who" of justice. The result is a set of sustained reflections on who should count with respect to what in a postwestphalian world. Let me elaborate.

Chapter 2, "Reframing Justice in a Globalizing World," aims to clarify present-day struggles over globalization. Revising my previous account of the "what" of justice, I introduce a third, *political* dimension alongside the economic and cultural dimensions I foregrounded earlier. Analytically distinct from redistribution and recognition, *representation* serves in part to account for "ordinary-political injustices," which arise internally, *within* bounded political communities, when skewed decision rules compromise the political voice of some who are already counted as members, impairing their ability to participate as peers in social interaction. This revision enriches our understanding of the "what" of justice, while also remedying a lacuna in my previous theory, which failed to appreciate the relative autonomy of inequities rooted in the political constitution of society, as opposed to the economic structure or the status order.

But that is not all. The addition of the third dimension also serves to account for "meta-political injustices," which arise when the division of political space *into* bounded polities works to misframe first-order questions of distribution, recognition, and representation – say, by casting what are actually transnational injustices as national matters. In that case, the "who" of justice is itself unjustly defined, as affected non-citizens are wrongly excluded from consideration. This is the case when, for example, the claims of the global poor are shunted into the domestic political arenas of weak or failed states and blocked from confronting the offshore sources of their dispossession. The result is a special, meta-political, kind of misrepresentation that I call *misframing.* Misframing, I claim, is an indispensable concept for critical theory, as it allows one to interrogate the mapping of political space from the standpoint of justice. Drawn from an expanded understanding of the "what," that notion enables critique of the "who." Engaging both the balance and the map, then, this chapter forges a conceptual link between those two images of *scales of justice*.

Chapter 3 elaborates, and complicates, that link. Here, however, the focus shifts from social reality to political philosophy, as I identify "Two Dogmas of Egalitarianism" in recent justice theorizing. The first dogma is the unexamined presupposition of the Westphalian "who." Deeply ingrained in the preceding period, even amid lively debates about the "what," the assumption that the national territorial state is the sole unit within which justice applies is no longer axiomatic today, as philosophers openly dispute the bounds of justice. Now, in intense exchanges sparked by John Rawls's *Law of Peoples*, the question of who counts as a subject of justice is receiving its due. Yet congratulations are, in my view, premature. Analyzing these debates, I uncover a second dogma of egalitarianism, stubbornly entrenched and possibly strengthening, despite (or perhaps because of) the decline of the first.

The second dogma is an unspoken methodological premise, concerning *how* one should determine the "who." Even as they disagree fiercely about the latter, cosmopolitans, internationalists, and liberal nationalists are tacitly agreed that disputes over the framing of justice can and should be resolved scientifically, by technical methods. That view follows from their shared supposition that what turns a collection of people into fellow subjects of justice is their co-imbrication in a common "basic structure," which determines their relative chances to live a good life. Although some identify that structure with the constitution of a bounded polity, while others equate it instead with the governance mechanisms of the global economy, nearly all look to social science to settle the issue, as if it could tell us, as a matter of fact, which structure is "basic." Here, accordingly, lies the second dogma of egalitarianism: the tacit, unargued assumption that normal social science can determine the "who" of justice. This chapter rejects that premise. Aiming to overcome the second dogma, I elaborate a "critical-democratic" alternative, which treats disputes about framing as *political* matters, to be settled by democratic debate and institutional decision-making on a transnational scale. A plea for transnational "meta-democracy," my argument serves as well to disclose a third parameter of justice, beyond the "what" and the "who." Absent a defensible approach to the "how," I conclude, we will never satisfactorily resolve the problems of the balance and the map.

Chapter 4 synthesizes the foregoing considerations into a programmatic reflection on "Abnormal Justice." Inspired by Richard Rorty, I suggest that most political theorists have tacitly conceived conflicts over justice on the model of "normal discourse." Presupposing the absence of deep disagreements about what well-formed justice claims look like, they have sought to elaborate normative principles that could resolve disputes in contexts where the grammar of justice was relatively settled. Whatever its merits for other historical eras, this approach is patently unsuitable today, when justice conflicts often assume the guise of "abnormal discourse." Absent a shared understanding of the "what," the "who," and the "how," not only first-order questions of normal justice, but the grammar of justice itself is up for grabs. What is needed today, accordingly, is a different sort of political theorizing, aimed at clarifying problems of "abnormal justice," in which first-order justice conflicts are interlaced with meta-disagreements. This chapter sketches such a theory. Neither celebrating abnormality nor rushing to instate a "new normal," I seek to accommodate both the positive and negative sides of abnormal justice – valorizing expanded contestation of previously overlooked harms, such as non-distributive inequities and transborder injustices, while also tracking reduced capacities for overcoming injustice, absent a stable framework in which claims can be equitably vetted and absent legitimate agencies by which they can be efficaciously redressed.

Chapter 5 assesses the capacity of public-sphere theory to advance such a project. Seeking to reimagine democracy for abnormal times, I ask: Can the ideal of inclusive, unrestricted political communication still play a critical, emancipatory role in the present era, when publics no longer coincide with territorial citizenries, economies are no longer national, and states no longer possess the necessary and sufficient capacity to solve many problems? Doubts arise because the critical force of public-sphere theory has always depended on a two-fold idealizing supposition: public opinion should be *normatively legitimate* and *politically efficacious*. However counterfactual, both ideas were arguably clear enough when viewed through the Westphalian lens: legitimacy required that fellow citizens be able to participate as peers in the formation of public opinion within their own polity, while efficacy required that national public opinion be strong enough to subject state power to citizen control. Today, however, matters are not so clear. What does it mean to speak of the legitimacy and efficacy of public opinion formed in *transnational* public spheres, which neither stage communication among fellow citizens, who enjoy the shared status of political peers, nor address it to sovereign states, which can implement the interlocutors' will and solve their problems? "Transnationalizing the Public Sphere" seeks an answer that can salvage the critical potential of this venerable concept. Explicating the implicit Westphalian presuppositions, not only of Jürgen Habermas's theory, but also of my own earlier effort to "rethink the public sphere," I propose to reconstruct the ideal of legitimate and efficacious publicity in a form suited to current conditions. A critique of actually existing democracy in the neoliberal era, this chapter, too, seeks to reimagine political space for a postwestphalian world.

Chapter 6 deploys the concepts developed so far to reflect on the trajectory of feminist movements. Highlighting shifts over several decades in gender-sensitive understandings of the "what" of justice, I plot the history of second-wave feminism in three phases. In the first phase, feminists joined other New Left democratizing forces to radicalize a social-democratic imaginary that had been largely restricted to class redistribution. In the second, with utopian energies in decline, feminists gravitated to a "postsocialist" imaginary, which foregrounded claims for the recognition of difference. Today, in an emergent third phase, feminists operating in transnational contexts are creating new, gender-conscious forms of political representation, which overflow territorial borders. "Mapping the Feminist Imagination" reconstructs this history to reveal the contours of an emergent "postwestphalian" feminist imaginary, which integrates redistribution and recognition with representation.

The next two chapters revisit major thinkers of the twentieth century in light of the changes in political space I have analyzed here. Chapter 7 rereads Michel Foucault "in the shadow of globalization." Written with the benefit of hindsight, "From Discipline to Flexibilization?" interprets the great works of Foucault's middle period, such as *Discipline and Punish*, as brilliant, if one-sided, accounts of social regulation in the era of *fordism*. Dating from the 1960s and 1970s, these works charted the political logic of the disciplinary society, like the Owl of Minerva, at the moment of its historical waning, when Keynesian social democracy was poised to mutate into a new *postfordist* regime in which nationally framed normalization is supplanted by transnationally framed "flexibilization." After sketching the contours of this new, neoliberal regime, this chapter ponders possibilities for developing a quasi-Foucauldian account of today's distinctive, *post-disciplinary*, modes of governmentality. That effort, I claim, would constitute a fitting tribute to one of the most original and important thinkers of the preceding century.

By any measure, Hannah Arendt also belongs in that company. Chapter 8 revisits her distinctive mode of political theorizing in order to envision ways of extending it in our own time. Situating Arendt as our greatest theorist of mid-twentieth-century catastrophe, "Threats to Humanity in Globalization" contemplates the extent to which her approach can illuminate looming menaces to human being in the twenty-first century. On the one hand, I find considerable power in Arendtian motifs to illuminate the epochal significance of 9/11 and the calamitous US response; on the other, I criticize quasi-Arendtian but deeply flawed efforts by Paul Berman, John Gray, and Michael Hardt and Antonio Negri to theorize the dangers of the present. Seeking to learn from their missteps, I conclude by sketching another way to appropriate her legacy, one that can clarify modes of negating humanity that she herself could not have imagined but that we must confront today.

Chapter 9 reprises this volume's central themes. In an interview originally published in *Theory, Culture & Society*, I join Kate Nash and Vikki Bell in a wide-ranging discussion of "The Politics of Framing." Stimulated by their thoughtful questions, I relate my ideas about justice to a diagnosis of the present conjuncture, on the one hand, and to a view of the role of the critical theorist, on the other. Situating my turn to representation vis-à-vis current struggles over globalization, I weigh prospects for transnational solidarity, democratic frame-setting, and emancipatory projects of social transformation. Engaging both the balance and the map, this interview offers some personal and conceptual reflections on the scales of justice.

If that problematic pervades the book as a whole, so, too, does a style of critical theorizing forged through encounters with several traditions, which are too often viewed as antithetical. Influenced both by analytic political philosophy and by European-style Critical Theory, I aspire throughout to relate normative theorizing concerning the "ought" to a *Zeitdiagnose* that captures the "is." Committed, too, both to structural-institutional critique and to the linguistic turn, I seek to link a critique of historically formed complexes of social power to a critique of political cultures and vocabularies of claims-making. Inspired, finally, both by agonistic poststructuralist theorizing and by Habermassian discourse ethics, I aim throughout to combine an interest in moments of opening, when hegemonic understandings are ruptured and occluded injustices disclosed, with an interest in moments of closure, when new understandings, forged through struggle and argument, galvanize public efforts to remedy injustice. Convinced that none of these approaches alone can adequately tackle the questions posed here, I seek to integrate the strong points of each in a more capacious genre of critical theorizing. My hope is that theorizing of this sort can serve both to clarify problems of scale and to advance the cause of justice in a globalizing world.

2

Reframing Justice in a Globalizing World

Globalization is changing the way we argue about justice. Not so long ago, in the heyday of social democracy, disputes about justice presumed what I shall call a "Keynesian-Westphalian frame." Typically played out within modern territorial states, arguments about justice were assumed to concern relations among fellow citizens, to be subject to debate within national publics, and to contemplate redress by national states. This was true for each of two major families of justice claims – claims for socioeconomic redistribution and claims for legal or cultural recognition. At a time when the Bretton Woods system of international capital controls facilitated Keynesian economic steering at the national level, claims for redistribution usually focused on economic inequities within territorial states. Appealing to national public opinion for a fair share of the national pie, claimants sought intervention by national states in national economies. Likewise, in an era still gripped by a Westphalian political imaginary, which sharply distinguished "domestic" from "international" space, claims for recognition generally concerned internal status hierarchies. Appealing to the national conscience for an end to nationally institutionalized disrespect, claimants pressed national governments to outlaw discrimination and accommodate differences among citizens. In both cases, the Keynesian-Westphalian frame was taken for granted. Whether the matter concerned redistribution or recognition, class differentials or status hierarchies, it went without saying that the unit within which justice applied was the modern territorial state.[1]

To be sure, there were always exceptions. Occasionally, famines and genocides galvanized public opinion across borders. And some cosmopolitans and anti-imperialists sought to promulgate globalist views.[2] But these were exceptions that proved the rule. Relegated to the sphere of "the international," they were subsumed within a problematic that was focused primarily on matters of security and humanitarian aid, as opposed to justice. The effect was to reinforce, rather than to challenge, the Keynesian-Westphalian frame. That framing of disputes about justice generally prevailed by default from the end of World War II to the 1970s.

Although it went unnoticed at the time, the Keynesian-Westphalian frame lent a distinctive shape to arguments about social justice. Taking for granted the modern territorial state as the appropriate unit, and its citizens as the pertinent subjects, such arguments turned on what precisely those citizens owed one another. In the eyes of some, it sufficed that citizens be formally equal before the law; for others, equality of opportunity was also required; for still others, justice demanded that all citizens gain access to the resources and respect they needed in order to be able to participate on a par with others, as full members of the political community. The argument focused, in other words, on what exactly should count as a just ordering of social relations within a society. Engrossed in disputing the "what" of justice, the contestants apparently felt no necessity to dispute the "who." With the Keynesian-Westphalian frame securely in place, it went without saying that the "who" was the national citizenry.

Today, however, the Keynesian-Westphalian frame is losing its aura of self-evidence. Thanks to heightened awareness of globalization, and to post-Cold War geopolitical instabilities, many observe that the social processes shaping their lives routinely overflow territorial borders. They note, for example, that decisions taken in one territorial state often impact the lives of those outside it, as do the actions of transnational corporations, international currency speculators, and large institutional investors. Many also note the growing salience of supranational and international organizations, both governmental and nongovernmental, and of transnational public opinion, which flows with supreme disregard for borders through global mass media and cybertechnology. The result is a new sense of vulnerability to transnational forces. Faced with global warming, the spread of HIV-AIDS, international terrorism, and superpower unilateralism, many believe that their chances for living good lives depend at least as much on processes that trespass the borders of territorial states as on those contained within them.[3]

Under these conditions, the Keynesian-Westphalian frame no longer goes without saying. For many, it has ceased to be axiomatic that the modern territorial state is the appropriate unit for thinking about issues of justice, and that the citizens of such states are the pertinent subjects. The effect is to destabilize the previous structure of political claims-making – and therefore to change the way we argue about social justice.

This is true for both major families of justice claims. In today's world, claims for redistribution increasingly eschew the assumption of national economies. Faced with transnationalized production, the outsourcing of jobs, and the associated pressures of the "race to the bottom," once nationally focused labor unions look increasingly for allies abroad.[4] Inspired by the Zapatistas, meanwhile, impoverished peasants and indigenous peoples link their struggles against despotic local and national authorities to critiques of transnational corporate predation and global neoliberalism.[5] Finally, anti-World Trade Organization protestors directly target the new governance structures of the global economy, which have vastly strengthened the ability of large corporations and investors to escape the regulatory and taxation powers of territorial states.[6]

In the same way, movements struggling for recognition increasingly look beyond the territorial state. Under the umbrella slogan "women's rights are human rights," for example, feminists throughout the world are linking struggles against local patriarchal practices to campaigns to reform international law.[7] Meanwhile, religious and ethnic minorities who face discrimination within territorial states are reconstituting themselves as diasporas and building transnational publics from which to mobilize international opinion.[8] Finally, transnational coalitions of human-rights activists are seeking to build new cosmopolitan institutions, such as the International Criminal Court, which can punish state violations of human dignity.[9]

In such cases, disputes about justice are exploding the Keynesian-Westphalian frame. No longer addressed exclusively to national states or debated exclusively by national publics, claims no longer focus solely on relations among fellow citizens. Thus, the grammar of argument has altered. Whether the issue is distribution or recognition, disputes that used to focus exclusively on the question of what is owed as a matter of justice to community members now turn quickly into disputes about who should count as a member and which is the relevant community. Not just the "what" but also the "who" is up for grabs.

Today, in other words, arguments about justice assume a double guise. On the one hand, they concern first-order questions of substance, just as before. How much economic inequality does justice permit, how much redistribution is required, and according to which principle of distributive justice? What constitutes equal respect, which kinds of differences merit public recognition, and by which means? But above and beyond such first-order questions, arguments about justice today also concern second-order, meta-level questions. What is the proper frame within which to consider first-order questions of justice? Who are the relevant subjects entitled to a just distribution or reciprocal recognition in the given case? Thus, it is not only the substance of justice, but also the frame, which is in dispute.

The result is a major challenge to our theories of social justice. Preoccupied largely with first-order issues of distribution and/or recognition, these theories have so far failed to develop conceptual resources for reflecting on the meta-issue of the frame. As things stand, therefore, it is by no means clear that they are capable of addressing the double character of problems of justice in a globalizing age.[10]

In this chapter, I shall propose a strategy for thinking about the problem of the frame. I shall argue, first, that theories of justice must become three-dimensional, incorporating the political dimension of representation alongside the economic dimension of distribution and the cultural dimension of recognition. I shall also argue that the political dimension of representation should itself be understood as encompassing three levels. The combined effect of these two arguments will be to make visible a third question, beyond those of the "what" and the "who," which I shall call the question of the "how." That question, in turn, inaugurates a paradigm shift: what the

Keynesian-Westphalian frame cast as the theory of social justice must now become a theory of *postwestphalian democratic justice*.

For a three-dimensional theory of justice: on the specificity of the political

Let me begin by explaining what I mean by justice in general and by its political dimension in particular. In my view, the most general meaning of justice is parity of participation. According to this radical-democratic interpretation of the principle of equal moral worth, justice requires social arrangements that permit all to participate as peers in social life. Overcoming injustice means dismantling institutionalized obstacles that prevent some people from participating on a par with others, as full partners in social interaction. Previously, I analyzed two distinct kinds of obstacles to participatory parity, which correspond to two distinct species of injustice.[11] On the one hand, people can be impeded from full participation by economic structures that deny them the resources they need in order to interact with others as peers; in that case they suffer from distributive injustice or maldistribution. On the other hand, people can also be prevented from interacting on terms of parity by institutionalized hierarchies of cultural value that deny them the requisite standing; in that case they suffer from status inequality or misrecognition.[12] In the first case, the problem is the class structure of society, which corresponds to the economic dimension of justice. In the second case, the problem is the status order, which corresponds to its cultural dimension. In modern capitalist societies, the class structure and the status order do not neatly mirror each other, although they interact causally. Rather, each has some autonomy vis-à-vis the other. As a result, misrecognition cannot be reduced to a secondary effect of maldistribution, as some economistic theories of distributive justice appear to suppose. Nor, conversely, can maldistribution be reduced to an epiphenomenal expression of misrecognition, as some culturalist theories of recognition tend to assume. Thus, neither recognition theory nor distribution theory can alone provide an adequate understanding of justice for capitalist society. Only a two-dimensional theory, encompassing both distribution and recognition, can supply the necessary levels of social-theoretical complexity and moral-philosophical insight.[13]

That, at least, is the view of justice I defended in the past. And this two-dimensional understanding of justice still seems right to me as far as it goes. But I now believe that it does not go far enough. Distribution and recognition could appear to constitute the sole dimensions of justice only so long as the Keynesian-Westphalian frame was taken for granted. Once the question of the frame becomes subject to contestation, the effect is to make visible a third dimension of justice, which was neglected in my previous work – as well as in the work of many other philosophers.[14]

The third dimension of justice is the political. Of course, distribution and recognition are themselves political in the sense of being contested and power-laden; and they have usually been seen as requiring adjudication by the state. But I mean political in a more specific, constitutive sense, which concerns the scope of the state's jurisdiction and the decision rules by which it structures contestation. The political in this sense furnishes the stage on which struggles over distribution and recognition are played out. Establishing criteria of social belonging, and thus determining who counts as a member, the political dimension of justice specifies the reach of those other dimensions: it tells us who is included in, and who excluded from, the circle of those entitled to a just distribution and reciprocal recognition. Establishing decision rules, the political dimension likewise sets the procedures for staging and resolving contests in both the economic and the cultural dimensions: it tells us not only who can make claims for redistribution and recognition, but also how such claims are to be mooted and adjudicated.

Centered on issues of membership and procedure, the political dimension of justice is concerned chiefly with representation. At one level, which pertains to the boundary-setting aspect of the political, representation is a matter of social belonging. What is at issue here is inclusion in, or exclusion from, the community of those entitled to make justice claims on one another. At another level, which pertains to the decision-rule aspect, representation concerns the procedures that structure public processes of contestation. Here, what is at issue are the terms on which those included in the political community air their claims and adjudicate their disputes.[15] At both levels, the question can arise as to whether the relations of representation are just. One can ask: Do the boundaries of the political community wrongly exclude some who are actually entitled to representation? Do the community's decision rules accord equal voice in public deliberations and fair representation in public decision-making to all members? Such issues of representation are specifically political. Conceptually distinct from both economic and cultural questions, they cannot be reduced to the latter, although, as we shall see, they are inextricably interwoven with them.

To say that the political is a conceptually distinct dimension of justice, not reducible to the economic or the cultural, is also to say that it can give rise to a conceptually distinct species of injustice. Given the view of justice as participatory parity, this means that there can be distinctively political obstacles to parity, not reducible to maldistribution or misrecognition, although (again) interwoven with them. Such obstacles arise from the political constitution of society, as opposed to the class structure or status order. Grounded in a specifically political mode of social ordering, they can only be adequately grasped through a theory that conceptualizes representation, along with distribution and recognition, as one of three fundamental dimensions of justice.

Two levels of political injustice: from ordinary-political misrepresentation to misframing

If representation is the defining issue of the political, then the characteristic political injustice is misrepresentation. Misrepresentation occurs when political boundaries and/or decision rules function wrongly to deny some people the possibility of participating on a par with others in social interaction – including, but not only, in political arenas. Far from being reducible to maldistribution or misrecognition, misrepresentation can occur even in the absence of the latter injustices, although it is usually intertwined with them.

At least two different levels of misrepresentation can be distinguished. Insofar as political decision rules wrongly deny some of the included the chance to participate fully, as peers, the injustice is what I call ordinary-political misrepresentation. Here, where the issue is intra-frame representation, we enter the familiar terrain of political science debates over the relative merits of alternative electoral systems. Do single-member-district, winner-take-all, first-past-the-post systems unjustly deny parity to numerical minorities? And if so, is proportional representation or cumulative voting the appropriate remedy?[16] Likewise, do gender-blind rules, in conjunction with gender-based maldistribution and misrecognition, function to deny parity of political participation to women?[17] And if so, are gender quotas an appropriate remedy? Such questions belong to the sphere of ordinary-political justice, which has usually been played out within the Keynesian-Westphalian frame.

Less obvious, perhaps, is a second level of misrepresentation, which concerns the boundary-setting aspect of the political. Here the injustice arises when the community's boundaries are drawn in such a way as to wrongly exclude some people from the chance to participate at all in its authorized contests over justice. In such cases, misrepresentation takes a deeper form, which I shall call misframing. The deeper character of misframing is a function of the crucial importance of framing to every question of social justice. Far from being of marginal significance, frame-setting is among the most consequential of political decisions. Constituting both members and non-members in a single stroke, this decision effectively excludes the latter from the universe of those entitled to consideration within the community in matters of distribution, recognition, and ordinary-political representation. The result can be a serious injustice. When questions of justice are framed in a way that wrongly excludes some from consideration, the consequence is a special kind of meta-injustice, in which one is denied the chance to press first-order justice claims in a given political community. The injustice remains, moreover, even when those excluded from one political community are included as subjects of justice in another – as long as the effect of the political division is to put some relevant aspects of justice beyond their reach. Still more serious, of course, is the case in which one is excluded from membership in any political community. Akin to the loss of what Hannah Arendt called "the right to have rights," that sort of misframing is a kind of "political death."[18] Those who suffer it may become objects of charity or benevolence. But deprived of the possibility of authoring first-order claims, they become non-persons with respect to justice.

It is the misframing form of misrepresentation that globalization has recently begun to make visible. Earlier, in the heyday of the postwar welfare state, with the Keynesian-Westphalian frame securely in place, the principal concern in thinking about justice was distribution. Later, with the rise of the new social movements and multiculturalism, the center of gravity shifted to recognition. In both cases, the modern territorial state was assumed by default. As a result, the political dimension of justice was relegated to the margins. Where it did emerge, it took the ordinary-political form of contests over the decision rules internal to the polity, whose boundaries were taken for granted. Thus, claims for gender quotas and multicultural rights sought to remove political obstacles to participatory parity for those who were already included in principle in the political community.[19] Taking for granted the Keynesian-Westphalian frame, they did not call into question the assumption that the appropriate unit of justice was the territorial state.

Today, in contrast, globalization has put the question of the frame squarely on the political agenda. Increasingly subject to contestation, the Keynesian-Westphalian frame is now considered by many to be a major vehicle of injustice, as it partitions political space in ways that block many who are poor and despised from challenging the forces that oppress them. Channeling their claims into the domestic political spaces of relatively powerless, if not wholly failed, states, this frame insulates offshore powers from critique and control.[20] Among those shielded from the reach of justice are more powerful predator states and transnational private powers, including foreign investors and creditors, international currency speculators, and transnational corporations. Also protected are the governance structures of the global economy, which set exploitative terms of interaction and then exempt them from democratic control.[21] Finally, the Keynesian-Westphalian frame is self-insulating: the architecture of the interstate system protects the very partitioning of political space that it institutionalizes, effectively excluding transnational democratic decision-making on issues of justice.[22]

From this perspective, the Keynesian-Westphalian frame is a powerful instrument of injustice, which gerrymanders political space at the expense of the poor and despised. For those persons who are denied the chance to press transnational first-order claims, struggles against maldistribution and misrecognition cannot proceed, let alone succeed, unless they are joined with struggles against misframing. It is not surprising, therefore, that some consider misframing the defining injustice of a globalizing age.

Under these conditions, of heightened awareness of misframing, the political dimension of justice is hard to ignore. Insofar as globalization is politicizing the question of the frame, it is also making visible an aspect of the grammar of justice that was often neglected in the previous period. It is now apparent that no claim for justice can avoid presupposing some notion of representation, implicit or explicit, insofar as none can avoid assuming a frame. Thus, representation is always already inherent in all claims for redistribution and recognition. The political dimension is implicit in, indeed required by, the grammar of the concept of justice. Thus, no redistribution or recognition without representation.[23]

In general, then, an adequate theory of justice for our time must be three-dimensional. Encompassing not only redistribution and recognition, but also representation, it must allow us to grasp the question of the frame as a question of justice. Incorporating the economic, cultural, and political dimensions, it must enable us to identify injustices of misframing and to evaluate possible remedies. Above all, it must permit us to pose, and to answer, the key political question of our age: How can we integrate struggles against maldistribution, misrecognition, and misrepresentation within a postwestphalian frame?

On the politics of framing: from state-territoriality to social effectivity?

So far I have been arguing for the irreducible specificity of the political as one of three fundamental dimensions of justice. And I have identified two distinct levels of political injustice: ordinary-political misrepresentation and misframing. Now, I want to examine the politics of framing in a globalizing world.

Distinguishing affirmative from transformative approaches, I shall argue that an adequate politics of representation must also address a third level: beyond contesting ordinary-political misrepresentation, on the one hand, and misframing, on the other, such a politics must also aim to democratize the process of frame-setting.

I begin by explaining what I mean by "the politics of framing." Situated at my second level, where distinctions between members and non-members are drawn, this politics concerns the boundary-setting aspect of the political. Focused on the issues of who counts as a subject of justice, and what is the appropriate frame, the politics of framing comprises efforts to establish and consolidate, to contest and revise, the authoritative division of political space. Included here are struggles against misframing, which aim to dismantle the obstacles that prevent disadvantaged people from confronting the forces that oppress them with claims of justice. Centered on the setting and contesting of frames, the politics of framing is concerned with the question of the "who."

The politics of framing can take two distinct forms, both of which are now being practiced in our globalizing world.[24] The first approach, which I shall call the affirmative politics of framing, contests the boundaries of existing frames while accepting the Westphalian grammar of frame-setting. In this politics, those who claim to suffer injustices of misframing seek to redraw the boundaries of existing territorial states or in some cases to create new ones. But they still assume that the territorial state is the appropriate unit within which to pose and resolve disputes about justice. For them, accordingly, injustices of misframing are not a function of the general principle according to which the Westphalian order partitions political space. They arise, rather, as a result of the faulty way in which that principle has been applied. Thus, those who practice the affirmative politics of framing accept that the principle of state-territoriality is the proper basis for constituting the "who" of justice. They agree, in other words, that what makes a given collection of individuals into fellow subjects of justice is their shared residence on the territory of a modern state and/or their shared membership in the political community that corresponds to such a state. Thus, far from challenging the underlying grammar of the Westphalian order, those who practice the affirmative politics of framing accept its state-territorial principle.[25]

Precisely that principle is contested, however, in a second version of the politics of framing, which I shall call the transformative approach. For proponents of this approach, the state-territorial principle no longer affords an adequate basis for determining the "who" of justice in every case. They concede, of course, that that principle remains relevant for many purposes; thus, supporters of transformation do not propose to eliminate state-territoriality entirely. But they contend that its grammar is out of synch with the structural causes of many injustices in a globalizing world, which are not territorial in character. Examples include the financial markets, "offshore factories," investment regimes, and governance structures of the global economy, which determine who works for a wage and who does not; the information networks of global media and cybertechnology, which determine who is included in the circuits of communicative power and who is not; and the bio-politics of climate, disease, drugs, weapons, and biotechnology, which determine who will live long and who will die young. In these matters, so fundamental to human well-being, the forces that perpetrate injustice belong not to "the space of places," but to "the space of flows."[26] Not locatable within the jurisdiction of any actual or conceivable territorial state, they cannot be made answerable to claims of justice that are framed in terms of the state-territorial principle. In their case, so the argument goes, to invoke the state-territorial principle to determine the frame is itself to commit an injustice. By partitioning political space along territorial lines, this principle insulates extra- and non-territorial powers from the reach of justice. In a globalizing world, therefore, it is less likely to serve as a remedy for misframing than as a means of inflicting or perpetuating it.

Postwestphalian framing

In general, then, the transformative politics of framing aims to change the deep grammar of frame-setting in a globalizing world. This approach seeks to supplement the state-territorial principle of the Westphalian order with one or more postwestphalian principles. The aim is to overcome injustices of misframing by changing not just the boundaries of the "who" of justice, but also the mode of their constitution, hence the way in which they are drawn. It is to establish a post-territorial mode of political differentiation.[27]

What might a postwestphalian mode of frame-setting look like? Doubtless it is too early to have a clear view. Nevertheless, the most promising candidate so far is the "all-affected principle." This principle holds that all those affected by a given social structure or institution have moral standing as subjects of justice in relation to it. On this view, what turns a collection of people into fellow subjects of justice is not geographical proximity, but their co-imbrication in a common structural or institutional framework, which sets the ground rules that govern their social interaction, thereby shaping their respective life possibilities in patterns of advantage and disadvantage.[28]

Until recently, the all-affected principle seemed to coincide in the eyes of many with the state-territorial principle. It was assumed, in keeping with the Westphalian world picture, that the common framework that determined patterns of advantage and disadvantage was precisely the constitutional order of the modern territorial state. As a result, it seemed that in applying the state-territorial principle, one simultaneously captured the normative force of the all-affected principle. In fact, this was never truly so, as the long history of colonialism and neo-colonialism attests. From the perspective of the metropole, however, the conflation of state-territoriality with social effectivity appeared to have an emancipatory thrust, as it served to justify the progressive incorporation, as subjects of justice, of the subordinate classes and status groups who were resident in the territory but excluded from active citizenship.

Today, however, the idea that state-territoriality can serve as a proxy for social effectivity is no longer plausible. Under current conditions, one's chances to live a good life do not depend wholly on the internal political constitution of the territorial state in which one resides. Although the latter remains undeniably relevant, its effects are mediated by other structures, both extra- and non-territorial, whose impact is at least as significant. In general, globalization is driving a widening wedge between state-territoriality and social effectivity. As those two principles increasingly diverge, the effect is to reveal the former as an inadequate surrogate for the latter. And so the question arises: Is it possible to apply the all-affected principle directly to the framing of justice, without going through the detour of state-territoriality?[29]

This is precisely what some practitioners of transformative politics are attempting to do. Seeking leverage against offshore sources of maldistribution and misrecognition, some globalization activists are appealing directly to the all-affected principle in order to circumvent the state-territorial partitioning of political space. Contesting their exclusion by the Keynesian-Westphalian frame, environmentalists and indigenous peoples are claiming standing as subjects of justice in relation to the extra- and non-territorial powers that impinge on their lives. Insisting that effectivity trumps state-territoriality, they have joined development activists, international feminists, and others in asserting their right to make claims against the structures that harm them, even when the latter cannot be located in the space of places. Casting off the Westphalian grammar of frame-setting, these claimants are applying the all-affected principle directly to questions of justice in a globalizing world.

Meta-political justice

In such cases, the transformative politics of framing proceeds simultaneously in multiple dimensions and on multiple levels. On one level, the social movements that practice this politics aim to redress first-order injustices of maldistribution, misrecognition, and ordinary-political misrepresentation. On a second level, these movements seek to redress meta-level injustices of misframing by reconstituting the "who" of justice. In those cases, moreover, where the state-territorial principle serves more to indemnify than to challenge injustice, transformative social movements appeal instead to the all-affected principle. Invoking a postwestphalian principle, they are seeking to change the very grammar of frame-setting – and thereby to reconstruct the meta-political foundations of justice for a globalizing world.

But the claims of transformative politics go further still. Above and beyond their other demands, these movements are also claiming a say in the process of frame-setting. Rejecting the standard view, which deems frame-setting the prerogative of states and transnational elites, they are effectively aiming to democratize the process by which the frameworks of justice are drawn and revised. Asserting their right to participate in constituting the "who" of justice, they are simultaneously transforming the "how" – by which I mean the accepted procedures for determining the "who." At their most reflective and ambitious, accordingly, transformative movements are demanding the creation of new democratic arenas for entertaining arguments about the frame. In some cases, moreover, they are creating such arenas themselves. In the World Social Forum, for example, some practitioners of transformative politics have fashioned a transnational public sphere where they can participate on a par with others in airing and resolving disputes about the frame. In this way, they are prefiguring the possibility of new institutions of postwestphalian democratic justice.[30]

The democratizing dimension of transformative politics points to a third level of political injustice, above and beyond the two already discussed. Previously, I distinguished first-order injustices of ordinary-political misrepresentation from second-order injustices of misframing. Now, however, we can discern a third-order species of political injustice, which corresponds to the question of the "how." Exemplified by undemocratic processes of frame-setting, this injustice consists in the failure to institutionalize parity of participation at the meta-political level, in deliberations and decisions concerning the "who." Because what is at stake here is the process by which first-order political space is constituted, I shall call this injustice meta-political misrepresentation. Meta-political misrepresentation arises when states and transnational elites monopolize the activity of frame-setting, denying voice to those who may be harmed in the process, and blocking creation of democratic arenas where the latter's claims can be vetted and redressed. The effect is to exclude the overwhelming majority of people from participation in the meta-discourses that determine the authoritative division of political space. Lacking any institutional arenas for such participation, and submitted to an undemocratic approach to the "how," the majority is denied the chance to engage on terms of parity in decision-making about the "who."

In general, then, struggles against misframing are revealing a new kind of democratic deficit. Just as globalization has made visible injustices of misframing, so transformative struggles against neoliberal globalization are making visible the injustice of meta-political misrepresentation. In exposing the lack of institutions where disputes about the "who" can be democratically aired and resolved, these struggles are focusing attention on the "how." By demonstrating that the absence of such institutions impedes efforts to overcome injustice, they are revealing the deep internal connections between democracy and justice. The effect is to bring to light a structural feature of the current conjuncture: struggles for justice in a globalizing world cannot succeed unless they go hand in hand with struggles for meta-political democracy. At this level, too, then, no redistribution or recognition without representation.

Monological theory and democratic dialogue

I have been arguing that what distinguishes the current conjuncture is intensified contestation concerning both the "who" and the "how" of justice. Under these conditions, the theory of justice is undergoing a paradigm shift. Earlier, when the Keynesian-Westphalian frame was in place, most philosophers neglected the political dimension. Treating the territorial state as a given, they endeavored to ascertain the requirements of justice theoretically, in a monological fashion. Thus, they did not envisage any role in determining these requirements for those who would be subject to them, let alone for those excluded by the national frame. Neglecting to reflect on the question of the frame, these philosophers never imagined that those whose fates would be so decisively shaped by framing decisions might be entitled to participate in making them. Disavowing any need for a dialogical democratic moment, they were content to produce monological theories of social justice.

Today, however, monological theories of social justice are becoming increasingly implausible. As we have seen, globalization cannot help but problematize the question of the "how," as it politicizes the question of the "who." The process goes something like this: as the circle of those claiming a say in frame-setting expands, decisions about the "who" are increasingly viewed as political matters, which should be handled democratically, rather than as technical matters, which can be left to experts and elites. The effect is to shift the burden of argument, requiring defenders of expert privilege to make their case. No longer able to hold themselves above the fray, they are necessarily embroiled in disputes about the "how." As a result, they must contend with demands for meta-political democratization.

An analogous shift is currently making itself felt in normative philosophy. Just as some activists are seeking to transfer elite frame-setting prerogatives to democratic publics, so some theorists of justice are proposing to rethink the classic division of labor between theorist and *demos*. No longer content to ascertain the requirements of justice in a monological fashion, these theorists are looking increasingly to dialogical approaches, which treat important aspects of justice as matters for collective decision-making, to be determined by the citizens themselves, through democratic deliberation. For them, accordingly, the grammar of the theory of justice is being transformed. What could once be called the "theory of social justice" now appears as the "theory of democratic justice."[31]

In its current form, however, the theory of democratic justice remains incomplete. To complete the shift from a monological to dialogical theory requires a further step, beyond those contemplated by most proponents of the dialogical turn.[32] Henceforth, democratic processes of determination must be applied not only to the "what" of justice, but also to the "who" and the "how." In that case, by adopting a democratic approach to the "how," the theory of justice assumes a guise appropriate to a globalizing world. Dialogical at every level, meta-political as well as ordinary-political, it becomes a theory of postwestphalian democratic justice.

The view of justice as participatory parity readily lends itself to such an approach. This principle has a double quality that expresses the reflexive character of democratic justice. On the one hand, the principle of participatory parity is an outcome notion, which specifies a substantive principle of justice by which we may evaluate social arrangements: the latter are just if and only if they permit all the relevant social actors to participate as peers in social life. On the other hand, participatory parity is also a process notion, which specifies a procedural standard by which we may evaluate the democratic legitimacy of norms: the latter are legitimate if and only if they can command the assent of all concerned in fair and open processes of deliberation, in which all can participate as peers. By virtue of this double quality, the view of justice as participatory parity has an inherent reflexivity. Able to problematize both substance and procedure, it renders visible the mutual entwinement of these two aspects of social arrangements. Thus, this approach can expose both the unjust background conditions that skew putatively democratic decision-making and the undemocratic procedures that generate substantively unequal outcomes. As a result, it enables us to shift levels easily, moving back and forth as necessary between first-order and meta-level questions. Making manifest the co-implication of democracy and justice, the view of justice as participatory parity supplies just the sort of reflexivity that is needed in a globalizing world.

All told, then, the norm of participatory parity suits the account of postwestphalian democratic justice presented here. Encompassing three dimensions and multiple levels, this account renders visible, and criticizable, the characteristic injustices of the present conjuncture. Conceptualizing misframing and meta-political misrepresentation, it discloses core injustices overlooked by standard theories. Focused not only on the "what" of justice, but also on the "who" and the "how," it enables us to grasp the question of the frame as the central question of justice in a globalizing world.

3

Two Dogmas of Egalitarianism

Until recently, struggles for justice proceeded against the background of a taken-for-granted frame: the modern territorial state. With that frame assumed by default, the scope of justice was rarely subject to explicit dispute in the post-World War II period. Whether the issue was socioeconomic distribution or legal-cultural recognition or political representation, it generally went without saying that the unit within which justice applied was a geographically bounded political community with a sovereign state. With that "Westphalian" assumption in place, another one followed in train: the subjects bound by obligations of justice were, by definition, fellow citizens of a territorial state. In the social-democratic era, these assumptions subtended even the fiercest political struggles. However strongly the antagonists disagreed about *what* justice required, nearly all agreed about *who* was entitled to claim it. For socialists and conservatives, liberals and communitarians, feminists and multiculturalists, the "who" of justice could only be the domestic-political citizenry.

Today, however, the "who" of justice is hotly contested. Epochal geopolitical developments – the fall of communism, the rise of neoliberalism, and the waning of US hegemony – are dislocating the postwar mapping of political space. At the same time, in this moment of destabilization, political struggles increasingly trespass the Westphalian frame. Human-rights activists and international feminists join critics of structural adjustment and the World Trade Organization in targeting injustices that cut across borders. Effectively exploding the territorial imaginary, these movements are seeking to re-map the bounds of justice on a broader scale. Challenging the view that justice can only be a domestic relation among fellow citizens, they are articulating new, "postwestphalian" understandings of "who counts." As their claims collide with those of nationalists and territorially oriented democrats, we witness new forms of "meta-political" contestation in which the "who" of justice is an object of explicit dispute.

As usual, theory scrambles to catch up with practice. Under these conditions, those who would theorize justice must face an issue that once seemed to go without saying: What is the proper frame for theorizing justice? How shall we frame issues of distributive justice, when the idea of a national economy is increasingly notional? How, too, shall we frame questions of recognition, when cultural and political flows regularly transgress national boundaries, fracturing older status hierarchies and creating new ones? How, finally, shall we frame questions of representation, when consequential decisions are increasingly made outside the precincts of territorially based government? How, in sum, shall we delimit the "who" of justice in a postwestphalian world?

In this chapter, I propose to address these questions in a roundabout way. To illuminate the problem's parameters, I shall examine some leading efforts to establish the appropriate frame for thinking about social justice in a postwestphalian world. Assessing the strengths and weaknesses of each, I shall consider what happens when mainstream political philosophers turn their attention from the "what" of justice to that of the "who." The result, to anticipate the argument, will be to bring to light a new question, over and above both the "what" and the "who." Thus, I shall suggest that in seriously considering those questions, one is led ineluctably to a third-order, *meta*-meta level question, which I shall call the question of the "how." Here the issue is in essence procedural: *How*, in a given case, should one determine the pertinent frame for reflecting on justice? By which criteria or decision procedure should one decide? And who is the "one" who should determine the relevant frame?

From the "what" to the "who" to the "how"

The previous chapter mapped a change in the grammar of struggles for justice. This one shifts the scene from public-sphere politics to political philosophy. Here, in the discourses of the academy, the grammar of arguments about justice is undergoing a parallel shift. Increasingly aware of transnational processes, political philosophers, too, are beginning to call into question the Keynesian-Westphalian frame, which they, too, had tacitly assumed in the preceding decades. As a result of this major new opening of philosophical discussion, they are overcoming the first of what I shall call, with apologies to W. V. O. Quine, "two dogmas of egalitarianism."[1] Let me explain.

Until recently, political philosophers were chiefly engrossed in debating their own specialized version of the question of the "what," which Amartya Sen called "equality of what?"[2] In the analytic tradition, theorists of distributive justice argued mostly about *what* should be fairly distributed, disputing the relative merits of rights, resources, primary goods, opportunities, real freedoms, and capabilities as alternative metrics for evaluating the justice of social relations.[3] Analogously, in the Hegelian tradition, theorists of recognition argued about *what* should be reciprocally recognized: group identity, individual achievement, or autonomous personhood; cultural distinctiveness, common humanity, or the claimant's standing as a partner in social interaction.[4] Focused intently on "equality of what?" philosophers in both traditions tended to overlook a second key question, which Deborah Satz poses as "equality among whom?"[5] Unwittingly replicating the grammar of public-sphere argument, they, too, simply assumed without critical reflection the Keynesian-Westphalian frame. Failing to justify that premise against possible alternatives, they succumbed to what I am calling the first dogma of egalitarianism: the unexamined presupposition of the national "who."[6]

Today, in contrast, philosophers openly argue about "equality among whom?," even as they continue to debate "equality of what?" Increasingly, the field is divided between cosmopolitans, internationalists, and liberal-nationalists. For those in the first camp, there are no morally compelling reasons to privilege concern for one's fellow nationals over others; thus, justice necessarily concerns relations among all human beings.[7] For those in the second camp, in contrast, the special character of bounded political communities justifies two distinct sets of justice requirements: one, more demanding set holds within such communities, while another, less demanding set holds among them.[8] For those in the third camp, finally, the requirements of justice apply only within communities possessing such morally relevant features as a common political constitution, a shared ethical horizon, or a historical self-identification as "a community of fate"; absent such special features, binding obligations of justice do not apply.[9]

That such disagreements are now explicit represents the overcoming of the first dogma of egalitarianism: the tacit presupposition of the national "who" in the absence of considered debate. To be sure, many theorists of justice still subscribe to the Keynesian-Westphalian frame, but now they must argue for it openly, against the alternatives. Overtly disputing the relative merits of alternative frames, political philosophers have finally awakened from their dogmatic slumbers concerning the "who".

Before we celebrate the lifting of repression, however, we should look more closely at these debates. Upon inspection, we shall see that while many philosophers have overcome this first dogma of egalitarianism, most still succumb to a second.

Consider current debates about the "who" among analytic theorists of distributive justice. Centered largely on John Rawls's 1999 book, *The Law of Peoples*, and on his earlier Amnesty Lecture of the same name, these debates pit egalitarian liberal-nationalists against proponents of global and international distributive justice.[10] On one side stands Rawls himself, who denied that norms of egalitarian distributive justice have any applicability at the global or international level. Drawing a sharp Westphalian distinction between the domestic and international spheres, he made the domestic sphere the sole and exclusive province of distributive justice, while conceiving international justice in a way that provided no basis for egalitarian economic claims.[11] On the other side, opposite Rawls, stand two other groups of philosophers, both of whom reject the Keynesian-Westphalian "who" in favor of larger, postwestphalian alternatives. For the first group, which defends a cosmopolitan "who," egalitarian distributive norms apply globally, among individuals, irrespective of nationality or citizenship; thus, impoverished individuals in, say, the Sudan have moral standing *qua* persons to make transborder claims for economic justice upon their fellow inhabitants of the globe.[12] For the second group, which defends an internationalist "who," egalitarian distributive norms apply internationally, among territorially bounded collectivities; here, impoverished "peoples," such as the Sudanese, have moral standing as corporate bodies to make transborder claims for economic justice upon other, more prosperous "peoples," such as the Dutch and the Americans.[13] For the cosmopolitans, accordingly, the "who" of distributive justice is the global set of individual persons; for the internationalists, in contrast, the "who" is the set of corporate political communities that possess territorial states.

The result is a three-way debate over the "who" among liberal-nationalists, egalitarian-internationalists, and cosmopolitans. Highly sophisticated and complex, this debate involves a major disagreement about the relation between justice and toleration in a liberal society.[14] Here, however, I leave aside that issue in order to focus on something else: namely, *how* exactly the participants go about determining the appropriate frame for distributive justice. Looking beneath their respective views of the "who," I propose to examine their underlying assumptions about the "how." The issue here is one of procedure: How do the various disputants envision the process of deciding between the Keynesian-Westphalian "who," on the one hand, and the global or internationalist "who," on the other? By reference to which criteria or decision pro-cedure does each choose? And whom exactly, as a consequence, does each philosopher effectively authorize to determine the frame?

Following Rawls, most participants in this debate justify their choice of a frame by invoking the device of the "original position." Although they differ as to how best to model and apply that device, they agree that principles of international justice are to be chosen by "parties" who are ignorant of some particular features of their own situation but who possess a general background knowledge of society and history.[15] They assume, specifically, that the parties choose in the light of an empirical social-scientific understanding of the nature and extent of the social structures that determine the relative life-chances of different individuals, an understanding that is supposed to be uncontroversial. Yet these philosophers disagree sharply as to the substantive content of the parties' knowledge. For the liberal-nationalists, the parties are assumed to "know" that a person's life prospects depend overwhelmingly on the domestic institutional framework of her or his own society.[16] For the cosmopolitans, in contrast, the parties "know" that the principal determinant of individual well-being is the basic structure of the global economy.[17] For the egalitarian-internationalists, finally, the parties "know" that one's life prospects are co-determined by institutional arrangements at both the domestic and international levels.[18]

These differences in the parties' social-scientific background knowledge bear importantly on their choice of principles of international justice. When, with Rawls, they assume high levels of national self-sufficiency, the parties adopt a "law of peoples" that includes no provision for transnational distributive justice.[19] When, with the internationalists, they assume that both national and international structures co-determine individuals' life-chances, the parties adopt an alternative "law of peoples" that authorizes redistribution across borders for the maximum benefit of the worst-off societies.[20] When, with the cosmopolitans, the parties assume the primacy of global structures, they choose a global difference principle, mandating the restructuring of the global economy for the maximum benefit of the worst-off individuals in the world.[21]

In this debate, therefore, the choice of the "who" comes down, in large measure, to how each philosopher answers the following questions: Does there exist a global economy with sufficient influence over the relative life-chances of individuals to count as a global "basic structure"? Or are the relative life-chances of different people determined exclusively or primarily by the constitutional structures of their respective domestic societies? Or, finally, are life-chances co-determined by domestic and international structures?[22]

In general, then, the choice of the "who" comes down in the end to a question of causal primacy: What precisely is the primary factor that determines people's life-chances in the current conjuncture? Yet this question is never adequately conceptualized in this debate. Far from engaging it directly, the disputants only broach it obliquely, as each philosopher presents what is actually a controversial view as if it were settled fact. Rawls, for example, justifies his choice of the Keynesian-Westphalian "who" in part by appealing to a putative social-scientific fact: that the principal cause of third-world poverty lies not in international political economy but in the deficient internal constitution of "burdened societies."[23] In the same way, his critics justify their choice of a postwestphalian "who" by insisting on a contrary social-scientific fact: that global and/or international structures play a substantial role in causing and reproducing such poverty, as well as in deforming the internal political constitution of third-world societies.[24] In each case, the controversial character of the postulated "fact" is disavowed, as is the latter's dependence on tacit social-theoretical assumptions and historical interpretations, which are themselves controversial. The effect is to posit an offstage "elsewhere," in which social scientists have supposedly already settled such difficult questions.[25]

In this debate, therefore, all sides determine the "who" in a similar way. All assume that the frame of distributive justice should match the reach of whatever structure proves to be "basic" in the sense of wielding causal primacy over people's life-chances. And all assume that the identity of that structure is an uncontroversial matter of empirical fact. As a result, all the philosophers in this debate effectively authorize the social scientist to determine the frame.

Here, accordingly, lies the second dogma of egalitarianism: the tacit, unargued assumption that normal social science can determine the "who" of justice. In the next section, I shall consider the relative merits of this assumption vis-à-vis an alternative. Here, in contrast, I wish only to draw attention to the unreflective way in which a particular view about the relation between normative theory and social science enters current debates. Insofar as philosophers simply assume this view, they fail to subject the procedural question to critical reflection. They fail to ask, in a methodologically self-reflective way: *How* should one determine the pertinent frame for reflecting on social justice in a globalizing world? What criterion or decision procedure should one invoke? And who in the end is the "one" who should decide?

In general, political philosophers have so far failed to reflect systematically on such questions. This is the case for the analytic theorists of distributive justice I have considered here.

But it is equally true of their Hegelian counterparts, whose theories of recognition also tend to glide over the question of the "how," even as they are now beginning in earnest to question the "who."[26] This situation may strike some as ironic: at the very moment when they are overcoming the first dogma of egalitarianism, philosophers in both traditions are succumbing to the second.

The effect is to leave those of us who argue about justice today in an awkward position. On the one hand, having left behind our dogmatic attachment to the Keynesian-Westphalian frame, we now have access to a range of possible answers to the question of the "who." On the other hand, absent considered reflection on the "how," we lack a defensible procedure for deciding among them. Thus, we still await a convincing answer to the burning question of our day: What is the pertinent frame within which to reflect on the requirements of justice in a globalizing world?

Beyond the second dogma: from the normal-social-scientific to the critical-democratic "how"

If we are ever to arrive at a satisfactory answer to that question, we need to overcome the second dogma of egalitarianism by beginning a new round of reflective discussion about the "how." I want now to sketch some parameters for such a discussion. I shall begin by canvassing some strengths and weaknesses of the approach just discussed, which I shall henceforth refer to as "the normal-social-science approach."[27] Then, I shall sketch an alternative, "critical-democratic," approach to the "how."

The normal-social-science approach finds at least initial support in three interrelated ideas. First, it appreciates the importance of situating arguments about justice in relation to the social circumstances in which they arise and the need to frame them in terms appropriate to those circumstances. Second, the versions of this approach that I have considered here posit a plausible conceptual link between one such circumstance, namely, the reach of the basic structure, and the "who" of distributive justice: they posit, that is, that what turns a collection of people into fellow subjects of distributive justice is their co-imbrication in a common framework, which sets the

terms of their social interaction, distributing benefits and bur-
dens among them, and shaping their respective life-chances.
Third, what underlies that idea, and lends this approach further
plausibility, is a version of the "all-affected" principle, which
holds that all those affected by a given social structure have
moral standing as subjects of justice in relation to it.

Together, these three ideas constitute a powerful conceptual
constellation. They suggest that current disputes over the
"who" can only be satisfactorily resolved in light of a well-
founded understanding of our social and historical circumstances, which comprehends the forces that shape people's
lives in a globalizing world. Stated thus, in the most general
terms, this suggestion appears unimpeachable. Any·acceptable
approach to the question of the "how" must incorporate defensible interpretations of the circumstances of justice, the major
causal forces, and the all-affected principle – while also theorizing the relations among them.

Everything depends, however, on how precisely one conceptualizes those ideas. Those who rely on the normal-social-
science approach construe them as settled matters of empirical
fact, which do not depend on controversial assumptions. On
their view, which is reminiscent of positivism, there is no need
for those of us who argue about justice to embroil ourselves in
social-theoretical disputes. Far from having to worry about the
relation between fact and value, causal explanation and historical interpretation, we need only consult the established fruits
of normal science.

In fact, however, none of the key concepts at issue can be
elaborated in this way. Far from being reducible to settled
matters of empirical fact, proposed accounts of the circumstances of justice are inherently theory-laden and value-laden,
which is why they are controversial. We need only recall current
disputes about the extent and reality of globalization to see that
efforts to specify those circumstances rest on normatively suffused interpretations and political judgments.[28] The task
of adjudicating rival characterizations cannot, accordingly, be
entrusted to a positivistically conceived social science. It must,
rather, be handled dialogically, in a multifaceted practical discourse that canvasses alternative conceptions, unpacks their
underlying assumptions, and weighs their relative merits –
all in full awareness of the internal relations between social

knowledge and normative reflection. The upshot is that we cannot settle arguments about the "who" by appealing to the "circumstances of justice," as if that were simply a matter of uncontroversial empirical fact. On the contrary, disagreements about what precisely should count as the relevant circumstances, and how exactly those circumstances should be characterized, should be opened up and made explicit, treated as part and parcel of broader political arguments about the "who" of social justice in a globalizing world.

The same is true for the concept of the "basic structure." That idea was originally developed by Rawls, in his 1970 book, *A Theory of Justice*, for a "closed society," which one entered only by birth and exited only by death.[29] Having excluded all transborder movements, Rawls posited a self-sufficient society, whose members' life-chances depended exclusively on their own internal institutional arrangements. Given those idealized assumptions, it made sense perhaps to imagine that those arrangements constituted a single structure with a uniform reach that determined the life-chances of an identifiable bounded population – and of no one else. But absent such counterfactual assumptions, the idea of a single basic structure with a uniform reach is hard to sustain. As soon as we introduce transborder interactions, we admit the possibility of multiple non-isomorphic structures, some local, some national, some regional, and some global, which mark out a variety of different "who's" for different issues. In the same breath, we admit the likelihood that people's life-chances are over-determined by multiple structures that partially overlap one another but differ in reach. How precisely such structures interact is by no means well understood by social scientists, whose accounts are mutually contradictory and controversial. Under these conditions, attempts to determine the "who" by appealing to bare social-scientific fact are highly implausible. To consider seriously what sense to make today of structural causation is to enter contested terrain, where rival social theories and historical interpretations must be assessed. Debates about these matters, too, need to be opened up and rendered explicit. No longer treated as external to the theory of justice, they should be brought into direct communication with normative reflection within broader arguments about the "who."

Analogous complexities surround the all-affected principle. It is intuitively plausible, to be sure, to hold that all those affected by a given structure should have moral standing as subjects of justice in relation to it. But it doesn't follow that we can operationalize that principle by appealing to uncontroversial social-scientific fact. The problem is that, given the so-called "butterfly effect," one can adduce empirical evidence that just about everyone is affected by just about everything. What is needed, therefore, is a way of distinguishing those levels and kinds of effectivity that are deemed sufficient to confer moral standing from those that are not. Normal social science, however, cannot supply such criteria. On the contrary, to operationalize the all-affected principle requires complex political judgments, which combine empirically informed normative reflection with historical interpretation and social theorizing. Inherently dialogical, such judgment involves weighing the relative merits of alternative interpretations of the all-affected principle, which generate alternative accounts of the "who."[30]

In general, then, the normal-social-science approach to the "how" positivistically misconstrues its own central concepts. In addition, this approach fails to recognize the performative dimension of framing decisions. Its adherents suppose that they can justify the choice of a "who" by referring to states of affairs in the world, concerning who is affected by what, which they take to be independent of framing decisions. In many cases, however, there is no fact of the matter about who is affected by a given structure that is independent of the decision to constitute that structure in a given way, with a given reach. In such cases, where structures have been designed expressly to mark out specific "who's," they themselves create "facts on the ground." Thus, the "empirical fact" of who is affected, far from being independent, is a performative artifact of prior design. To appeal to normal social science to determine the "who" in such cases is not to introduce independent epistemic considerations. It is, rather, uncritically to ratify a previous framing decision.

Then, too, this approach misconstrues the subjects of justice. Those who would determine the "who" by appealing to normal science tend to treat the subjects of justice as if they were objects. Focused on discovering the facts as to who is affected by what, they construe human beings primarily as passive objects under the sway of structural forces. Granted, their ultimate aim is to enhance the private autonomy of individual persons, their equal freedom to devise and pursue their own life plans. But the effect is to neglect the importance of public autonomy, the freedom of associated social actors to participate with one another in framing the norms that bind them. Insofar as this approach confers the authority to determine the frame on social-scientific experts, it denies the public autonomy of those whom it subjects to those experts' determinations. Thus, it deprives decisions concerning the frame of democratic legitimacy.

Taken together, these shortcomings of the normal social-scientific approach suggest the need to rethink the question of "how" we should determine the "who" in a globalizing world. A viable approach requires new conceptualizations of the circumstances of justice, structural causation, and the all-affected principle. The task is to reconstruct each of those concepts in the light of a post-positivist understanding of social knowledge.

The starting point must be a frank acknowledgment that we currently lack a settled, uncontroversial account of these crucial concepts. This meta-premise differs in kind from the sort of first-order premises assumed by the philosophers discussed in the previous section. Whereas they began by assuming the settled truth of one or another substantive claim about causal primacy, I propose to begin by assuming the contested character of all such claims.[31] The effect is to suggest another, more complex, view of the process by which disputes about the "who" should be resolved.

On this view, which I shall call the "critical-democratic" approach to the "how," arguments over the "who" have a double character, simultaneously epistemic and political. In their epistemic aspect, these arguments deploy knowledge claims about the nature of vulnerability and the extent of interdependence in a globalizing world, which cannot, however, be vindicated by normal science. To adjudicate them, rather, requires a wide-ranging, open-ended mode of reasoning, in which the argument shifts back and forth among different levels and kinds of questions, some evidentiary, some interpretive, some normative, some historical, some conceptual. At each level, the disputants offer reasons and counter-reasons, although they lack any settled consensus about what counts as a good reason. Often, accordingly, their arguments become reflexive, scrutinizing previously taken-for-granted aspects of their own processes. In this approach, therefore, arguments over the frame exhibit the sort of dialogic, communicative rationality that goes with a post-positivist understanding of social knowledge. Far from appealing to normal science, then, the critical-democratic approach to the "how" incorporates modes of reasoning that are associated with Critical Theory.

But the epistemic dimension does not exhaust the nature of disputes over the "who." On the critical-democratic view, these disputes also have a political dimension. Fraught with controversy on multiple levels, the arguments implicate the evaluative and interpretive commitments of the disputants. Far from concealing this political aspect by appealing to normal science, this approach proposes to bring it into the open, encouraging interlocutors to publicly disclose, and frankly contest, the interests and value commitments suffusing their claims. At present, however, the disputants do not participate on terms of parity in arguments about the frame. Situated in unequally favorable social and geographic locations, they find their contests shot through with disparities of power. These, too, should be rendered explicit. Drawing once more on the reflexive capacity of communicative reason, the critical-democratic approach encourages participants to problematize the power disparities that taint their disputes. The aim, in other words, is to make a virtue of necessity. Recognizing their irreducible political aspect, this approach seeks insofar as possible to democratize arguments over the "who."[32]

In general, then, the critical-democratic approach to the "how" combines two fundamental ideas: on the one hand, a critical-theoretical conception of the relation between social knowledge and normative reflection; on the other, a democratic political interest in fair public contestation. Thanks to this combination of epistemic and political commitments, this approach should be able to remedy the deficits of the normal-scientific approach – without throwing out the baby with the bathwater. Important notions, such as "the circumstances of justice," "structural determination," and the "all-affected" principle, are not discarded, but rather dialogized, opened up to critical reflection through democratic debate. Far from excluding social knowledge of our globalizing world, the effect is to reclaim it from the experts and to resituate it within a wide-ranging democratic debate about the "who." Acknowledging the irreducibly performative dimension of every determination of the frame, this approach construes the subjects of justice not only as causal objects but also as social and political actors. Appreciating the importance of public autonomy, it aims to foster procedures for deciding the "who" of justice that can claim democratic legitimacy.

Democratizing disputes over the "who": institutional and conceptual issues

In several respects, then, the critical-democratic approach to the "how" improves on the normal-social-science alternative. But its full implications still need to be worked out. Institutionally, this approach points to the need to create new transnational arenas for democratically mooting, and resolving, arguments about the "who." Such arenas would be discursive spaces for hearing the claims of those who contend that existing territorially based frames unjustly exclude them. The point, however, is not to replace the Keynesian-Westphalian frame with a single all-encompassing global frame. Insofar as globalization involves the interpenetration of multiple structures of injustice, the point is rather to generate, through democratic debate of the claims of the excluded, a more adequate, intersubjectively defensible understanding of who is entitled to consideration in a given case. The probable result would be a set of multiple, functionally defined frames, corresponding to the multiple, functionally defined "who's" that emerge through such debates and are judged entitled to consideration with respect to various issues. Nevertheless, the critical-democratic approach to the "how" does not envision the abolition of territorially defined frames, or their wholesale replacement by functionally defined alternatives. It is likely, rather, that territorially defined frames and "who's" will remain important for many purposes, and that they will continue to exist alongside functionally defined frames and "who's."

The key point, in any case, is this: whatever configuration of frames emerges as provisionally justified must itself be open to future revision, as new claims of exclusion emerge to challenge that configuration. Assuming that disputes over the frame will not be susceptible of any definitive, final resolution, the critical-democratic approach to the "how" views them as an enduring feature of political life in a globalizing world. Thus, it proposes new, permanent institutions for staging and provisionally resolving such disputes democratically.

Certainly, there remain many difficult, unanswered questions about how to institutionalize this approach. One issue is how to ensure adequate representation and equal voice for those who claim standing vis-à-vis a given issue but who are excluded by existing territorially based frames. Another issue is how to envision an appropriate division of labor between weak publics, which merely debate alternative frames, and strong publics, which provisionally resolve such debates by taking binding decisions.[33] Yet another issue concerns the possible role of impartial, third-party judges or arbitrators in hearing and resolving disputes about the frame.[34] A further issue is how to deal with knee-jerk, ideological nationalism, which refuses to enter into good-faith dialogue with those who plead for a postwestphalian "who." To handle these and related issues requires institutional imagination in the spirit of realistic utopianism.

In addition, the critical-democratic approach faces at least three strong conceptual challenges. One such challenge is the specter of an infinite regress, given that this approach introduces a new, meta-meta-level question: namely, *who* should participate in the democratic process of determining the frame? Insofar as the critical-democratic approach requires a second-order democratic "who" or meta-*demos*, it seems to court a version of "the democratic paradox," which holds that boundaries and frames cannot be determined democratically, as the *demos* cannot determine the *demos*.[35] Although it is sometimes considered a knockdown argument, I do not find this objection convincing. Whatever force it may have had in the Keynesian-Westphalian era, when the need for a non-democratically determined (national) "who" was widely accepted, seems to me to have dissipated today, when democratic expectations are higher, territorially bounded "who's" are contested, and many are demanding a say in the reframing of questions of justice. Because disputes about the frame are unlikely to go away any time soon, we should treat them not only as a challenge but also as an opportunity – a spur to creative institutional thinking. Thus, instead of throwing up our hands in the face of a logical paradox, we should try to envision ways to finesse it, by imagining institutional arrangements for resolving such arguments democratically.[36]

A second conceptual challenge to the critical-democratic approach to the "how" arises from the circularity of the relations between justice and democracy. Insofar as this approach seeks to resolve arguments about the frame democratically, it seems to presuppose as a prior background condition the very outcome it seeks to promote: namely, social arrangements that are sufficiently just to permit all to participate as peers in democratic discussion and decision-making. This objection rightly notes the internal conceptual links between democracy and justice, not to mention the real-world disparities in resources and status that taint existing deliberations that are claimed to be democratic. Nevertheless, the objection applies quite generally, to all democratic processes, including those at the level of territorial states. Just as democrats do not cravenly bow down before this objection at that level, so, too, we should not do so here. Rather, we should try to envision ways to transform what looks like a vicious circle into a virtuous spiral. The idea is to begin by establishing what could be called, with apologies to D. W. Winnicott, "good-enough deliberation."[37] Although such deliberation would fall considerably short of participatory parity, it would be good enough to legitimate some social reforms, however modest, which would in turn, once institutionalized, bring the next round of deliberation closer to participatory parity. This next round, accordingly, would be "good enough" to legitimate additional, slightly less modest reforms that would in turn improve the quality of the following round – and so on.[38] In the case of this challenge, then, as for one just discussed, the solution is to draw on democracy's reflexive capacity: its ability to problematize and revise previously taken-for-granted aspects of its own procedures and frames.

A third conceptual challenge concerns the distinction between the moral and the political. That distinction assumed a sharp guise within the Keynesian-Westphalian frame, which contrasted political obligations, owed to fellow citizens, with moral obligations, owed to human beings as such. The approach proposed here, in contrast, appears to collapse the distinction, and thus threatens to moralize politics, by suggesting that all questions of justice should become political in a globalizing world. Or so the argument goes. In fact, however, the objection is misplaced. Granted, the critical-democratic approach entails building new political institutions for handling trans-territorial problems of justice, which appeared to be "merely" moral from the older perspective. But it doesn't entail that every question of justice becomes political in exactly the same way. A more likely outcome is that the sharp Westphalian contrast between the moral and the political will give way to a continuum encompassing "thicker," territorially framed political questions, at one end, and "thinner," non-territorially framed political questions, at the other. In that case, the result will not be to moralize politics, but rather to nuance it, disclosing a range of different forms of the political. From this perspective, moreover, the sharp distinction between the political and the moral is revealed to be an artifact of the Keynesian-Westphalian frame, which wrongly denied the possibility of transnational political institutions. But it does not on that account follow that that distinction can no longer be drawn. What does follow is that the distinction must henceforth be drawn in a different way. Treated as contestable and subject to revision, it, too, must be adjudicated dialogically. Thus, the question of where and when to distinguish the political from the moral now appears as a political question, subject to democratic debate.[39]

In general, then, the critical-democratic approach to the "how" need not in principle be stymied by conceptual objections. I would like to conclude, accordingly, by suggesting that it is well worth the effort to develop this approach in a form that can satisfactorily resolve the outstanding institutional and conceptual problems. Three considerations in particular are worth stressing.

First, by developing this approach we can make significant strides in overcoming the second dogma of egalitarianism. By articulating a plausible and attractive critical-democratic alternative, we can help dissolve the unjustified aura of self-evidence that currently insulates the normal-social-science approach to the "how" from critical reflection.

Second, by developing this approach we can deepen the connections between justice and democracy. At present our most robust egalitarian theories of postwestphalian justice proceed largely in isolation from democratic theory, while our most ambitious theories of postwestphalian democracy have yet to develop the strongly egalitarian conceptions of social justice that they require as a necessary complement. The critical-democratic approach to the "how" promises to connect these two bodies of political-theoretical reflection, while opposing the current *de facto* alliance of egalitarianism with technocracy, on the one hand, and that of democracy with nationalism, on the other.

Finally, and most importantly, unless we develop a defensible critical-democratic approach to the "how," we will never arrive at a defensible answer to the question of the "who." And that means we will still be in no position to answer the burning question of our day: How shall we frame questions of justice in a globalizing world?

4

Abnormal Justice

in memory of Richard Rorty,
an inspiration in more ways than one

In some contexts, public debates about justice assume the guise of normal discourse. However fiercely they disagree about what exactly justice requires in a given case, the contestants share some underlying presuppositions about what an intelligible justice claim looks like. These include ontological assumptions about the kind(s) of actors who are entitled to make such claims (usually, individuals) and about the kind of agency from which they should seek redress (typically, a territorial state). Also shared are assumptions about scope, which fix the circle of interlocutors to whom claims for justice should be addressed (usually, the citizenry of a bounded political community) and which delimit the universe of those whose interests and concerns deserve consideration (ditto). Finally, the disputants share social-theoretical assumptions about the space in which questions of justice can intelligibly arise (often, the economic space of distribution) and about the social cleavages that can harbor injustices (typically, class and ethnicity). In such contexts, where those who argue about justice share a set of underlying assumptions, their contests assume a relatively regular, recognizable shape. Constituted through a set of organizing principles, and manifesting a discernible grammar, such conflicts take the form of "normal justice."[1]

Of course, it is doubtful that justice discourse is ever fully normal in the sense just described. There may well be no real-world context in which public debates about justice remain wholly within the bounds set by a given set of constitutive assumptions. And we may never encounter a case in which every participant shares every assumption. Whenever a situation approaching normality *does* appear, moreover, one may well suspect that it rests on the suppression or marginalization of those who dissent from the reigning consensus.

Nevertheless, and notwithstanding these caveats, we may still speak of "normal justice" in a meaningful sense. By analogy with Thomas Kuhn's understanding of normal science, justice discourse is normal just so long as public dissent from, and disobedience to, its constitutive assumptions remains contained.[2] So long as deviations remain private or appear as anomalies, so long as they do not cumulate and destructure the discourse, then the field of public-sphere conflicts over justice retains a recognizable, hence a "normal," shape.

By this standard, the present context is one of "abnormal justice."[3] Even as public debates about justice proliferate, they increasingly lack the structured character of normal discourse. Today's disputants often lack any shared understanding of what the authors of justice claims should look like, as some countenance groups and communities, while others admit only individuals. Likewise, those who argue about justice today often share no view of the agency of redress, as some envision new transnational or cosmopolitan institutions, while others restrict their appeals to territorial states. Often, too, the disputants hold divergent views of the proper circle of interlocutors, as some address their claims to international public opinion, while others would confine discussion within bounded polities. In addition, present-day contestants often disagree about who is entitled to consideration in matters of justice, as some accord standing to all human beings, while others restrict concern to their fellow citizens. Then, too, they frequently disagree about the conceptual space within which claims for justice can arise, as some admit only (economic) claims for redistribution, while others would also admit (cultural) claims for recognition and (political) claims for representation. Finally, today's disputants often disagree as to which social cleavages can harbor injustices, as some admit only nationality and class, while others also accept gender and sexuality.

The result is that current debates about justice have a freewheeling character. Absent the ordering force of shared presuppositions, they lack the structured shape of normal discourse. This is patently true for informal contests over justice in civil society, where it has always been possible in principle to problematize *doxa* – witness the affair of the Danish cartoons of the Prophet Muhammad, which is better grasped as a species of abnormal discourse about justice than as a clash of civilizations, on the one hand, or as an exercise in liberal public reason, on the other. But abnormality also swirls around institutionalized arenas of argument, such as courts and arbitration bodies, whose principal *raison d'être* is to normalize justice – witness the dispute among the Justices of the US Supreme Court in a recent death penalty case over whether it is proper to cite opinions of foreign courts.[4] As such contests over basic premises proliferate, deviation becomes less the exception than the rule. Far from appearing in the guise of anomalies within a relatively stable field of argument, abnormality invades the central precincts of justice discourse. No sooner do first-order disputes arise than they become overlain with meta-disputes over constitutive assumptions, concerning who counts and what is at stake. Not only substantive questions, but also the grammar of justice itself is up for grabs.

This situation is by no means unprecedented. Even the most cursory reflection suggests some historical parallels. One prior era of abnormal justice in Europe is the period leading up to the Treaty of Westphalia, when the feudal political imaginary was unraveling, but the system of territorial states had not yet been consolidated.[5] Another is the period following World War I, when nascent internationalisms collided with resurgent nationalisms amidst the ruins of three major empires.[6] In those cases, absent a secure and settled hegemony, competing paradigms clashed, and efforts to normalize justice did not succeed. Such cases are scarcely exceptional. It is likely, in fact, that normal justice is historically abnormal, while abnormal justice represents the historical norm.

Nevertheless, today's abnormalities are historically specific, reflective of recent developments, including the break-up of the Cold War order, contested US hegemony, the rise of neo-liberalism, and the new salience of globalization. Under these conditions, established paradigms have tended to unsettle, and claims for justice have easily become unmoored from pre-existing islands of normalcy. This is the case for each of three major families of justice claims: claims for socioeconomic redistribution, claims for legal or cultural recognition, and claims for political representation. Thus, in the wake of transnationalized production, globalized finance, and neoliberal trade and investment regimes, redistribution claims increasingly trespass the bounds of state-centered grammars and arenas of argument. Likewise, given transnational migration and global media flows, the claims for recognition of once distant "others" acquire a new proximity, destabilizing horizons of cultural value that were previously taken for granted. Finally, in an era of contested superpower hegemony, global governance, and transnational politics, claims for representation increasingly break the previous frame of the modern territorial state. In this situation of de-normalization, justice claims immediately run up against counterclaims, whose underlying assumptions they do not share. Whether the issue is redistribution, recognition, or representation, current disputes evince a heteroglossia of justice discourse, which lacks any semblance of normality.

In this situation, our familiar theories of justice offer little guidance. Formulated for contexts of normal justice, they focus largely on first-order questions. What constitutes a just distribution of wealth and resources? What counts as reciprocal recognition or equal respect? What constitute fair terms of political representation and equal voice? Premised upon a shared grammar, these theories do not tell us how to proceed when we encounter conflicting assumptions concerning moral standing, social cleavage, and agency of redress. Thus, they fail to provide the conceptual resources for dealing with problems of abnormal justice, so characteristic of the present era.

What sort of theory of justice could provide guidance in this situation? What type of theorizing could handle cases in which first-order disputes about justice are overlain with meta-disputes about what counts as an intelligible first-order claim? In this chapter, I shall suggest a way of approaching questions of (in)justice in abnormal times. What I have to say divides into three parts. First, I shall identify three nodes of abnormality in contemporary disputes about justice. Then, I shall formulate three corresponding conceptual strategies for clarifying these abnormalities. Finally, I shall consider some implications for the theory and practice of struggles against injustice in abnormal times.

Nodes of abnormality in a globalizing world

I begin by sketching a recent dispute over social justice:

> *Claiming to promote justice for workers at home and abroad, labor unions in developed countries seek to block imports whose production conditions do not meet domestic environmental, health, and safety standards. Organizations representing workers in the developing world object that, in imposing standards they cannot possibly meet at the present time, this seemingly progressive approach is actually a species of unjust protectionism. Debated in both domestic and transnational public spheres, the first position finds support among those who advocate the pursuit of justice through democratic politics at the level of the territorial state, while the second is championed both by proponents of global justice and by free-marketeers. Meanwhile, corporations and states dispute related issues in international legal arenas. For example, a North American Free Trade Agreement arbitration panel hears arguments from a US-based multinational, which contends that Canada's relatively stringent environmental and labor laws constitute an illegal restraint on trade. The US representative on the three-judge panel finds for the corporation, on free-trade grounds. The Canadian representative finds against, invoking the self-government rights of the Canadian citizenry. The Mexican representative casts the deciding vote: finding for the corporation, and thus siding with the United States, he invokes poor nations' right to development. At the same time, however, the legitimacy of these proceedings is disputed. In transnational civil society, demonstrators protest against NAFTA, the World Trade Organization, and other governance structures of the global economy. Pronouncing these structures unjust and undemocratic, activists meeting at the World Social Forum debate the contours of an alternative "globalization from below."*

This is an example of "abnormal justice." Traversing multiple discursive arenas, some formal, some informal, some mainstream, some subaltern, the locus of argument shifts with dizzying speed. And far from going without saying, the topography of debate is itself an object of dispute. Offshore contestants strive to pierce the bounds of domestic debates, even as nationalists and country-level democrats seek to territorialize them. Meanwhile, states and corporations work to contain disputes within regional juridical institutions, even as transnational social movements strain to widen them. Thus, the very shape of controversy, uncontested in normal discourse, is here a focus of explicit struggle. Even as they dispute substantive issues, then, the contestants also rehearse deep disagreements about who is entitled to address claims to whom concerning what; about where and how such claims should be vetted; and about who is obliged to redress them, if and when they are vindicated.

The abnormalities are not wholly random, however, as they constellate around three principal nodes. The first node reflects the absence of a shared view of the "what" of justice. At issue here is the matter of justice, the substance with which it is concerned. Given that justice is a comparative relation, what is it that justice compares? What social-ontological presuppositions distinguish well-formed from ill-formed claims? Such matters go without saying in normal justice – as, for example, when all parties conceive justice in distributive terms, as concerned with the allocation of divisible goods, which are typically economic in nature. In abnormal contexts, by contrast, the "what" of justice is in dispute. Here we encounter claims that do not share a common ontology. Where one party perceives distributive injustice, another sees status hierarchy, and still another political domination.[7] Thus, even those who agree that the status quo is unjust disagree as to how to describe it.

Divergent assumptions concerning the "what" suffuse the example just sketched. There, offshore workers' economic claims, aimed at dismantling protectionist barriers, which maintain distributive injustice, collide with a territorial citizenry's political claims, aimed at repulsing neoliberal encroachments, which imperil the democratic sovereignty of a bounded polity. The effect is a bewildering lack of consensus, even among professed democrats and egalitarians, as to how to understand the injustice, let alone how to redress it. The very "what" of justice is up for grabs.

A second node of abnormality reflects the lack of a shared understanding of the "who" of justice. At issue here is the scope of justice, the frame within which it applies: *Who* counts as a subject of justice in a given matter? Whose interests and needs deserve consideration? Who belongs to the circle of those entitled to equal concern? Such matters go without saying in normal justice – as, for example, when all parties frame their disputes as matters internal to territorial states, thereby equating the "who" of justice with the citizenry of a bounded polity. In abnormal justice, by contrast, the "who" is up for grabs. Here we encounter conflicting framings of justice disputes. Where one party frames the question in terms of a domestic, territorial "who," others posit "who's" that are regional, transnational, or global.[8]

Divergent assumptions about these matters, too, pervade the example just sketched, which encompasses conflicting frames. There, some of the disputants evaluate Canadian labor regulations in terms of their domestic effects, while others consider the effects on the larger North American region, and still others look further afield, to the interests of workers in the developing world or of global humanity. The result is a lack of consensus as to "who" counts. Not just the "what" of justice but also the "who" is in dispute.

The third node of abnormality reflects the lack of a shared understanding of the "how" of justice. Here the issue is in essence procedural: *How*, in a given case, should one determine the pertinent grammar for reflecting on justice? By which criteria or decision procedure should one resolve disputes about the "what" and the "who"? In normal justice, such questions do not arise by definition, as the "what" and the "who" are not in dispute. In abnormal contexts, by contrast, with both those parameters up for grabs, disagreements about the "how" are bound to erupt. Here we encounter conflicting scenarios for resolving disputes. Where one party invokes the authority of an interstate treaty, others appeal to the United Nations, the balance of power, or the institutionalized procedures of a cosmopolitan democracy that remains to be invented.[9]

Uncertainty about the "how" suffuses the argument just sketched. There, states and corporations look to NAFTA for resolution, while anti-neoliberalism activists look instead to transnational popular struggle aimed at influencing global public opinion. Whereas the former appeal to a treaty-based regional arena of dispute resolution, the latter appeal to a "World Social Forum" that lacks institutionalized authority to make and enforce binding decisions. Here, then, there is no agreement as to how disputes about the grammar of justice should be resolved. Not just the "what" and the "who," but also the "how" of justice is up for grabs.

Together, these three nodes of abnormality reflect the destabilization of the previous hegemonic grammar. Today's uncertainty about the "what" reflects the decentering of that grammar's definition of the substance of justice. What has been problematized here is the view that identifies justice exclusively with fair economic distribution. That understanding organized the lion's share of argument in the decades following World War II. Subtending the otherwise disparate political cultures of first-world social democracy, second-world communism, and third-world "developmentalism," the distributive interpretation of the "what" tended to marginalize non-economic wrongs. Casting maldistribution as the quintessential injustice, it obscured injustices of misrecognition, rooted in hierarchies of status, as well as injustices of misrepresentation, rooted in the political constitution of society.[10]

Analogously, today's uncertainty about the "who" reflects the destabilization of the previous grammar's frame. In this case, what has been problematized is the Westphalian view that the modern territorial state is the sole unit within which justice applies. That view framed most justice discourse in the postwar era. In conjunction with the distributive conception, it organized otherwise disparate political cultures throughout the world, notwithstanding lip service to human rights, proletarian internationalism, and third-world solidarity.[11] Effectively territorializing justice, the Westphalian frame equated the scope of concern with the citizenry of a bounded political community. The effect was to drastically limit, if not wholly to exclude, binding obligations of justice that cut across borders. Constructing a set of territorially bounded domestic "who's," discrete and arrayed side-by-side, this frame obscured transborder injustices.[12]

Finally, today's uncertainty concerning the "how" reflects the new salience of a previously unspoken feature of the postwar grammar. What has become visible, and therefore contestable, is a hidden hegemonic assumption. So long as the lion's share of justice discourse was governed by Westphalian-distributivist assumptions, there was little overtly perceived

need for institutions and procedures for resolving disputes
about the "what" and the "who." On those occasions when such
a need *was* perceived, it was assumed that powerful states and
private elites would resolve those disputes, in intergovernmental organizations or smoke-filled back rooms. The effect was
to discourage open democratic contestation of the "what" and
the "who."

Today, however, none of these three normalizing assumptions goes without saying. The hegemony of the distributive
"what" has been challenged from at least two sides: first, by
diverse practitioners of the politics of recognition, ranging
from multiculturalists who seek to accommodate differences
to ethno-nationalists who seek to eliminate them; and, second,
by diverse practitioners of the politics of representation, ranging
from feminists campaigning for gender quotas on electoral lists
to national minorities demanding power-sharing arrangements.
As a result, there are now in play at least three rival conceptions of the "what" of justice: redistribution, recognition, and
representation.

Meanwhile, the hegemony of the Westphalian "who" has
been challenged from at least three directions: first, by localists
and communalists, who seek to locate the scope of concern in
subnational units; second, by regionalists and transnationalists,
who propose to identify the "who" of justice with larger, though
not fully universal, units, such as "Europe" or "Islam"; and,
third, by globalists and cosmopolitans, who propose to accord
equal consideration to all human beings. Consequently, there
are now in play at least four rival views of the "who" of justice:
Westphalian, local-communalist, transnational-regional, and
global-cosmopolitan.

Finally, the silent sway of the hegemonic "how" has been
challenged by a general rise in democratic expectations, as
mobilized movements of all these kinds demand a say about
the "what" and the "who." Contesting hegemonic institutions
and frames, such movements have effectively challenged the
prerogative of states and elites to determine the grammar of
justice. Inciting broad debates about the "what" and the "who,"
they have put in play, alongside the hegemonic presumption,
populist and democratic views of the "how" of justice.

The appearance of rival views of the "what," the "who," and
the "how" poses a major problem for anyone who cares about

injustice today. Somehow, we must work through these meta-disputes without losing sight of pressing problems of first-order justice. But with all three parameters in play simultaneously, we have no firm ground on which to stand. Abnormality confronts us at every turn.

Strategies for theorizing justice in abnormal times

What sort of theory of justice could provide guidance in this situation? To find a convincing answer, one must start with a balanced view of the matter at hand. The key, I think, is to appreciate both the positive and negative sides of abnormal justice. The positive side is an expansion of the field of contestation, hence the chance to challenge injustices that the previous grammar elided. For example, the decentering of the distributive "what" renders visible, and criticizable, non-economic harms of misrecognition and misrepresentation. Likewise, the de-normalization of the Westphalian "who" makes conceivable a hitherto obscure type of meta-injustice, call it "misframing," in which first-order questions of justice are unjustly framed – as when the national framing of distributive issues forecloses the claims of the global poor.[13] If we assume, as I think we should, that misrecognition, misrepresentation, and misframing belong in principle in the catalogue of genuine injustices, then the destabilization of a grammar that obscured them must rank as a positive development. Here, then, is the good side of abnormal justice: expanded possibilities for contesting injustice.

But abnormal justice also has a negative side. The problem is that expanded contestation cannot by itself overcome injustice. Overcoming injustice requires at least two additional conditions: first, a relatively stable framework in which claims can be equitably vetted; and, second, institutionalized agencies and means of redress. Both these conditions are absent in abnormal justice. How can demands be fairly evaluated and injustices be legitimately rectified in contexts in which the "what," the "who," and the "how" are in dispute? Here, then, is the negative side of abnormal justice: amidst expanded contestation, reduced means for corroborating and redressing injustice.

Those who would theorize justice in abnormal times must keep both sides of this equation in view. What sort of theorizing could simultaneously valorize expanded contestation and strengthen diminished capacities of adjudication and redress? Without pretending to present a full answer, I propose to hunt for clues by re-examining the three nodes of abnormality just described. Considered in turn, each can tell us something important about how to think about justice in abnormal times.

The "what" of justice: participatory parity in three dimensions

Consider, first, the problem of the "what." Here, the question is: What sort of approach can validate contestation of reductive distributivism while also clarifying prospects for resolving disputes that encompass rival understandings of the matter of justice? The short answer is: an approach that combines a multidimensional social ontology with normative monism. Let me explain.

In order to validate expanded contestation, a theory of justice must hold out the prospect of a fair hearing for disputants' claims. If it is to avoid foreclosing demands in advance, the theory must be able to entertain claims that presuppose non-standard views of the "what" of justice. Erring on the side of inclusiveness, then, it should begin by assuming that injustice comes in more than one form and that no single view of the "what" can capture them all. Rejecting social-ontological monism, it should conceive justice as encompassing multiple dimensions, each of which is associated with an analytically distinct genre of injustice and revealed through a conceptually distinct type of social struggle.

Consider three possibilities I have already alluded to. As seen, first, from the standpoint of labor struggles, justice comprises an economic dimension, rooted in political economy, whose associated injustice is *maldistribution* or class inequality. As seen, second, from the perspective of struggles over multiculturalism, justice encompasses a cultural dimension, rooted in the status order, whose corresponding injustice is *misrecognition* or status hierarchy. As seen, finally, through the lens of democratization struggles, justice includes a political dimension, rooted in the political constitution of society, whose associated injustice is *misrepresentation* or political voicelessness.

Here, then, are three different views of the "what" of justice. Insofar as each of them corresponds to a bonafide form of injustice that cannot be reduced to the others, none can be legitimately excluded from contemporary theorizing. Thus, ontological monism with respect to injustice is deeply misguided.[14] Contra those who insist on a single monistic account of the "what," justice is better viewed as a multidimensional concept that encompasses the three dimensions of *redistribution, recognition,* and *representation.*[15] Such a conception is especially useful in abnormal times. Only by assuming at the outset that claims in all three dimensions are in principle intelligible can one provide a fair hearing to all claimants in disputes that harbor multiple views of the "what."

But why only three? The examples just given suggest that, rather than being given all at once, the dimensions of justice are disclosed historically, through the medium of social struggle. On this view, social movements disclose new dimensions of justice when they succeed in establishing as plausible claims that transgress the established grammar of normal justice, which will appear retrospectively to have obscured the disadvantage their members suffer. But in the moment before a novel understanding of the "what" becomes broadly intelligible, the irruption of transgressive claims sparks abnormal discourse.[16] At such times, it remains unclear whether a new dimension of justice is being disclosed. It follows that any attempt to theorize justice in these conditions must allow for that possibility. Whoever dogmatically forecloses the prospect declares his or her thinking inadequate to the times.

What follows for a theory of justice for abnormal times? At the outset, one should practice hermeneutical charity with respect to claimants' non-standard views of the "what," according them the presumption of intelligibility and potential validity. At the same time, the theory should test such views by considering whether they do in fact render visible genuine forms of injustice that the previous grammar foreclosed; and if so, whether these newly disclosed forms are rooted in hitherto overlooked dimensions of social ordering.[17] In today's context, this means accepting as well-formed and intelligible in principle claims premised on at least three distinct views of the "what" of justice: namely, redistribution, recognition and representation.[18] Provisionally embracing a three-dimensional view of justice, centered on economy, culture, and politics, the theory should nevertheless remain open to the disclosure of further dimensions through social struggle.

By itself, however, a multidimensional social ontology is not a solution. As soon as we admit multiple genres of injustice, we need a way to bring them under a common measure. Thus, we need a normative principle that overarches them all. Absent such a commensurating principle, we have no way to evaluate claims across different dimensions, hence no way to process disputes that encompass multiple views of the "what."

What might such a principle look like? My proposal is to submit claims in all three dimensions to the overarching normative principle of *parity of participation*. According to this principle, justice requires social arrangements that permit all to participate as peers in social life.[19] On the view of justice as participatory parity, overcoming injustice means dismantling institutionalized obstacles that prevent some people from participating on a par with others, as full partners in social interaction. As the foregoing discussion suggests, such obstacles can be of at least three types. First, people can be impeded from full participation by economic structures that deny them the resources they need in order to interact with others as peers; in that case they suffer from distributive injustice or maldistribution. Second, people can be prevented from interacting on terms of parity by institutionalized hierarchies of cultural value that deny them the requisite standing; in that case they suffer from status inequality or misrecognition.[20] Third, people can be impeded from full participation by decision rules that deny them equal voice in public deliberations and democratic decision-making; in that case they suffer from political injustice or misrepresentation.[21]

Here, then, is an account in which three different types of injustice lead to a common result: in each case, some social actors are prevented from participating on a par with others in social interaction.[22] Thus, all three injustices violate a single principle, the principle of participatory parity. That principle overarches the three dimensions and serves to make them commensurable.[23]

The exact details of this account are less important than its overall conceptual structure. What is paramount here is that this view of the "what" of justice combines a multidimensional social ontology with normative monism. As a result, it reckons with both sides of abnormal justice, the negative as well as the positive. Thanks to its ontological multidimensionality, it validates contestation of normalizing distributivism. Stipulating that misrecognition and misrepresentation are genuine injustices in principle, it provides a fair hearing for claims that transgress the previous grammar. At the same time, thanks to its normative monism, this approach brings the three genres of injustice under a common measure. Submitting claims for redistribution, recognition, and representation to the overarching principle of participatory parity, it creates a single discursive space that can accommodate them all. Thus, this approach offers the prospect of evaluating claims under conditions of abnormal discourse, where multiple views of the "what" of justice are in play.

And yet: a major question remains. Parity of participation *among whom? Who* exactly is entitled to participate on a par *with whom* in *which* social interactions? Unless we can find a suitable way of addressing the "who" of justice, this approach to the "what" will not be of any use.

The "who" of justice: misframing and subjection

I turn, accordingly, to the second node of abnormal justice, concerning the "who." For this issue, too, the pressing need is to reckon with both the positive and negative sides of abnormal justice. What sort of theorizing can valorize contestation of the Westphalian frame, while also clarifying disputes that encompass conflicting views about who counts? The short answer is: theorizing that is simultaneously reflexive and determinative. Let me explain.

In order to valorize expanded contestation, reflection on abnormal justice must be open to claims that first-order questions of justice have been wrongly framed. To ensure that such claims receive a fair hearing, one should assume at the outset that injustices of misframing could exist in principle. Thus, the theorizing of abnormal justice must be reflexive. In order to apply the principle of participatory parity to first-order questions of distribution, recognition, and representation, one must be able to jump to the next level, where the frame itself is in dispute. Only by becoming reflexive can one grasp the question of the "who" *as* a question of justice.

How can one generate the reflexivity needed in abnormal justice? The strategy I propose draws on a distinctive conception of the political dimension. So far, I have considered this dimension in the usual way, as concerned exclusively with injustices of "ordinary-political misrepresentation." These are political injustices that arise within a political community whose boundaries and membership are widely assumed to be settled. Thus, ordinary-political misrepresentation occurs when a polity's rules for decision-making deny some who are counted in principle as members the chance to participate fully, as peers. Recently, such injustices have given rise to demands for changes in the mode of ordinary-political representation – ranging from demands for gender quotas on electoral lists, multicultural rights, indigenous self-government, and provincial autonomy, on the one hand, to demands for campaign finance reform, redistricting, proportional representation, and cumulative voting, on the other.[24]

Important as such matters are, they make up only half the story. In addition to ordinary-political injustice, which arises *within* the frame of a bounded polity, we can also conceptualize another level, call it "meta-political injustice," which arises as a result of the division of political space *into* bounded polities. This second level comprehends injustices of *misframing*. Such injustices occur when a polity's boundaries are drawn in such a way as to wrongly deny some people the chance to participate *at all* in its authorized contests over justice. In such cases, those who are constituted as non-members are wrongly excluded from the universe of those entitled to consideration within the polity in matters of distribution, recognition, and ordinary-political representation. The injustice remains, moreover, even when those excluded from one polity are included as subjects of justice in another – as long as the effect of the political division is to put some relevant aspects of justice beyond their reach. An example is the way in which the international system of supposedly equal sovereign states gerrymanders political space at the expense of the global poor.

Although they do not use the term, the notion of misframing implicitly informs the claims of many "alternative globalization" activists, associated with the World Social Forum. In their eyes, the Westphalian frame is unjust, as it prevents the global poor from challenging perpetrators of transborder injustices. Shunting their claims into the domestic political arenas of weak or failed states, this frame effectively immunizes extra-domestic malefactors, be they more powerful marauding states, foreign investors and creditors, international currency speculators, and/or transnational corporations.[25] Equally important, it precludes challenge to the background structures that enable foreign predation: above all, the exploitative governance structures of the global economy and the undemocratic design of the interstate system.[26]

Such, at any rate, are the claims of some World Social Forum activists. Their concerns pertain to our second level of justice, the meta-political level, which encompasses wrongs of misframing. Oriented to the possibility that first-order framings of justice may themselves be unjust, this level grasps the question of the frame *as* a question of justice. As a result, it provides the reflexivity needed to parse disputes about the "who" in abnormal justice.

By itself, however, reflexivity is not a solution. As soon as we accept that injustices of misframing can exist in principle, we require some means of deciding when and where they exist in reality. Thus, a theory of justice for abnormal times requires a determinative normative principle for evaluating frames. Absent such a determinative principle, we have no way to assess the alternatives, hence no way to clarify disputes that encompass conflicting understandings of the "who."

What might a determinative principle for evaluating frames look like? Currently, there are three major candidates on offer. Proponents of the *membership principle* propose to resolve disputes concerning the "who" by appealing to criteria of political belonging. For them, accordingly, what turns a collection of individuals into fellow subjects of justice is shared citizenship or shared nationality.[27] Because this approach delimits frames on the basis of political membership, it has the advantage of being grounded in existing institutional reality and/or in widely held collective identifications. Yet that strength is also its weakness. In practice, the membership principle serves all too easily to ratify the exclusionary nationalisms of the privileged and powerful – hence, to shield established frames from critical scrutiny.

No wonder, then, that some philosophers and activists look instead to the *principle of humanism*. Seeking a more inclusive standard, they propose to resolve disputes concerning the "who" by appealing to criteria of personhood. For them, accordingly, what turns a collection of individuals into fellow subjects of justice is common possession of distinguishing features of humanity, such as autonomy, rationality, language use, capacity to form and pursue an idea of the good, or vulnerability to moral injury.[28] Because this approach delimits frames on the basis of personhood, it provides a critical check on exclusionary nationalism. Yet its lofty abstraction is also its weakness. Cavalierly oblivious to actual or historical social relations, it accords standing indiscriminately to everyone in respect to everything. Adopting the one-size-fits-all frame of global humanity, it forecloses the possibility that different issues require different frames or scales of justice.

Understandably, then, yet another group of philosophers and activists rejects both the exclusionary nationalism of membership and the abstract globalism of humanism. Aiming to conceptualize *transnational* justice, proponents of the *all-affected principle* propose to resolve disputes about the "who" by appealing to social relations of interdependence. For them, accordingly, what makes a group of people fellow subjects of justice is their objective co-imbrication in a web of causal relationships.[29] This approach has the merit of providing a critical check on self-serving notions of membership, while also taking cognizance of social relations. Yet, by conceiving relations objectivistically, in terms of causality, it effectively relegates the choice of the "who" to mainstream social science. In addition, the all-affected principle falls prey to the *reductio ad absurdum* of the butterfly effect, which holds that everyone is affected by everything. Unable to identify *morally relevant* social relations, it has trouble resisting the one-size-fits-all globalism it sought to avoid. Thus, it, too, fails to supply a defensible standard for determining the "who" in abnormal times.

Given the respective deficiencies of membership, humanism, and affectedness, what sort of determinative principle can help us evaluate rival frames in abnormal justice? I propose to submit allegations of misframing to what I shall call the *all-subjected principle*. According to this principle, all those who are subject to a given governance structure have moral standing as subjects of justice in relation to it. On this view, what turns a collection of people into fellow subjects of justice is neither shared citizenship or nationality, nor common possession of abstract personhood, nor the sheer fact of causal interdependence, but rather their joint subjection to a structure of governance that sets the ground rules that govern their interaction. For any such governance structure, the all-subjected principle matches the scope of moral concern to that of subjection.[30]

Of course, everything depends on how we interpret the phrase "subjection to structure of governance." I understand this expression broadly, as encompassing relations to powers of various types. Not restricted to states, governance structures also comprise non-state agencies that generate enforceable rules that structure important swaths of social interaction. The most obvious examples are the agencies that set the ground rules of the global economy, such as the World Trade Organization and the International Monetary Fund. But many other examples could also be cited, including transnational agencies governing environmental regulation, atomic and nuclear power, policing, security, health, intellectual property, and the administration of civil and criminal law. Insofar as such agencies regulate the interaction of large transnational populations, they can be said to subject the latter, even though the rule-makers are not accountable to those whom they govern. Given this broad understanding of governance structures, the term "subjection" should be understood broadly as well. Not restricted to formal citizenship, or even to the broader condition of falling within the jurisdiction of such a state, this notion also encompasses the further condition of being subject to the coercive power of non-state and trans-state forms of governmentality.

Understood in this way, the all-subjected principle affords a critical standard for assessing the (in)justice of frames. An issue is justly framed if and only if everyone subjected to the governance structure(s) that regulate the relevant swath(s) of social interaction is accorded equal consideration. To deserve such consideration, moreover, one need not already be an officially accredited member of the structure in question; one need only be subjected to it. Thus, sub-Saharan Africans who have been involuntarily disconnected from the global economy as a result of the rules imposed by its governance structures count as subjects of justice in relation to it, even if they are not officially recognized as participating in it.[31]

The all-subjected principle remedies the major defects of the previous principles. Unlike membership, it pierces the self-serving shield of exclusionary nationalism so as to contemplate injustices of misframing. Unlike humanism, it overcomes abstract, all-embracing globalism by taking notice of social relationships. Unlike affectedness, it avoids the indiscriminateness of the butterfly effect by identifying the morally relevant type of social relation, namely, joint subjection to a governance structure. Far from substituting a single global "who" for the Westphalian "who," the all-subjected principle militates against any one-size-fits-all framing of justice. In today's world, all of us are subject to a plurality of different governance structures, some local, some national, some regional, and some global. The need, accordingly, is to delimit a variety of different frames for different issues. Able to mark out a plurality of "who's" for different purposes, the all-subjected principle tells us when and where to apply which frame – and, thus, who is entitled to parity of participation with whom in a given case.

For this proposal, too, however, the details are less important than the overall conceptual structure. What is crucial here is that this approach combines the reflexive questioning of justice frames with a determinative evaluative principle. In this way, it pays heed to both sides of abnormal justice, the negative as well as the positive. Thanks to its reflexivity, the concept of misframing validates contestation of the Westphalian frame. Because it is pitched to the meta-level, this concept permits us to entertain the possibility that first-order questions of justice have been unjustly framed. At the same time, thanks to its determinative character, this approach offers a way of assessing the justice of various "who's." By submitting proposed frames to the all-subjected principle, it enables us to weigh their relative merits. Thus, this approach holds considerable promise for clarifying disputes about the "who" in abnormal times.

And yet: another major question remains: *How* exactly ought we to implement the all-subjected principle? By way of what procedures and processes can that principle be applied to resolve disputes about who counts in abnormal times? Unless we can find a suitable way of addressing the "how" of justice, this approach to the "who" will not be of any use.

The "how" of justice: institutionalizing meta-democracy

This brings me, finally, to the problem of the "how." For this issue, too, the trick is to reckon with both the positive and negative sides of abnormal justice. What sort of justice theorizing can valorize expanded contestation, while also clarifying disputes in which there is no shared understanding of the "how" of justice? The short answer is: theorizing that is at once dialogical and institutional. Let me elaborate.

In order to valorize expanded contestation, a theory of justice for abnormal times must abjure two approaches that have already surfaced in the previous considerations. First, it must suspend the hegemonic presumption that powerful states and private elites should determine the grammar of justice. As we saw, this view went without saying in normal justice, when disputes about the "who" were sufficiently rare and restricted to be settled in smoke-filled back rooms. Today, however, as social movements contest the Westphalian frame, they are challenging such prerogatives – by the mere fact of treating the question of the frame as a proper subject of broad public debate. Asserting their right to a say in determining the "who," they are simultaneously problematizing the hegemonic "how." Above and beyond their other demands, then, these movements are effectively demanding something more: the creation of new, non-hegemonic procedures for handling disputes about the framing of justice in abnormal times. This demand, too, deserves a fair hearing. In order to avoid foreclosing it in advance, a theory of justice for times such as these must entertain non-standard views of the "how."

Second, a theory of justice for abnormal times must reject what I shall call "the scientistic presumption." Presupposed by some proponents of the all-affected principle, this understanding of the "how" of justice holds that decisions about the frame should be determined by normal social science, which is presumed to possess uncontroversial facts concerning who is affected by what, and thus who deserves consideration in respect of which issues. In abnormal justice, however, disputes about the frame are not reducible to simple questions of empirical fact, as the historical interpretations, social theories, and normative assumptions that necessarily underlie factual claims are themselves in dispute.[32] Under conditions of *in*justice, moreover, what passes in the mainstream for social "science" may well reflect the perspectives, and entrench the blindspots, of the privileged. In these conditions, to adopt the scientistic presumption is to risk foreclosing the claims of the disadvantaged. Thus, a theory committed to expanded contestation must reject this presumption. Without denying the relevance of social knowledge, it must refuse any suggestion that disputes about the "who" be settled by "justice technocrats."[33]

What other possibilities remain? Despite the differences between them, the hegemonic presumption and the scientistic presumption share a common premise. Both propose to settle framing disputes monologically, by appeal to an authority (in one case power, in the other case science) that is not accountable to the discursive give-and-take of political debate. A theory of justice for abnormal times must reject this monological premise. To validate contestation, it must treat framing disputes *dialogically*, as political conflicts whose legitimate resolution requires unconstrained, inclusive public discussion. Rejecting appeals to authority, abnormal justice theorizing must envision a dialogical process for applying the all-subjected principle to disputes about the "who."

Thus, a theory of justice for abnormal times must be dialogical. By itself, however, dialogue is not a solution. As soon as we accept that conflicts concerning the frame must be handled discursively, we need to envision a way in which public debates concerning the "who" could eventuate in binding resolutions. Absent an account of the relation between contestation and legitimate decision-making, we have no way to implement the all-subjected principle, hence no way to process disputes in abnormal justice.

How should one conceive this relation? One approach, call it "populism," would situate the nexus of contest and decision in civil society. Thus, this approach would assign the task of applying the all-subjected principle to social movements or discursive arenas like the World Social Forum.[34] Although it appears to fulfill the dialogism requirement, populism is nevertheless unsatisfactory, for at least two reasons. First, even the best civil society formations are neither sufficiently representative nor sufficiently democratic to legitimate their proposals to reframe justice. Second, these formations lack the capacity to convert their proposals into binding political decisions. Put differently, although they can introduce novel claims into public debate, by themselves civil society actors can neither *warrant claims* nor *make binding decisions.*

These limitations suggest the need for a second track of the dialogical process, a formal institutional track. This second track should stand in a dynamic interactive relation to the first track. Conceived as one pole of a two-way communicative process, the formal institutional track must be responsive to the civil-society track.[35] But it should differ from the latter in two respects. First, the institutional track requires fair procedures and a representative structure to ensure the democratic legitimacy of its deliberations. Second, the representatives, while accountable via publicity and elections, must have the capacity to make binding decisions about the "who" that reflect their communicatively generated judgment as to who is in fact subjected to a given structure of governance.

The upshot is that abnormal justice requires the invention of new global democratic institutions where disputes about framing can be aired and resolved. Assuming that such disputes will not go away anytime soon, and may not be susceptible to any definitive, final resolution, the approach I propose views them as an enduring feature of political life in a globalizing world. Thus, it advocates new institutions for staging and provisionally resolving such disputes democratically, in permanent dialogue with transnational civil society.

Certainly, much more needs to be said about the design and workings of such arrangements. But for the purposes of my argument here, the details are less important than the overall conceptual structure of the proposal. What is paramount here is that this view of the "how" of justice combines dialogical and institutional features. As a result, it pays heed to both sides of abnormal justice, the negative as well as the positive. Thanks to its dialogism, it validates contestation of previously taken-for-granted parameters of justice. Rejecting monologism, it seeks a fair hearing for claims that hegemonism and scientism foreclose. At the same time, thanks to its two-track character, it overcomes the legitimacy and decisional deficits of populism. Submitting meta-claims for the reframing of justice to a process of two-way communication between civil society and new global representative institutions, it envisions procedures for implementing the all-subjected principle in contexts of disagreement about the "who." Thus, this approach holds out the prospect of provisionally resolving conflicts over framing in abnormal justice.

But that is not all. By providing a means to sort out meta-problems, this proposal clears a path to the pressing first-order problems with which we began. Coming to terms with injustices of misframing, it simultaneously opens the way to tackling injustices of maldistribution, misrecognition, and misrepresentation. Thus, this approach enables us to envision political scenarios for overcoming or reducing injustice in abnormal times.

It is with the aim of fostering that end that I have devised the argument of this section. I have argued here that a theory of justice suited to conditions of abnormal discourse should combine three features. First, such a theory should encompass an account of the "what" of justice that is multidimensional in social ontology and normatively monist – for example, an account that submits claims for redistribution, recognition, and ordinary-political representation to the principle of participatory parity. Second, such a theory should encompass a view of the "who" that is simultaneously reflexive and determinative – for example, a view that submits claims against injustices of misframing to the all-subjected principle. Finally, a theory of justice for abnormal times should encompass a view of the "how" that is simultaneously dialogical and institutional – for example, a view that envisions new global representative institutions where meta-political claims can be submitted to deliberative-democratic decision procedures.

More important than these specifics, however, is the general problem I have outlined here. Under conditions of abnormal justice, previously taken-for-granted assumptions about the "what," the "who," and the "how" no longer go without saying. Thus, these assumptions must themselves be subject to critical discussion and re-evaluation. In such discussions, the trick is to avoid two things. On the one hand, one must resist the reactionary and ultimately futile temptation to cling to assumptions that are no longer appropriate to our globalizing world, such as reductive distributivism and *passé* Westphalianism. On the other hand, one should avoid celebrating abnormality for its own sake, as if contestation were itself liberation. In this section, I have tried to model an alternative stance, which acknowledges abnormal justice as the horizon within which all struggles against injustice must currently proceed. Only by appreciating both the perils and prospects of this condition can we hope to reduce the vast injustices that now pervade our world.

A new normal? On reflexivity, agonism, and hegemony

Before closing, I want to consider some of the conceptual and political implications of my overall argument. To this point, my discussion has encompassed two heterogeneous parts, one diagnostic, the other reconstructive. In the first, diagnostic, section, I characterized the present as an era of abnormal justice, in which the basic parameters of political contestation are up for grabs; identifying three distinct nodes of abnormality, I mapped the contours of a (Westphalian-distributivist) discursive formation in the throes of de-normalization. In the second, reconstructive, section, I proposed three corresponding strategies for reflecting on justice in abnormal times; noting that our familiar theories of justice presuppose conditions of normal discourse, I sought to develop alternative models of theorizing better suited to contexts in which there is no agreement as to the "what," the "who," and the "how" of justice. Given the heterogeneity of these two parts of my argument, a question arises as to the relation between them. What conceptual logic and political aspiration links my *Zeitdiagnose* of the present conjuncture with my attempts at theoretical reconstruction?[36]

Two possibilities suggest themselves. On one reading, the negative features of abnormal justice are sufficiently disabling of struggles against injustice to warrant efforts aimed at renormalization. This view stresses the impossibility of emancipatory change in the absence of a relatively stable framework

for vetting and redressing claims. Given that premise, the goal
should be to reconstruct such a framework for the current
conjuncture. The result, were things to go well, would be a
new paradigm of normal discourse about justice, premised on
new interpretations of the "what," the "who," and the "how,"
more appropriate to a globalizing world. On this reading,
therefore, my specific proposals would be aimed at constructing such a paradigm. The point of the overall exercise would
be to develop a "new normal."

Certainly, one could do a lot worse than devise a new normal
able to reframe justice conflicts in forms suited to a globalizing
world. Yet there are reasons to doubt that such an approach
could be fully adequate to the present situation. For one thing,
re-normalization risks prematurely closing down new avenues
of contestation, before they have had a fair shot at establishing
their plausibility. For another, it risks instating a new, restrictive
predefinition of what counts as an intelligible claim for justice,
thereby entrenching new exclusions. Finally, the proposal to
establish a "new normal" risks enshrining a fixed set of justice
assumptions at a historical juncture when the circumstances of
justice are in flux and demand flexibility. For all these reasons,
it is worth considering another reading of the overall argument
presented here.

The second reading I have in mind envisions an outcome
that unsettles the distinction between normal and abnormal
justice. Underlining the respective shortcomings of each of
those genres of discourse, this reading seeks an alternative
model that avoids their defects, while incorporating the best
features of each. Unlike abnormal discourse, the desired model
would have sufficient structuring capacities to stage today's
justice struggles as *arguments*, in which the parties *confront* one
another, compelling the attention and *judgment* of those looking
on. Unlike normal discourse, however, the hoped-for model
would have sufficient self-problematizing capacities to entertain novel claims about the "what," the "who," and the "how."
Combining features of normal and abnormal discourse, the
result would be a grammar of justice that incorporates an orientation to closure, necessary for political argument, but that
treats every closure as *provisional* – subject to question, possible
suspension, and thus to reopening. Cultivating responsiveness
to emergent exclusions, such a model would feature concepts,

such as *misframing*, that invite reflexive self-problematization, with the aim of disclosing injustices that were previously occluded. On this reading, the point of the overall exercise would be neither to revel in abnormality nor to rush to instate a new normal. The point, rather, would be to develop a third genre of discourse that we might call *reflexive justice*.

The idea of reflexive justice is well suited to the present context of abnormal discourse. In this context, disputes about the "what," the "who," and the "how" are unlikely to be settled soon. Thus, it makes sense to regard these three nodes of abnormality as persistent features of justice discourse for the foreseeable future. On the other hand, given the magnitude of first-order injustice in today's world, the worst conceivable response would be to treat ongoing meta-disputes as a license for paralysis. Thus, it is imperative not to allow discursive abnormalities to defer or dissipate efforts to remedy injustice. The expression "reflexive justice" expresses that dual commitment, signaling a genre of theorizing that works at two levels at once: entertaining urgent claims on behalf of the disadvantaged, while also parsing the meta-disagreements that are interlaced with them. Because these two levels are inextricably entangled in abnormal times, reflexive justice theorizing cannot ignore either one of them. Working at their intersection, and tacking back and forth between them, such theorizing mobilizes the corrective capacities of each to mitigate the defects of the other. In this way, it scrambles the distinction between normal and abnormal discourse.[37]

For these reasons, I prefer to understand the *telos* of my overall argument not as a new normal, but as a species of reflexive justice.[38] That reading has two additional implications that are worth considering. The first concerns the well-known opposition in political philosophy between discourse-ethical approaches, on the one hand, and agonistic approaches, on the other. Rightly or wrongly, the first are sometimes portrayed as objectionably normalizing, while the second are often seen as irresponsibly reveling in abnormality.[39] Without pretending to assess the merits of these charges and counter-charges, I propose that the idea of reflexive justice scrambles this opposition as well. Like agonistic models, reflexive justice valorizes the moment of opening, which breaches the exclusions of normal justice, embracing claimants the latter has silenced, and disclosing injustices the latter has occluded – all of which it holds essential for contesting injustice. Like discourse ethics, however, reflexive justice also valorizes the moment of closure, which enables political argument, collective decision-making, and public action – all of which it deems indispensable for remedying injustice. Seeking to accommodate both moments, the moment of opening and the moment of closure, reflexive justice views the standard opposition between agonism and discourse ethics as a false antithesis. Refusing to absolutize either model and thus to exclude the insights of the other, it draws on elements of each to fashion a new genre of theorizing for abnormal times.

The second implication concerns the relation between the problematic of abnormal justice and that of hegemony. As is well known, hegemony theory conceptualizes a second, discursive, face of power, alongside that of brute repression. This second face includes the capacity to construct a "common sense" for a diverse array of constituencies, whom the hegemon thereby inducts into a shared political universe. Within that universe, each constituency can constitute itself as a political subject and formulate its interests and goals in a way that is intelligible to others.[40] Seen this way, hegemony includes the capacity to define the legitimate universe of political disagreement, while simultaneously constituting the latter's exterior as a region of unintelligibility.[41] The point can also be put like this: by instituting a structuring set of background assumptions, which itself largely goes without saying, hegemony predetermines what will count as a plausible claim for justice – and what will not.

Understood this way, hegemony theory has clear affinities with the problematic elaborated here. In its terms, episodes of normal justice would correspond to periods of relatively secure, uncontested hegemony, in which extra-commonsensical claims remain dispersed, failing to coalesce into a counter-hegemonic bloc. In contrast, episodes of abnormality would correlate with periods of overt struggles for hegemony, in which counter-hegemonic formations achieve sufficient cohesion to problematize what had previously passed for common sense. Affinities aside, however, the hegemony problematic suggests a different historical account of today's abnormalities. Through its lens, the latter are traceable less to the subjectless process of "globalization" than to the decline of US hegemony since the collapse of the USSR in 1989. Insofar as US hegemony was based on the Cold War, the demise of that geopolitical order presented a challenge to the (Westphalian-distributivist) grammar of justice that defined "the Free World." Having failed to articulate a plausible post-Cold-War commonsense centered on the "war on terror," the US has so far proved unable to perpetuate its hegemony. The result is a glaring discrepancy between the two faces of power: US military supremacy is not matched by any comparable capacity to constitute a shared commonsense that could normalize conflicts over justice. No wonder, then, that justice discourse is undergoing denormalization and that disputes about the "what," the "who," and the "how" are proliferating.

Compelling as this story is, it is not in fact a rival to the one I have developed here. On the contrary, the hegemony perspective complements the problematic of abnormal/normal discourse. Whereas the former views justice discourse historically and strategically, aiming to understand shifts in power, the latter interrogates it philosophically and normatively, aiming to disclose present possibilities for emancipatory change. Thus, far from being mutually incompatible, these two perspectives enrich one another. Like hegemony theory, the abnormal/normal framework acknowledges the historicity and power-laden character of justice discourse. What it adds, however, is an interest in emancipation, an insistence that the grammar of justice be reconstituted so as to enable the subaltern to speak *in authoritative terms*. In this way, the perspective developed here supplies a crucial ingredient of critical theorizing, which hegemony theory taken alone does not provide: the elusive but inspiring vision of a discourse of justice that could reveal contemporary injustices for the moral outrages they surely are. It supplies, in Richard Rorty's terms, the otherwise missing ingredient of "social hope."[42]

5

Transnationalizing the Public Sphere

On the Legitimacy and Efficacy of Public Opinion in a Postwestphalian World

It is commonplace nowadays to speak of "transnational public spheres," "diasporic public spheres," "Islamic public spheres," and even an emerging "global public sphere." And such talk has a clear point. A growing body of media studies literature is documenting the existence of discursive arenas that overflow the bounds of both nations and states. Numerous scholars in cultural studies are ingeniously mapping the contours of such arenas and the flows of images and signs in and through them.[1] The idea of a "transnational public sphere" is intuitively plausible, then, and seems to have purchase on social reality.

Nevertheless, this idea raises a problem. The concept of the public sphere was developed not simply to understand communication flows but also to contribute to a critical theory of democracy. In that theory, a public sphere is conceived as a space for the communicative generation of public opinion. Insofar as the process is inclusive and fair, publicity is supposed to discredit views that cannot withstand critical scrutiny and to assure the legitimacy of those that do. Thus, it matters who participates and on what terms. In addition, a public sphere is conceived as a vehicle for marshaling public opinion as a political force. Mobilizing the considered sense of civil society, publicity is supposed to hold officials accountable and to assure that the actions of the state express the will of the citizenry. Thus, a public sphere should correlate with a sovereign power. Together, these two ideas – the *normative legitimacy* and *political efficacy* of public opinion – are essential to the concept of the public sphere in critical theory.[2] Without them, the concept loses its critical force and its political point.

Yet these two features are not easily associated with the discursive arenas that we today call "transnational public spheres." It is difficult to associate the notion of legitimate public opinion with communicative arenas in which the inter-locutors are not fellow members of a political community, with equal rights to participate in political life. And it is hard to associate the notion of efficacious communicative power with discursive spaces that do not correlate with sovereign states. Thus, it is by no means clear what it means today to speak of "transnational public spheres." From the perspective of critical theory, at least, the phrase sounds a bit like an oxymoron.

Nevertheless, we should not rush to jettison the notion of a "transnational public sphere." Such a notion is indispensable, I think, to those who aim to reconstruct critical theory in the current "postnational constellation." But it will not be sufficient merely to refer to such public spheres in a relatively casual commonsense way, as if we already knew what they were. Rather, it will be necessary to return to square one, to prob-lematize public-sphere theory – and ultimately to reconstruct its conceptions of the normative legitimacy and political effi-cacy of communicative power. The trick will be to walk a narrow line between two equally unsatisfactory approaches. On the one hand, one should avoid an empiricist approach that simply adapts the theory to the existing realities, as that approach risks sacrificing its normative force. On the other hand, one should also avoid an externalist approach that invokes ideal theory to condemn social reality, as that approach risks forfeiting critical traction. The alternative, rather, is a critical-theoretical approach that seeks to locate normative standards and emancipatory political possibilities precisely within the historically unfolding constellation.

This project faces a major difficulty, however. At least since its 1962 adumbration by Jürgen Habermas, public-sphere theory has been implicitly informed by a Westphalian political imaginary: it has tacitly assumed the frame of a bounded politi-cal community with its own territorial state.[3] The same is true for nearly every subsequent egalitarian critique of public-sphere theory, including those of feminists, multiculturalists, and anti-racists. Only very recently, in fact, have the theory's Westphalian underpinnings been problematized. Only recently, thanks to post-Cold-War geopolitical instabilities, on the one hand, and to the increased salience of transnational phenomena associated with "globalization," on the other, has it become possible – and necessary – to rethink public-sphere theory in a transnational frame. Yet these same phenomena force us to face the hard question: Is the concept of the public sphere so thoroughly Westphalian in its deep conceptual structure as to be unsalvageable as a critical tool for theorizing the present? Or can the concept be reconstructed to suit a postwestphalian frame? In the latter case, the task would not simply be to conceptualize transnational public spheres as actually existing institutions. It would rather be to reformulate *the critical theory of the public sphere* in a way that can illuminate the emancipatory possibilities of the present constellation.

In this chapter I sketch the parameters for such a discussion. I shall be mapping the terrain and posing questions rather than offering definitive answers. But I start with the assumption that public-sphere theory is in principle an important critical-conceptual resource that should be reconstructed rather than jettisoned, if possible. My discussion will proceed in three parts. First, I shall explicate the implicit Westphalian presuppositions of Habermas's public-sphere theory and show that these have persisted in its major feminist, anti-racist, and multicultural critiques. Second, I shall identify several distinct facets of transnationality that problematize both traditional public-sphere theory and its critical counter-theorizations. Finally, I shall propose some strategies whereby public-sphere theorists might begin to respond to these challenges. My overall aim is to repoliticize public-sphere theory, which is currently in danger of being depoliticized.

Classical public-sphere theory and its radical critique: thematizing the Westphalian frame

Let me begin by recalling some analytic features of public-sphere theory, drawn from the *locus classicus* of all discussions, Jürgen Habermas's *Structural Transformation of the Public*

Sphere. In this early work, Habermas's inquiry proceeded simultaneously on two levels, one empirical and historical, the other ideological-critical and normative. On both levels, the public sphere was conceptualized as coextensive with a bounded political community and a sovereign territorial state, often a nation-state. To be sure, this was not always fully explicit. Tacitly, however, Habermas's account of the public sphere rested on at least six social-theoretical presuppositions, all of which took for granted the Westphalian framing of political space:

1   *Structural Transformation* correlated the public sphere with a modern state apparatus that exercised sovereign power over a bounded territory. Thus, Habermas assumed that public opinion was addressed to a Westphalian state that was capable in principle of regulating its inhabitants' affairs and solving their problems.[4]
2   *Structural Transformation* conceived the participants in public-sphere discussion as fellow members of a bounded political community. Casting the *telos* of their discussions as the articulated general interest of a *demos*, which should be translated into binding laws, Habermas tacitly identified members of the public with the citizenry of a democratic Westphalian state.[5]
3   *Structural Transformation* conceived a principal *topos* of public-sphere discussion as the proper organization of the political community's economic relations. The latter, in turn, it located in a capitalist market economy that was legally constituted and subject in principle to state regulation. In effect, Habermas assumed that a primary focus of the public's concern was a national economy, contained by a Westphalian state.[6]
4   *Structural Transformation* associated the public sphere with modern media that, in enabling communication across distance, could knit spatially dispersed interlocutors into a public. Tacitly, however, Habermas territorialized publicity by focusing on national media, especially the national press and national broadcasting. Thus, he implicitly assumed a national communications infrastructure, contained by a Westphalian state.[7]

5 *Structural Transformation* took for granted that public-
   sphere discussion was fully comprehensible and lingui-
   stically transparent. Tacitly presupposing a single shared
   linguistic medium of public communication, Habermas
   effectively assumed that public debate was conducted in a
   national language.[8]

6 Finally, *Structural Transformation* traced the cultural origins
   of the public sphere to the letters and novels of eighteenth-
   and nineteenth-century print capitalism. It credited those
   bourgeois genres with creating a new subjective stance,
   through which private individuals envisioned themselves as
   members of a public.[9] Thus, Habermas grounded the structure of public-sphere subjectivity in the very same vernacular literary forms that also gave rise to the imagined
   community of the nation.[10]

These six social-theoretical presuppositions tie Habermas's
early account of the public sphere to the Westphalian framing
of political space. In *Structural Transformation*, publics correlate with modern territorial states and national imaginaries. To
be sure, the national aspect went largely unthematized in this
work. But its presence there as an implicit subtext betrays a
point that Habermas has since made explicit: historically, the
rise of modern publicity coincided with the rise of the nation-
state, in which the Westphalian territorial state became fused
with the imagined community of the nation.[11] It may be true,
as Habermas now claims, that present-day democratic states
can dispense with national identity as a basis of social integration.[12] But it remains the case that *Structural Transformation*'s
conception of publicity had a national subtext. That work's
account of the public sphere presupposed a nationally inflected
variant of the Westphalian frame.

But that is not all. Thanks to its (national) Westphalian
presuppositions, *Structural Transformation* conceptualized the
public sphere from the standpoint of a historically specific
political project: the democratization of the modern territorial (nation-)state. Far from putting in question that project's Westphalian frame, Habermas envisioned a deliberative
model of democracy that was situated squarely within it. In this
model, democracy requires the generation, through territorially
bounded processes of public communication, conducted in the

national language and relayed through the national media, of a body of national public opinion. This opinion should reflect the general interest of the national citizenry concerning the organization of their territorially bounded common life, especially the national economy. The model also requires the mobilization of public opinion as a political force. Effectively empowering the national citizenry, publicity should influence lawmakers and hold state officials accountable. Serving thus to "rationalize" national political domination, it should ensure that the actions and policies of the Westphalian state reflect the discursively formed political will of the national citizenry. In *Structural Transformation*, therefore, the public sphere is a key institutional component of (national) Westphalian democracy.

Empirically, then, *Structural Transformation* highlighted historical processes, however incomplete, of the democratization of the Westphalian nation-state. Normatively, it articulated a model of deliberative democracy for a territorially bounded polity. Accordingly, the public sphere served as a benchmark for identifying, and critiquing, the democratic deficits of actually existing Westphalian states. Thus, Habermas's early theory enabled us to ask: Are all citizens really full members of the national political public? Can all participate on equal terms? In other words, is what passes as national public opinion genuinely *legitimate*? Moreover, does that opinion attain sufficient political force to rein in private powers and to subject the actions of state officials to citizen control? Does the communicative power generated in Westphalian civil society effectively translate into legislative and administrative power in the Westphalian state? In other words, is national public opinion politically *efficacious*? By inviting us to explore such questions, *Structural Transformation* constituted a contribution to the critique of actually existing democracy in the modern Westphalian state.

Some readers found the critique insufficiently radical. In the discussion that followed the work's belated translation into English, the objections tended to divide into two distinct streams. One stream interrogated the *legitimacy* of public opinion along lines beyond those pursued by Habermas. Focused on relations within civil society, exponents of what I shall call "the legitimacy critique" contended that *Structural*

Transformation obscured the existence of systemic obstacles
that deprive some who are nominally members of the public
of the capacity to participate on a par with others, as full partners in public debate. Highlighting class inequalities and status
hierarchies in civil society, these critics analyzed their effects
on those whom the Westphalian frame included in principle,
but excluded or marginalized in practice: propertyless workers,
women, the poor; ethno-racial, religious, and national minorities.[13] Thus, this critique questioned the legitimacy of what
passes for public opinion in democratic theory and in social
reality.

A second stream of criticism radicalized Habermas's prob-
lematization of the *efficacy* of public opinion. Focused on relations between civil society and the state, proponents of "the
efficacy critique" maintained that *Structural Transformation*
failed to register the full range of systemic obstacles that deprive
discursively generated public opinion of political muscle. Not
convinced that these had been adequately captured by
Habermas's account of the "refeudalization" of the public
sphere, these critics sought to theorize the structural forces
that block the flow of communicative power from civil society
to the state. Highlighting the respective roles of private economic power and entrenched bureaucratic interests, their critique served to deepen doubt about the efficacy of public
opinion as a political force in capitalist societies.[14]

Notwithstanding the difference in focus, the two streams of
criticism shared a deeper assumption. Like *Structural Transformation*, both the legitimacy critics and the efficacy critics took
for granted the Westphalian framing of political space. To be
sure, some proponents of the legitimacy critique exposed the
national subtext of publicity that had largely gone without
saying in Habermas's account. Analyzing its exclusionary effects
on national minorities, multiculturalist critics sought to purge
the public sphere of majority national privilege in hopes of
reducing disparities of participation in public debate. The point,
however, was not to question the territorial basis of the public
sphere. Far from casting doubt on the Westphalian frame, the
critics sought to enhance the legitimacy of public opinion
within it. An analogous objective informed the efficacy critique. Taking for granted that public opinion was addressed to
a territorial state, proponents of this critique hoped to subject

the latter more firmly to the discursively formed will of its *demos*. Like Habermas, then, if arguably more radically, both sets of critics placed their reflections on the public sphere within the Westphalian frame.

My own earlier effort to "rethink the public sphere" was no exception. In an article originally published in 1991, I directed criticisms of both types against what I called, following Habermas, "the liberal model of the bourgeois public sphere." In its legitimacy aspect, my critique focused on the effects on public opinion of inequality within civil society. Rebutting the liberal view that it was possible for interlocutors in a public sphere to bracket status and class differentials and to deliberate "as if" they were peers, I argued that social equality is a necessary condition for political democracy. Under real-world conditions of massive *in*equality, I reckoned, the only way to reduce disparities in political voice was through social movement contestation that challenged some basic features of bourgeois publicity. Complicating the standard liberal picture of a single comprehensive public sphere, I claimed that the proliferation of subaltern counterpublics could enhance the participation of subordinate strata in stratified societies. Exposing, too, the bourgeois masculinist bias in standard liberal views of what counts as a public concern, I endorsed efforts by movements such as feminism to redraw the boundaries between public and private. Yet this critique presupposed the national-territorial understanding of publicity. Far from challenging the Westphalian frame, it aimed to enhance the legitimacy of public opinion within it.[15]

My article also propounded an efficacy critique, which interrogated the capacity of public opinion to achieve political force. Identifying forces that block the translation of communicative power into administrative power, I questioned the standard liberal view that a functioning public sphere always requires a sharp separation between civil society and the state. Distinguishing the "weak publics" of civil society, which generate public opinion but not binding laws, from the "strong publics" within the state, whose deliberations issue in sovereign decisions, I sought to envision institutional arrangements that could enhance the latter's accountability to the former. Aiming, too, to open space for imagining radical-democratic alternatives, I questioned the apparent foreclosure by Habermas of hybrid forms, such as "quasi-strong" decision-making publics in civil society. Yet here, too, I neglected to challenge the Westphalian frame. The thrust of my argument was, on the contrary, to enhance the efficacy of public opinion vis-à-vis the Westphalian state.[16]

Both the legitimacy critique and the efficacy critique still seem right to me as far as they went. But I now believe that neither went far enough. Neither critique interrogated, let alone modified, the social-theoretical underpinnings of *Structural Transformation*, which situated the public sphere in a Westphalian frame. Still oriented to the prospects for deliberative democracy in a bounded political community, both critiques continued to identify the public with the citizenry of a territorial state. Neither abandoned the assumption of a national economy, whose proper steering by the democratic state remained a principal *topos* of public-sphere debate, which was itself still envisioned as being conducted in the national language through the national media. Thus, neither the legitimacy critique nor the efficacy critique challenged the Westphalian frame. Animated by the same political project as *Structural Transformation*, both sought to further deliberative democracy in the modern territorial state.

The same is true for Habermas's subsequent discussion of publicity in *Between Facts and Norms*. Among other things, that work revisited the public sphere and incorporated elements of the two critiques. Stressing the "co-implication of private and public autonomy," Habermas valorized the role of emancipatory social movements, such as second-wave feminism, in promoting democracy by pursuing equality, and vice versa.[17] By thus acknowledging the mutual dependence of social position and political voice, he grappled here with previously neglected aspects of the legitimacy deficits of public opinion in democratic states. In addition, *Between Facts and Norms* was centrally concerned with the problem of efficacy. Theorizing law as the proper vehicle for translating communicative into administrative power, the work distinguished an "official," democratic circulation of power, in which weak publics influence strong publics, which in turn control administrative state apparatuses, from an "unofficial," undemocratic one, in which private social powers and entrenched bureaucratic interests control lawmakers and manipulate public opinion. Acknowledging that the unofficial circulation usually prevails, Habermas here provided a fuller account of the efficacy deficits of public opinion in democratic states.[18]

One may question, to be sure, whether Habermas fully succeeded in addressing his critics' concerns on either point.[19] But even if we grant him the benefit of that doubt, the fact remains that *Between Facts and Norms* continued to assume the Westphalian frame. Its many departures from *Structural Transformation* notwithstanding, the later work still conceived the addressee of public opinion as a sovereign territorial state, which could steer a national economy in the general interest of the national citizenry; and it still conceived the formation of public opinion as a process conducted in the national media via a national communications infrastructure. Granted, Habermas did advocate a postnationalist form of social integration, namely "constitutional patriotism," with the aim of emancipating the democratic state from its nationalist integument.[20] But in this he effectively endorsed a more purely Westphalian, because more exclusively territorial, conception of publicity.

In general, then, the publicity debate in critical theory contains a major blindspot. From *Structural Transformation* through *Between Facts and Norms*, virtually all the participants, including me, correlated public spheres with territorial states. Despite their other important disagreements, all assumed the Westphalian framing of political space – at precisely the moment when epochal historical developments seemed to be calling that frame into question.

The postnational constellation: problematizing the Westphalian frame

Today, the Westphalian blindspot of public-sphere theory is hard to miss. Whether the issue is global warming or immigration, women's rights or the terms of trade, unemployment or the "war on terror," current mobilizations of public opinion seldom stop at the borders of territorial states. In many cases, the interlocutors do not constitute a *demos* or political citizenry. Often, too, their communications are neither addressed to a Westphalian state nor relayed through national media. Frequently, moreover, the problems debated are inherently trans-territorial and can neither be located within Westphalian space nor be resolved by a Westphalian state. In such cases, current formations of public opinion scarcely respect the parameters of the Westphalian frame. Thus, assumptions that previously went without saying in public-sphere theory now cry out for critique and revision.

No wonder, then, that expressions like "transnational public spheres," "diasporic public spheres," and "the global public sphere" figure so prominently in current discussions. Views about these phenomena divide into two camps. One camp treats transnational publicity as a new development, associated with late twentieth-century globalization. Claiming that the modern interstate system previously channeled most political debate into state-centered discursive arenas, this camp maintains that the Westphalian frame was appropriate for theorizing public spheres until very recently.[21] The second camp insists, in contrast, that publicity has been transnational at least since the origins of the interstate system in the seventeenth century. Citing Enlightenment visions of the international "republic of letters" and cross-national movements such as abolitionism and socialism, not to mention world religions and modern imperialism, this camp contends that the Westphalian frame has always been ideological, obscuring the inherently unbounded character of public spheres.[22] Undoubtedly, both interpretations have some merit. Whereas the first accurately captures the hegemonic division of political space, the second rightly reminds us that metropolitan democracy arose in tandem with colonial subjection, which galvanized transnational flows of public opinion. For present purposes, therefore, I propose to split the difference between them. Granting that transnational publicity has a long history, I shall assume that its present configuration is nevertheless new, reflecting yet another "structural transformation of the public sphere." On this point, all parties can surely agree: the current constitution of public opinion bursts open the Westphalian frame.

Yet the full implications remain to be drawn. Focusing largely on cultural aspects of transnational flows, such as "hybridization" and "glocalization," many students of transnational publicity neglect to pose the questions of greatest importance for a *critical* theory: If public opinion now overflows the Westphalian frame, what becomes of its *critical* function of checking domination and democratizing governance? More specifically, can we still meaningfully interrogate the *legitimacy* of public opinion when the interlocutors do not constitute a *demos* or political citizenry? And what could legitimacy mean in such a context? Likewise, can we still meaningfully interrogate the *efficacy* of public opinion when it is not addressed to a sovereign state that is capable in principle of regulating its territory and solving its citizens' problems in the public interest? And what could efficacy mean in this situation? Absent satisfactory answers to these questions, we lack a usable *critical* theory of the public sphere.[23]

To clarify the stakes, I propose to revisit the six constitutive presuppositions of public-sphere theory. I shall consider, in the case of each presupposition, how matters stand empirically and what follows for the public sphere's status as a *critical* category.

1   Consider, first, the assumption that the addressee of public opinion is a modern Westphalian state, with exclusive, undivided sovereignty over a bounded territory. Empirically, this view of sovereignty is highly questionable – and not just for poor and weak states. Today, even powerful states share responsibility for many key governance functions with international institutions, intergovernmental networks, and nongovernmental organizations. This is the case not only for relatively new functions, such as environmental regulation, but also for classical ones, such as defense, policing, and the administration of civil and criminal law – witness the International Atomic Energy Agency, the International Criminal Court, and the World Intellectual Property Organization.[24] Certainly, these institutions are dominated by hegemonic states, as was the interstate system before them. But the mode in which hegemony is exercised today is evidently new. Far from invoking the Westphalian model of exclusive, undivided state sovereignty, hegemony increasingly operates through a *postwestphalian model of disaggregated sovereignty*.[25] Empirically, therefore, the first presupposition of public-sphere theory does not stand up.

But what follows for public-sphere theory? The effect, I submit, is not simply to falsify the theory's underpinnings, but also to jeopardize the *critical* function of public opinion. If states do not fully control their own territories, if they lack the sole and undivided capacity to wage war, secure order, and administer law, then how can their citizenries' public opinion be politically effective? Even granting, for the sake of argument, that national publicity is fairly generated and satisfies criteria of legitimacy; even granting, too, that it influences the will of parliament and the state administration; how, under conditions of disaggregated sovereignty, can it be *implemented*? How, in sum, can public opinion be *efficacious* as a critical force in a postwestphalian world?

2   Consider, next, the assumption that a public coincides with a national citizenry, resident on a national territory, which formulates its common interest as the general will of a bounded political community. This assumption, too, is counterfactual. For one thing, the equation of citizenship, nationality, and territorial residence is belied by such phenomena as migrations, diasporas, dual- and triple-citizenship arrangements, indigenous community membership, and patterns of multiple residency. Every state now has non-citizens on its territory; most are multicultural and/or multinational; and every nationality is territorially dispersed.[26] Equally confounding, however, is the fact that public spheres today are not coextensive with political membership. Often the interlocutors are neither co-nationals nor fellow citizens. The opinion they generate, therefore, represents neither the common interest nor the general will of any *demos*. Far from institutionalizing debate among citizens who share a common status as political equals, postwestphalian publicity appears in the eyes of many observers to empower transnational elites, who possess the material and symbolic prerequisites for global networking.[27]

Here, too, the difficulty is not just empirical but also conceptual and political. If the interlocutors do not constitute a *demos*, how can their collective opinion be translated into binding laws and administrative policies? If, moreover, they are not fellow citizens, putatively equal in participation rights, status, and voice, then how can the opinion they generate be considered legitimate? How, in sum, can the *critical* criteria of *efficacy* and *legitimacy* be meaningfully applied to transnational public opinion in a postwestphalian world?

3   Consider, now, the assumption that a principal *topos* of public-sphere discussion is the proper regulation by a territorial state of a national economy. That assumption, too, is belied by present conditions. We need only mention outsourcing, transnational corporations, and offshore business registry to appreciate that territorially based national production is now largely notional. Thanks, moreover, to the dismantling of the Bretton Woods capital controls and the emergence of 24/7 global electronic financial markets, state control over national currency is presently quite limited. Finally, as those who protest policies of the World Trade Organization, the International Monetary Fund, the North American Free Trade Agreement, and the World Bank have insisted, the ground rules governing trade, production, and finance are set transnationally, by agencies more accountable to global capital than to any public.[28] In these conditions, the presupposition of a national economy is counterfactual.

As before, moreover, the effect is to imperil the critical function of public spheres. If states cannot in principle steer economies in line with the articulated general interest of their populations, how can national public opinion be an effective force? Then, too, if economic governance is in the hands of agencies that are not locatable in Westphalian space, how can it be made accountable to public opinion? Moreover, if those agencies are invalidating national labor and environmental laws in the name of free trade, if they are prohibiting domestic social spending in the name of structural adjustment, if they are institutionalizing neoliberal governance rules that would once and for all remove major matters of public concern from any possibility of political regulation, if in sum they are systematically reversing the democratic project, using markets to tame politics instead of politics to tame markets, then how can citizen public opinion have any impact? Lastly, if the world capitalist system operates to the massive detriment of the global poor, how can what passes for transnational public opinion be remotely legitimate, when those affected by current policies cannot possibly debate their merits as peers? In general, then, how can public opinion concerning the economy be either *legitimate* or *efficacious* in a postwestphalian world?

4   Consider, as well, the assumption that public opinion is conveyed through a national communications infrastructure, centered on print and broadcasting. This assumption implies that communicative processes, however decentered, are sufficiently coherent and politically focused to coalesce in "public opinion." But it, too, is rendered counterfactual by current conditions. Recall the profusion of niche media, some subnational, some transnational, which do not in any case function as national media, focused on subjecting the exercise of state power to the test of publicity. Granted, one can also note the parallel emergence of global media, but these market-driven, corporately owned outlets are scarcely focused on checking transnational power. In addition, many countries have privatized government-operated media, with decidedly mixed results: on the one hand, the prospect of a more independent press and TV and more inclusive populist programming; on the other hand, the further spread of market logic, advertisers' power, and dubious amalgams like talk radio and "infotainment." Finally, we should mention instantaneous electronic, broadband, and satellite communications technologies, which permit direct transnational communication, bypassing state controls. Together, all these developments signal the denationalization of communicative infrastructure.[29]

The effects here, too, pose threats to the critical functioning of public spheres. Granted, we see some new opportunities for critical public opinion formation. But these go along with the disaggregation and complexification of communicative flows. Given a field divided between corporate global media, restricted niche media, and decentered internet networks, how could critical public opinion possibly be generated on a large scale and mobilized as a political force? Given, too, the absence of even the sort of formal equality associated with common citizenship, how could those who comprise transnational media audiences deliberate together as peers? How, once again, can public opinion be normatively *legitimate* or politically *efficacious* under current conditions?

5   Consider, too, the presupposition of a single national language, which was supposed to constitute the linguistic medium of public-sphere communication. As a result of the population mixing already noted, national languages do not map onto

states. The problem is not simply that official state languages were consolidated at the expense of local and regional dialects, although they were. It is also that existing states are *de facto* multilingual, while language groups are territorially dispersed, and many more speakers are multilingual. Meanwhile, English has become the *lingua franca* of global business, mass entertainment, and academia. Yet language remains a political fault-line, threatening to explode countries like Belgium, if no longer Canada, while complicating efforts to democratize countries like South Africa and to erect transnational formations like the European Union.[30]

These developments, too, pose threats to the critical function of public opinion. Insofar as public spheres are monolingual, how can they constitute an inclusive communications community of all those affected? Conversely, insofar as public spheres correspond to linguistic communities that straddle political boundaries and do not correspond to any citizenry, how can they mobilize public opinion as a political force? Likewise, insofar as new transnational political communities, such as the EU, are multi-linguistic, how can they constitute public spheres that can encompass the entire *demos*? Finally, insofar as transnational publics conduct their communications in English, which favors global elites and Anglophone post-colonials at the expense of others, how can the opinion they generate be viewed as legitimate? For all these reasons, and in all these ways, language issues compromise both the *legitimacy* and *efficacy* of public opinion in a postwestphalian world.

6   Consider, finally, the assumption that a public sphere rests on a national vernacular literature, which supplies the shared social imaginary needed to underpin solidarity. This assumption, too, is today counterfactual. Consider the increased salience of cultural hybridity and hybridization, including the rise of "world literature." Consider also the rise of global mass entertainment, whether straightforwardly American or merely stylistically informed by American entertainment. Consider, finally, the spectacular rise of visual culture, or, better, of the enhanced salience of the visual within culture, and the relative decline of print and the literary.[31] In all these cases, it is difficult to recognize the sort of (national) literary cultural formation seen by Habermas (and by Benedict Anderson) as underpinning

the subjective stance of public-sphere interlocutors.[32] On the contrary, insofar as public spheres require the cultural support of shared social imaginaries, rooted in national literary cultures, it is hard to see them functioning effectively today.

In general, then, public spheres are increasingly transnational or postnational with respect to each of the constitutive elements of public opinion.[33] The "who" of communication, previously theorized as a Westphalian-national citizenry, is often now a collection of dispersed interlocutors, who do not constitute a *demos*. The "what" of communication, previously theorized as a Westphalian-national interest rooted in a Westphalian-national economy, now stretches across vast reaches of the globe, in a transnational community of risk, which is not, however, reflected in concomitantly expansive solidarities and identities. The "where" of communication, once theorized as the Westphalian-national territory, now increasingly occupies deterritorialized cyberspace. The "how" of communication, once theorized as Westphalian-national print media, now encompasses a vast translinguistic nexus of disjoint and overlapping visual cultures. Finally, the "to whom" or addressee of communication, once theorized as a sovereign territorial state, which should be made answerable to public opinion, is now an amorphous mix of public and private transnational powers that is neither easily identifiable nor rendered accountable.

Rethinking the public sphere – yet again

These developments raise the question of whether and how public spheres today could conceivably perform the democratic political functions with which they have been associated historically. Could public spheres today conceivably generate *legitimate* public opinion, in the strong sense of considered understandings of the general interest, filtered through fair and inclusive argumentation, open to everyone potentially affected? And if so, how? Likewise, could public spheres today conceivably render public opinion sufficiently *efficacious* to constrain the various powers that determine the conditions of the interlocutors' lives? And if so, how? What sorts of changes (institutional, economic, cultural, and communicative) would be required even to imagine a genuinely *critical* and democratizing role for transnational public spheres under current conditions? Where are the sovereign powers that public opinion today should constrain? Which publics are relevant to which powers? Who are the relevant members of a given public? In what language(s) and through what media should they communicate? And via what communicative infrastructure?

These questions well exceed the scope of the present inquiry. And I shall not pretend to try to answer them here. I want to conclude, rather, by suggesting a conceptual strategy that can clarify the issues and point the way to possible resolutions.

My proposal centers on the two features that together constituted the *critical* force of the concept of the public sphere in the Westphalian era: namely, the *normative legitimacy* and *political efficacy* of public opinion. As I see it, these ideas are intrinsic, indispensable elements of *any* conception of publicity that purports to be critical, regardless of the socio-historical conditions in which it obtains. The present constellation is no exception. Unless we can envision conditions under which current flows of transnational publicity could conceivably become legitimate and efficacious, the concept loses its critical edge and its political point. Thus, the only way to salvage the critical function of publicity today is to rethink legitimacy and efficacy. The task is to detach those two ideas from the Westphalian premises that previously underpinned them and to reconstruct them for a postwestphalian world.

Consider, first, the question of *legitimacy*. In public-sphere theory, as we saw, public opinion is considered legitimate if and only if all who are potentially affected are able to participate as peers in deliberations concerning the organization of their common affairs. In effect, then, the theory holds that the legitimacy of public opinion is a function of two analytically distinct characteristics of the communicative process, namely, the extent of its *inclusiveness* and the degree to which it realizes *participatory parity*. In the first case, which I shall call the inclusiveness condition, discussion must in principle be open to all with a stake in the outcome. In the second, which I shall call the parity condition, all interlocutors must, in principle, enjoy roughly equal chances to state their views, place issues on the agenda, question the tacit and explicit assumptions of others, switch levels as needed, and generally receive a fair hearing. Whereas the inclusiveness condition concerns the question of *who* is authorized to participate in public discussions, the parity condition concerns the question of *how*, in the sense of on what terms, the interlocutors engage one another.[34]

In the past, however, these two legitimacy conditions of public opinion were not always clearly distinguished. Seen from the perspective of the Westphalian frame, both the inclusiveness condition and the parity condition were yoked together under the ideal of *shared citizenship in a bounded community*. As we saw, public-sphere theorists implicitly assumed that citizenship set the legitimate bounds of inclusion, effectively equating those affected with the members of an established polity. Tacitly, too, theorists appealed to citizenship in order to give flesh to the idea of parity of participation in public deliberations, effectively associating communicative parity with the shared status of political equality in a territorial state. Thus, citizenship supplied the model for both the "who" and the "how" of legitimate public opinion in the Westphalian frame.

The effect, however, was to truncate discussions of legitimacy. Although it went unnoticed at the time, the Westphalian frame encouraged debate about the parity condition, while deflecting attention away from the inclusiveness condition. Taking for granted the modern territorial state as the appropriate unit, and its citizens as the pertinent subjects, that frame foregrounded the question of *how* precisely those citizens should relate to one another in the public sphere. The argument focused, in other words, on what should count as a relation of participatory parity among the members of a bounded political community. Engrossed in disputing the "how" of legitimacy, the contestants apparently felt no necessity to dispute the "who." With the Westphalian frame securely in place, it went without saying that the "who" was the national citizenry.

Today, however, the question of the "who" can no longer be swept under the carpet. Under current conditions of transnationality, the inclusiveness condition of legitimacy cries out for explicit interrogation. We must ask: If political citizenship no longer suffices to demarcate the members of the public, then how should the inclusiveness requirement be understood? By what alternative criterion should we determine who counts as a bonafide interlocutor in a postwestphalian public sphere?

Public-sphere theory already offers a clue. In its classical Habermasian form, the theory associates the idea of inclusiveness with the "all-affected principle." Applying that principle to publicity, it holds that all potentially affected by political decisions should have the chance to participate on terms of parity in the informal processes of opinion formation to which the decision-takers should be accountable. Everything depends, accordingly, on how one interprets the all-affected principle. Previously, public-sphere theorists assumed, in keeping with the Westphalian frame, that what most affected people's life conditions was the constitutional order of the territorial state of which they were citizens. As a result, it seemed that in correlating publics with political citizenship, one simultaneously captured the force of the all-affected principle. In fact, this was never truly so, as the long history of colonialism and neocolonialism attests. From the perspective of the metropole, however, the conflation of membership with affectedness appeared to have an emancipatory thrust, as it served to justify the progressive incorporation, as active citizens, of the subordinate classes and status groups who were resident in the territory but excluded from full political participation.

Today, however, the idea that citizenship can serve as a proxy for affectedness is no longer plausible. Under current conditions, one's conditions of living do not depend wholly on the internal constitution of the political community of which one is a citizen. Although the latter remains undeniably relevant, its effects are mediated by other structures, both extra- and non-territorial, whose impact is at least as significant.[35] In general, globalization is driving a widening wedge between affectedness and political membership. As those two notions increasingly diverge, the effect is to reveal the former as an inadequate surrogate for the latter. And so the question arises: Why not apply the all-affected principle directly to the framing of publicity, without going through the detour of citizenship?

Earlier, I considered this a promising path for reconstructing a critical conception of inclusive public opinion in a postwestphalian world. Today, however, I prefer the alternative, "all-subjected principle" introduced in chapter 4.[36] Although I cannot explore this alternative fully here, let me recall the essential point: the all-subjected principle holds that what turns a collection of people into fellow members of a public is not shared citizenship, or co-imbrication in a causal matrix, but rather their joint subjection to a structure of governance that set the ground rules for their interaction. For any given problem, accordingly, the relevant public should match the reach of the governance structure that regulates the relevant swath of social interaction. Where such structures transgress the borders of states, the corresponding public spheres must be transnational. Failing that, the opinion that they generate cannot be considered legitimate.

With respect to the legitimacy of public opinion, then, the challenge is clear. In order for public-sphere theory to retain its critical orientation in a postwestphalian world, it must reinterpret the meaning of the inclusiveness requirement. Renouncing the automatic identification of the latter with political citizenship, it must redraw publicity's boundaries by applying the all-subjected principle directly to the question at hand. In this way, the question of the "who" emerges from under its Westphalian veil. Along with the question of the "how," which remains as pressing as ever, it, too, becomes an explicit focus of concern in the present constellation. In fact, the two questions, that of inclusiveness and that of parity, now go hand in hand. Henceforth, public opinion is legitimate if and only if it results from a communicative process in which all who are jointly subjected to the relevant governance structure(s) can participate as peers, *regardless of political citizenship*. Demanding as it is, this new, postwestphalian understanding of legitimacy constitutes a genuinely critical standard for evaluating existing forms of publicity in the present era.

Let me turn, now, to the second essential feature of a critical conception of publicity, namely, the political *efficacy* of public opinion. In public-sphere theory, as we saw, public opinion is considered efficacious if and only if it is mobilized as a political force to hold public power accountable, ensuring that the latter's exercise reflects the considered will of civil society. In effect, therefore, the theory treats publicity's efficacy as a function of two distinct elements, which I shall call the *translation* condition and the *capacity* condition. According to the translation condition, the communicative power generated in civil society must be translated first into binding laws and then into administrative power. According to the capacity condition, the public power must be able to implement the discursively formed will to which it is responsible. Whereas the translation condition concerns the flow of communicative power from civil society to an instituted public power, the capacity condition concerns the ability of an administrative power to realize its public's designs, both negatively, by reining in private powers, and positively, by solving its problems and organizing common life in accord with its wishes.

In the past, these two efficacy conditions were understood in the light of the Westphalian frame. From that perspective, both the translation condition and the capacity condition were linked to the idea of the sovereign territorial state. As we saw, public-sphere theorists assumed that the addressee of public opinion was the Westphalian state, which should be constituted democratically, so that communication flows unobstructed from weak publics to strong publics, where it can be translated into binding laws. At the same time, these theorists also assumed that the Westphalian state had the necessary administrative capacity to implement those laws so as to realize its citizens' aims and solve their problems. Thus, the Westphalian state was considered the proper vehicle for fulfilling both the translation and capacity conditions of public-sphere efficacy.

Here, too, however, the result was to truncate discussions of efficacy. Although the Westphalian frame fostered interest in the translation condition, it tended to obscure the capacity condition. Taking for granted that the sovereign territorial state was the proper addressee of public opinion, that frame foregrounded the question of whether the communicative power generated in the national public sphere was sufficiently strong to influence legislation and constrain state administration. The argument focused, accordingly, on what should count as a democratic circulation of power between civil society and the state. What was not much debated, in contrast, was the state's capacity to regulate the private powers that shaped its citizens' lives. That issue went without saying, as public-sphere theorists assumed, for example, that economies were effectively national and could be steered by national states in the interest of national citizens. Engrossed in debating the translation condition, they apparently felt no necessity to dispute the capacity condition. With the Westphalian frame in place, the latter became a non-issue.

Today, however, these assumptions no longer hold. Under current conditions of transnationality, the capacity condition demands interrogation in its own right. We must ask: If the modern territorial state no longer possesses the administrative ability to steer "its" economy, ensure the integrity of "its" national environment, and provide for the security and well-being of "its" citizens, then how should we understand the capacity component of efficacy today? By what means can the requisite administrative capacity be constituted and where precisely should it be lodged? If not to the sovereign territorial state, then to what or whom should public opinion on transnational problems be addressed?

With respect to these questions, alas, existing public-sphere theory affords few clues. But it does suggest that the problem of publicity's efficacy in a postwestphalian world is doubly complicated. A critical conception can no longer restrict its attention to the direction of communicative flows in established polities, where publicity should constrain an already known and constituted addressee. In addition, it must consider the need to construct new addressees for public opinion, in the sense of new, transnational public powers that possess the administrative capacity to solve transnational problems. The challenge, accordingly, is twofold: on the one hand, to create new, transnational public powers; on the other, to make them accountable to new, transnational public spheres. Both those elements are necessary; neither alone is sufficient. Only if it thematizes both conditions (capacity as well as translation) will public-sphere theory develop a postwestphalian conception of communicative efficacy that is genuinely critical.

In general, then, the task is clear: if public-sphere theory is to function today as a *critical* theory, it must revise its account of the normative legitimacy and political efficacy of public opinion. No longer content to leave half the picture in the shadows, it must treat each of those notions as comprising two analytically distinct but practically entwined critical requirements. Thus, the legitimacy critique of existing publicity must now interrogate not only the "how" but also the "who" of existing publicity. Or, rather, it must interrogate parity and inclusiveness together, by asking: *participatory parity among whom?* Likewise, the efficacy critique must now be expanded to encompass both the translation and capacity conditions of existing publicity. Putting those two requirements together, it must envision new transnational public powers, which can be made accountable to new democratic transnational circuits of public opinion.

Granted, the job is not easy. But only if public-sphere theory rises to the occasion can it serve as a *critical* theory in a post-westphalian world. For that purpose, it is not enough for cultural studies and media studies scholars to map existing communications flows. Rather, critical social and political theorists will need to rethink the theory's core premises concerning the legitimacy and efficacy of public opinion. Only then will the theory recover its critical edge and its political point. Only then will public-sphere theory keep faith with its original promise to contribute to struggles for emancipation.

6

Mapping the Feminist Imagination

From Redistribution to Recognition to Representation

For many years, feminists throughout the world looked to the United States for the most advanced theory and practice. Today, however, US feminism finds itself at an impasse, stymied by the hostile, post-9/11 political climate. Unsure how to pursue gender justice under current conditions, we are now returning the favor, by looking to feminists elsewhere for inspiration and guidance. Today, accordingly, the cutting edge of gender struggle has shifted away from the United States, to transnational spaces, such as "Europe" and the World Social Forum, where the room for maneuver appears greater. The consequence is a major shift in the geography of feminist energies.

What lies behind this geographical shift? And what are its political implications for the future of the feminist project? In what follows, I will propose an account of the historical trajectory of second-wave feminism aimed at illuminating these matters. My strategy will be to relate geographical shifts in feminist energies to shifts of two other kinds. On the one hand, I will identify some major transformations in the way feminists have imagined gender justice since the 1970s. On the other hand, I will situate changes in the feminist imaginary in the context of broader shifts in the political *Zeitgeist* and in postwar capitalism. The result will be a historically elaborated *Zeitdiagnose* through which we can assess the political prospects of feminist struggles for the coming period.

In general, then, the point of this exercise is political. By historicizing shifts in the geography of feminist energies, I aim to gain some insight as to how we might reinvigorate the theory and practice of gender equality under current conditions. Likewise, by mapping transformations of the feminist imagination, I aim to determine what should be discarded, and what preserved, for the struggles ahead. By situating those shifts, finally, in the context of changes in postwar capitalism and post-communist geopolitics, I aim to stimulate discussion as to how we might reinvent the project of feminism for a globalizing world.

Historicizing second-wave feminism

How should we understand the history of second-wave feminism? The narrative I propose differs importantly from the standard one told in US academic feminist circles. The standard story is a narrative of progress, according to which we have moved from an exclusionary movement, dominated by white, middle-class, heterosexual women, to a broader, more inclusive movement that better allows for the concerns of lesbians, women of color, and/or poor and working-class women.[1] Naturally, I support efforts to broaden and diversify feminism, but I do not find this narrative satisfactory. From my perspective, it is too internal to feminism. Preoccupied exclusively with developments inside the movement, it fails to situate interior changes in relation to broader historical developments and the larger political context. Thus, I will propose an alternative story, which is more historical and less self-congratulatory.

For my purposes, the history of second-wave feminism divides into three phases. In a first phase, feminism stood in a close relation to the various "new social movements" that emerged from the ferment of the 1960s. In a second phase, it was drawn into the orbit of identity politics. In a third phase, finally, feminism is increasingly practiced as a transnational politics, in emerging transnational spaces. Let me explain.

The history of second-wave feminism presents a striking trajectory. Nourished by the radicalism of the New Left, this wave of feminism began life as one of the new social movements that challenged the normalizing structures of post-World War II social democracy. It originated, in other words, as part of a broad effort to transform an economistic political imaginary that had narrowed political attention to problems of class distribution. In this first (new social movements) phase, feminists sought to burst open that imaginary. Exposing a broad range of forms of male dominance, they propounded an expanded view of the political as encompassing "the personal." Later, however, as the utopian energies of the New Left declined, feminism's anti-economistic insights were resignified, selectively incorporated into an emerging new political imaginary, which foregrounded cultural issues. Effectively captured by this culturalist imaginary, feminism reinvented itself as a politics of recognition. In its second phase, accordingly, feminism became preoccupied with culture and was drawn into the orbit of identity politics. Although it was not often noticed at the time, feminism's identity-politics phase coincided with a broader historical development, the fraying of nationally based social democracy under pressure from global neoliberalism. Under these conditions, a culture-centered politics of recognition could not succeed. To the extent that it neglected political economy and geopolitical developments, this approach could not effectively challenge either the depredations of free-market policies or the rising tide of rightwing chauvinism that emerged in their wake. US feminism especially was unprepared for the dramatic alteration of the political landscape following 9/11. In Europe and elsewhere, however, feminists have discovered, and are skillfully exploiting, new political opportunities in the transnational political spaces of our globalizing world. Thus, they are reinventing feminism yet again – this time as a project and process of transnational politics. Although this third phase is still very young, it portends a change in the scale of feminist politics that could make it possible to integrate the best aspects of the previous two phases in a new and more adequate synthesis.

That, in a nutshell, is the story I intend to elaborate here. Before I proceed to unpack it, however, I need to introduce two caveats. The first concerns the narrative's highly stylized character. In order to clarify the overall trajectory, I am drawing overly sharp lines between phases that in reality overlapped one another in many places and at many points. The risk of distortion will be worth it, however, if the narrative generates some intellectual and political insights for the period ahead.

My second caveat concerns the geography of feminism's three phases. As I understand it, the first (new social movements) phase encompassed North American, and Western European feminisms – and possibly currents elsewhere as well. In contrast, the second (identity-politics) phase found its fullest expression in the United States, although it was not without resonance in other regions. Finally, the third phase is most developed, as its name suggests, in transnational political spaces, paradigmatically those associated with "Europe."

Engendering social democracy: a critique of economism

To understand phase one, accordingly, let's recall conditions in what could then still be meaningfully called "the First World." When second-wave feminism first erupted on the world stage, the advanced capitalist states of Western Europe and North America were still enjoying the unprecedented wave of prosperity that followed World War II. Utilizing new tools of Keynesian economic steering, they had apparently learned to counteract business downturns and to guide national economic development so as to secure near full employment for men. Incorporating once unruly labor movements, they had built extensive welfare states and institutionalized national cross-class solidarity. To be sure, this historic class compromise rested on a series of gender and racial-ethnic exclusions, not to mention external neocolonial exploitation. But those potential fault-lines tended in the main to remain latent in a social-democratic imaginary that foregrounded class redistribution. The result was a prosperous North Atlantic belt of mass-consumption societies, which had apparently tamed social conflict.[2]

In the 1960s, however, the relative calm of this Golden Age was suddenly shattered. In an extraordinary international explosion, radical youth took to the streets – at first to oppose racial segregation in the US, and the Vietnam War. Soon thereafter they began to question core features of capitalist modernity that social democracy had hitherto naturalized: sexual repression, sexism, and heteronormativity; materialism, corporate culture, and "the achievement ethic"; consumerism, bureaucracy, and "social control." Breaking through the normalized political routines of the previous era, new social actors formed new social movements, with second-wave feminism among the most visionary.[3]

Along with their comrades in other movements, the feminists of this era recast the political imaginary. Transgressing a political culture that had privileged actors who cast themselves as nationally bounded and politically tamed classes, they challenged the gender exclusions of social democracy. Problematizing welfare paternalism and the bourgeois family, they exposed the deep androcentrism of capitalist society. Politicizing "the personal," they expanded the boundaries of contestation beyond socioeconomic redistribution – to include housework, sexuality, and reproduction.[4]

Radical as it was, the feminism of this first phase stood in an ambivalent relation to social democracy. On the one hand, much of the early second wave rejected the latter's *étatism* and its tendency, especially in Europe, to marginalize social divisions other than class, and social problems other than those of distribution. On the other hand, most feminists presupposed key features of the socialist imaginary as a basis for more radical designs. Taking for granted the welfare state's solidaristic ethos and prosperity-securing steering capacities, they, too, were committed to taming markets and promoting egalitarianism. Acting from a critique that was at once radical and immanent, early second-wave feminists sought less to dismantle the welfare state than to transform it into a force that could help to remedy male domination.[5]

By 1989, however, history seemed to have bypassed that political project. A decade of conservative rule in much of Western Europe and North America, capped by the fall of communism in the East, miraculously breathed new life into free-market ideologies previously given up for dead. Resurrected from the historical dustbin, "neoliberalism" authorized a sustained assault on the very idea of egalitarian redistribution. The effect, amplified by accelerating globalization, was to cast doubt on the legitimacy and viability of Keynesian steering of national economies. With social democracy on the defensive, efforts to broaden and deepen its promise naturally fell by the wayside. Feminist movements that had earlier taken the welfare state as their point of departure, seeking to extend its egalitarian ethos from class to gender, now found the ground cut out from under their feet. No longer able to assume social democracy as a basis for radicalization, they gravitated to newer grammars of political claims-making, more attuned to the postsocialist *Zeitgeist*.

From redistribution to recognition: the unhappy marriage of culturalism and neoliberalism

Enter the politics of recognition. If the first phase of postwar feminism sought to "engender" the socialist imaginary, the second phase stressed the need to "recognize difference." "Recognition," accordingly, became the chief grammar of feminist claims-making in the *fin de siècle*. A venerable category of Hegelian philosophy, resuscitated by political theorists, this notion captured the distinctive character of postsocialist struggles, which often took the form of identity politics, aimed more at valorizing difference than at promoting equality. Whether the question was violence against women or gender disparities in political representation, feminists increasingly resorted to the grammar of recognition to press their claims. Unable to make headway against injustices of political economy, they preferred to target harms resulting from androcentric patterns of cultural value or status hierarchies. The result was a major shift in the feminist imaginary: whereas the previous generation pursued an expanded ideal of social equality, this one invested the bulk of its energies in cultural change.[6]

Let me be clear. The project of cultural transformation has been integral to every phase of feminism, including the new social movements phase. What distinguished the identity-politics phase was the relative autonomization of the cultural project – its decoupling from the project of political-economic transformation and distributive justice.

Unsurprisingly, the effects of phase two were mixed. On the one hand, the new orientation to recognition focused attention on forms of male dominance that were rooted in the status order of capitalist society. Had it been combined with the earlier focus on socioeconomic inequalities, our understanding of gender justice would have been deepened. On the other hand, the figure of the struggle for recognition so thoroughly captured the feminist imagination that it served more to displace than to deepen the socialist imaginary. The tendency was to subordinate social struggles to cultural struggles, the politics of redistribution to the politics of recognition. That was not, to be sure, the original intention. It was assumed, rather, by proponents of the cultural turn that a feminist politics of identity and difference would synergize with struggles for social equality. But that assumption fell prey to the larger *Zeitgeist*. In the *fin de siècle* context, the turn to recognition dovetailed all too neatly with a hegemonic neoliberalism that wanted nothing more than to repress all memory of social egalitarianism. The result was a tragic historical irony. Instead of arriving at a broader, richer paradigm that could encompass both redistribution and recognition, we effectively traded one truncated paradigm for another – a truncated economism for a truncated culturalism.

The timing, moreover, could not have been worse. The shift to a culturalized politics of recognition occurred at precisely the moment when neoliberalism was staging its spectacular comeback. Throughout this period, academic feminist theory was largely preoccupied with debates about "difference." Pitting "essentialists" against "antiessentialists," these disputes usefully served to reveal hidden exclusionary premises of earlier theories, and they opened gender studies to many new voices. Even at their best, however, they tended to remain on the terrain of recognition, where subordination was construed as a problem of culture and dissociated from political economy. The effect was to leave us defenseless against free-market fundamentalism, which had meanwhile become hegemonic. Effectively mesmerized by the politics of recognition, we unwittingly diverted feminist theory into culturalist channels at precisely the moment when circumstances required redoubled attention to the politics of redistribution.[7] I shall return to this point shortly.

Geographies of recognition: postcommunism, postcolonialism, and the Third Way

First, however, I need to clarify one point. In recounting the shift from phase one to phase two, I have been describing an epochal shift in the feminist imaginary. But the shift was not limited to feminism *per se*. On the contrary, analogous shifts can be found in virtually every progressive social movement, as well as in the worldwide decline and/or co-optation of trade unions and socialist parties, and in the corresponding rise of identity politics, in both its progressive and chauvinist forms. Linked to the fall of communism, on the one hand, and to the rise of neoliberalism, on the other, this "shift from redistribution to recognition" (as I have called it) is part of the larger historical transformation associated with corporate globalization.[8]

It might be objected that this *Zeitdiagnose* reflects a limited first-world, American perspective. But I do not believe that is so. On the contrary, the tendency for recognition claims to eclipse distribution claims was quite general, even worldwide, even though the content of such claims differed widely. In Western Europe, the social-democratic focus on redistribution largely gave way in the 1990s to various versions of the Third Way. This approach adopted a neoliberal orientation to labor-market "flexibility," while seeking to maintain a progressive political profile. To the extent that it succeeded in the latter effort, it was by seeking not to mitigate economic inequalities but rather to overcome status hierarchies – through anti-discrimination and/or multicultural policies. Thus, in Western Europe, too, the currency of political claims-making shifted from redistribution to recognition, albeit in a milder form than in the United States.

Analogous shifts also occurred in the former Second World. Communism had enshrined its own version of the economistic paradigm, which shunted political claims into distributive channels, effectively muting recognition issues, which were cast as mere subtexts of "real" economic problems. Postcommunism shattered that paradigm, fueling the broad delegitimation of economic egalitarianism and unleashing new struggles for recognition – especially around nationality and religion. In that context, the development of feminist politics was retarded by its association, both real and symbolic, with a discredited communism.

Related processes, too, occurred in the so-called "Third World." On the one hand, the end of bipolar competition between the Soviets and the West reduced flows of aid to the periphery. On the other hand, the US-led dismantling of the Bretton Woods financial regime encouraged the new neoliberal policy of structural adjustment, which threatened the post-colonial developmental state. The result was to greatly reduce the scope for egalitarian redistributive projects in the South. And the response was an enormous surge of identity politics in the postcolony, much of it communalist and authoritarian. Thus, postcolonial feminist movements, too, were forced to operate without a background political culture that guides popular aspirations into egalitarian channels. Caught between downsized state capacities, on the one hand, and burgeoning communalist chauvinisms, on the other, they, too, felt pressure to recast their claims in forms more in keeping with the post-socialist *Zeitgeist*.

In general, then, the shift in feminism from phase one to phase two occurred within the larger matrix of postcommunism and neoliberalism. Insofar as feminists failed to understand this larger matrix, they were slow to develop the resources needed to fight for gender justice under new conditions.

US gender politics, post-9/11

That was especially the case in the United States. There, feminists were surprised to find that, while we had been arguing about essentialism, an unholy alliance of free-marketeers and fundamentalist Christians had taken over the country. Because this development has proved so momentous for the world at large, I want to pause to consider it briefly, before turning to the emergence of phase three.

The decisive issues in the 2004 US election were the so-called "war on terror," on the one hand, and (to a lesser extent) the so-called "family values" issues, especially abortion rights and gay marriage, on the other. In both cases, the strategic manipulation of gender was a crucial instrument of Bush's victory. The winning strategy invoked a gender-coded politics of recognition to hide a regressive politics of redistribution.

Let me explain. The Bush campaign's strategy painted the "war on terror" as a problem of leadership, which it addressed in explicitly gendered terms. Mobilizing masculinist stereotypes, Bush cultivated the image of a reassuringly steady and determined commander-in-chief, a protector who never doubts and never wavers – in short, a real man. In contrast, the Republicans presented the Democratic challenger, John Kerry, as a "girlie man," to use Arnold Schwarzenegger's memorable phrase, an effeminate "flip-flopper" who could not be trusted to protect American women and children from the crazed violence of bearded fanatics.[9]

Despite its distance from reality, this gender-coded rhetoric proved immensely powerful – to male and female voters alike. So powerful in fact that it appeared to neutralize what everyone agreed was the Bush campaign's weak point: its regressive politics of redistribution, which was bringing significant hardship to many Americans. Already in his first term, Bush had engineered an enormous upward redistribution of wealth to corporate interests and the propertied classes. By eliminating inheritance taxes, and lowering the tax rates of the wealthy, he had obliged the working classes to pay a far greater share of the national budget than before. The effect was to turn the politics of redistribution upside down, to promote increased social *injustice*. But none of that seemed to matter in the face of the "war on terror." Thus, a gender-coded politics of recognition effectively trumped a regressive politics of redistribution.[10]

A similar dynamic underlay the strategic deployment of "family values" rhetoric in the election campaign. The decisive issue in Ohio, which turned out to be the crucial state in the election, may have been "the defense of marriage." This issue was deliberately chosen by conservatives for a ballot referendum in that state (and others) as a strategy to ensure a high turnout of fundamentalist Christian voters. The theory was that once you got them to the polls to vote against gay marriage, then they would go ahead and also vote for Bush. And it seems to have worked.

In any case, "family values" proved to be a powerful electoral campaign theme. But here lies a major irony. The real tendencies that are making family life so difficult for the working and lower-middle classes stem from the neoliberal, corporate capitalist agenda that Bush supports. These policies include reduced taxes on corporations and the wealthy, diminished social-welfare and consumer protections, and very low wages and precarious employment. Thanks to these and related trends, it is no longer possible to support a family on one paycheck, and often not even on two. Far from being voluntary or supplemental, then, women's wage work is obligatory, an indispensable pillar of the neoliberal economic order. So, too, is the practice of "moonlighting," whereby working- and lower middle-class family members must work at more than one job in order to make ends meet. Those are the real forces that are threatening family life in the United States.[11] Feminists understand this, but they have not succeeded in convincing many who are harmed by these policies. On the contrary, the Right has managed to persuade them that it is abortion rights and gay rights that threaten their way of life. Here, too, in other words, the Republicans successfully used an anti-feminist politics of recognition to conceal an anti-working-class politics of redistribution.

In this scenario you can see the whole problem of phase two. Although it was not widely understood at the time, US feminists shifted their focus from redistribution to recognition, just as the Right was perfecting its own strategic deployment of a regressive cultural politics to distract attention from its regressive politics of redistribution. The coincidence was truly unfortunate. The relative neglect of political economy by US feminists and other progressive movements ended up playing into the hands of the Right, which reaped the principal benefits of the cultural turn.

Evangelicalism: a neoliberal technology of the self

But why were Americans so easily fooled by this obvious trick? And why were so many American women so susceptible to the Republicans' gender-coded appeals? Many observers have noted that the Right had some success in portraying US feminists as elite professionals and secular humanists, who have nothing but contempt for ordinary women, especially religious and working-class women. At one level, that view of feminism as elitist is patently false, of course, but the fact remains that feminism has failed to reach a large stratum of working- and lower-class women who have been attracted over the past decade to evangelical Christianity. Focused too one-sidedly on the politics of recognition, we have failed to understand how their religious orientation responds to their social class position.

Let me explain. At first sight, the situation of evangelical Christian women in the United States appears contradictory. On the one hand, they subscribe to a conservative ideology of traditional domesticity. On the other hand, these women do not in fact live patriarchal lives: most are active in the labor market and relatively empowered in family life.[12] The mystery is clarified when we understand that evangelicalism responds to the emergence in the United States of a new kind of society, which I call "the insecurity society." This society is the successor to the "welfare society" that was associated with social democracy in the previous period. Unlike the latter, the new society institutionalizes increased insecurity in the living conditions of most people. As I noted before, it weakens social welfare protections, even as it institutionalizes more precarious forms of wage labor, including subcontracting, temp work, and non-unionized work, which are low-waged and do not carry benefits. The result is a great sense of insecurity, to which evangelical Christianity responds.

Interestingly, evangelicalism does not actually give people security. Rather, it gives them a discourse and a set of practices through which they can manage insecurity. It says to them: "You are a sinner, you are going to fail, you may lose your job, you may drink too much, you may have an affair, your husband may leave you, your children may use drugs. But that's okay. God still loves you, and your church still accepts you." The effect is in part to convey acceptance but also to prepare people for trouble in hard times. Constantly invoking the likelihood of trouble, evangelicalism stokes its followers' feelings of insecurity, even as it seems to offer them a way of coping with it. Perhaps one needs the late Foucault to understand this: evangelicalism is a "care of the self" technology that is especially suited to neoliberalism, insofar as the latter is always generating insecurity. As I said, many working-class women in the United States are deriving something significant from this ideology, something that confers meaning on their lives. But feminists have not succeeded in understanding what it is and how it works. Nor have we figured out how to talk to them or what feminism can offer them in its place.

A different but related gender dynamic emerged in the 2008 Democratic Party Presidential primary contest, in which Barack Obama defeated Hillary Clinton.[13] These American examples have a larger, epochal significance. All of us are living in an age of declining security, thanks to neoliberal pressures to increase "flexibility" and curtail welfare protections amid increasingly precarious labor markets. For less integrated strata, including immigrants, these pressures are compounded when class inequalities of distribution are overlain with status inequalities of recognition; and the latter can easily be blamed on "secular feminism." In such cases, it behooves all feminists, in Europe as well as in the United States, to revisit the relationship between the politics of redistribution and the politics of recognition. Today, as we move into a third phase of feminist politics, we need to reintegrate these two indispensable dimensions of feminist politics, which were not adequately balanced in phase two.

Reframing feminism: a transnational politics of representation

Fortunately, something like this is already beginning to happen in those strands of feminist politics that are now operating in transnational spaces. Sensitized to the growing power of neoliberalism, these currents are crafting a new and promising synthesis of redistribution and recognition. In addition, they are changing the scale of feminist politics. Aware of women's vulnerability to transnational forces, they find that they cannot adequately challenge gender injustice if they remain within the previously taken-for-granted frame of the modern territorial state. Because that frame limits the scope of justice to intra-state institutions that organize relations among fellow citizens, it systematically obscures transborder forms and sources of gender injustice. The effect is to shield from the reach of justice all those forces shaping gender relations that routinely overflow territorial borders.

Today, accordingly, many transnational feminists reject the state-territorial frame. They note that decisions taken in one territorial state often impact the lives of women outside it, as do the actions of supranational and international organizations, both governmental and nongovernmental. They also note the force of transnational public opinion, which flows with supreme disregard for borders through global mass media and cybertechnology. The result is a new appreciation of the role of transnational forces in maintaining gender injustice. Faced with global warming, the spread of HIV-AIDS, international terror-ism, and superpower unilateralism, feminists in this phase believe that women's chances for living good lives depend at least as much on processes that trespass the borders of territorial states as on those contained within them.

Under these conditions, important currents of feminism are challenging the state-territorial framing of political claims-making. As they see it, that frame is a major vehicle of injustice, as it prevents many women from confronting the forces that oppress them. Imposing a kind of political purdah, it sequesters their claims in the domestic spheres of weak or powerless states, thereby insulating offshore agents of sexist domination from critique and control. The result is to shield many large-scale malefactors from the reach of gender justice. Left unaccount-able are not only the obvious suspects (powerful predator states, foreign investors and creditors, international currency speculators, and transnational corporations), but also the back-ground structures that enable them to operate with impunity – especially, the governance structures of the global econ-omy and the interstate system. The overall effect of the state-territorial frame is to exclude democratic consideration of transborder gender injustice.

Today, accordingly, feminist claims for redistribution and recognition are linked increasingly to struggles to change the frame. Faced with transnationalized production, many femi-nists eschew the assumption of national economies. In Europe, for example, feminists target the economic policies and struc-tures of the European Union, while feminist currents among the anti-World Trade Organization protestors are challenging the governance structures of the global economy. Analogously, feminist struggles for recognition increasingly look beyond the territorial state. Under the umbrella slogan "women's rights are human rights," feminists throughout the world are linking struggles against local patriarchal practices to campaigns to reform international law.[14]

The result is a new phase of feminist politics in which gender justice is being reframed. In this phase, a major concern is to challenge interlinked injustices of maldistribution and mis-recognition. Above and beyond those first-order injustices, however, feminists are also targeting a newly visible meta-injustice, which I have called *misframing*.[15] Misframing arises when the state-territorial frame is imposed on transnational sources of injustice. The effect is to gerrymander political space at the expense of the poor and despised, who are denied the chance to press transnational claims. In such cases, struggles against maldistribution and misrecognition cannot proceed, let alone succeed, unless they are joined with struggles against misframing. Misframing, accordingly, is emerging as a central target of feminist politics in its transnational phase.

By confronting misframing, this phase of feminist politics is making visible a third dimension of gender justice, beyond redistribution and recognition. I call this third dimension *representation*. As I understand it, representation is not only a matter of ensuring equal political voice for women in already constituted political communities; in addition, it requires reframing disputes about justice that cannot be properly contained within established polities. In contesting misframing, therefore, transnational feminism is reconfiguring gender justice as a three-dimensional problem, in which redistribution, recognition, and representation must be integrated in a balanced way.[16]

The developing transnational political space surrounding the European Union promises to be one important site for this third phase of feminist politics. In Europe, the task is to somehow do three things at once. First, feminists must work with other progressive forces to create egalitarian, gender-sensitive social-welfare protections at the transnational level. In addition, they must join with allies to integrate such redistributive policies with egalitarian, gender-sensitive recognition policies that can do justice to European cultural heterogeneity. Finally, they must do all that without hardening external borders, ensuring that transnational Europe does not become fortress Europe, so as not to replicate injustices of misframing on a broader scale.

Europe, however, is by no means the only site for this third phase of feminist politics. Equally important are the transnational spaces surrounding the various United Nations agencies and the World Social Forum. There, too, feminists are joining other progressive transnational actors, including environmentalists, development activists, and indigenous peoples, in challenging linked injustices of maldistribution, misrecognition, and misrepresentation. There, too, the task is to develop a three-dimensional politics that appropriately balances and integrates those concerns.

Developing such a three-dimensional politics is by no means easy. Yet it holds out tremendous promise for a third phase of feminist struggle. On the one hand, this approach could overcome the chief weakness of phase two, by rebalancing the politics of recognition and the politics of redistribution. On the other hand, it could overcome the blindspot of both of the previous phases of feminist politics, by explicitly contesting injustices of misframing. Above all, such a politics could permit us to pose, and eventually to answer, the key political question of our age: How can we integrate claims for redistribution, recognition, and representation so as to challenge the full range of gender injustices in a globalizing world?

7

From Discipline to Flexibilization?

Rereading Foucault in the Shadow of Globalization

Michel Foucault was the great theorist of the fordist mode of social regulation. Writing at the zenith of the postwar Keynesian welfare state, he taught us to see the dark underside of even its most vaunted achievements. Viewed through his eyes, social services became disciplinary apparatuses, humanist reforms became panoptical surveillance regimes, public health measures became deployments of biopower, and therapeutic practices became vehicles of subjection. From his perspective, the components of the postwar social state constituted a carceral archipelago of disciplinary domination, all the more insidious because self-imposed.

Granted, Foucault did not himself understand his project as an anatomy of fordist regulation. Positing a greater scope for his diagnosis, he preferred to associate disciplinary power with "modernity." And most of his readers, including me, followed suit. As a result, the ensuing debates turned on whether the Foucauldian picture of modernity was too dark and one-sided, neglecting the latter's emancipatory tendencies.[1]

Today, however, circumstances warrant a narrower reading. If we now see ourselves as standing on the brink of a new, postfordist epoch of globalization, then we should reread Foucault in that light. No longer an interpreter of modernity *per se*, he becomes a theorist of the fordist mode of social regulation, grasping its inner logic, like the Owl of Minerva, at the moment of its historical waning. From this perspective, it is significant that his great works of social analysis – *Madness and Civilization, The Birth of the Clinic, Discipline and Punish, The History of Sexuality*, volume I – were written in the 1960s and 1970s, just as the OECD countries abandoned Bretton Woods, the international financial framework that undergirded national Keynesianism and thus made possible the welfare state. In other words, Foucault mapped the contours of the disciplinary society just as the ground was being cut out from under it. And although it is only now with hindsight becoming clear, this was also the moment at which discipline's successor was struggling to be born. The irony is plain: whether we call it postindustrial society or neoliberal globalization, a new regime oriented to "deregulation" and "flexibilization" was about to take shape just as Foucault was conceptualizing disciplinary normalization.

Of course, to read Foucault in this way is to problematize his relevance to the present. If he theorized fordist regulation, then how does his diagnosis relate to postfordism? Is his account of the disciplinary society *dépassé*? Or does the regulatory grammar of fordism also subtend neoliberal globalization? In what follows, I shall examine such questions, while steering clear of both of those hypotheses. Proposing a third, "transformationalist," interpretation, I shall maintain that while the emerging postfordist mode of social regulation diverges sufficiently from the fordist one to preclude simple extension of the Foucauldian analysis of discipline, that analysis can still serve to illuminate it. More precisely, it can inspire us to creatively transform Foucauldian categories to account for new modes of "governmentality" in the era of neoliberal globalization.

Conceptualizing fordist discipline

To conceptualize discipline as the fordist mode of social regulation is to bring together Foucauldian and Marxian categorizations. Whether or not Foucault himself would have countenanced these associations is a question that could well be debated, as one can find textual support for both sides.[2] Here, however, I pass over that issue, as my intention is not to be faithful to Foucault. I seek, rather, to historicize him, just as he himself sought to historicize many others, not least among them Marx. In my effort, as in his, historicization means recontextualization, rereading texts in light of categories and problems not available to their authors. And so in this sense I shall be faithful to him after all.

So: discipline as the fordist mode of social regulation. Let me begin to unpack the meaning of that hypothesis by explaining what I mean by fordism. As I use the term, "fordism" covers the period of "the short twentieth century," from World War I to the fall of communism. In this period, capitalism generated a distinctive mode of accumulation, premised on mass industrial production, mass commodity consumption, and the vertically integrated corporation. But fordism was not simply a matter of economics. Rather, fordist accumulation mechanisms were embedded in, and dependent upon, a facilitating shell of social, cultural, and political arrangements. In the First World, one such arrangement was the family wage, which linked labor markets to emerging gender norms and family forms, while fostering an orientation to privatized domestic consumption. Another was a burgeoning consumer culture, adumbrated through advertising, mass media, and mass entertainment. Importantly, some of fordism's most characteristic first-world institutions did not fully develop until after World War II: the "class compromise" that incorporated labor as a major player in national polities; the Keynesian welfare state, which stabilized national markets and afforded social entitlements to national citizens; and, as mentioned above, an international financial system that enabled national state steering of national economies. Finally, as these last points suggest, fordism was an international phenomenon organized along national lines. Disproportionately benefiting the wealthy countries of the North Atlantic, while depending on colonial (and, later, postcolonial) labor and materials, it fostered national aspirations and institutional forms in the Third World, even as it stunted development there of the economic and political capacities needed to realize them. Also central to the fordist conjuncture were anti-fascism and anti-communism. In a century of virtually unending hot and cold world wars, fordist states fatefully commixed private industry with publicly financed military production, while also creating international organizations pledged to respect their national sovereignty. The result was a multifaceted social formation. A historically specific phase of capitalism, yet not simply an economic category, fordism was an international configuration that embedded mass production and mass consumption in national frames.

Understood in this way, what does fordism have to do with Foucault? To establish the link, we must assume that fordism was not just a set of mutually adapted institutions. We must posit, rather, that subtending those institutions was a distinctive set of regulatory mechanisms, which suffused them with a common ethos. Widely diffused throughout society, these small-scale techniques of coordination organized relations on the "capillary" level: in factories and hospitals, in prisons and schools, in state welfare agencies and in private households, in the formal associations of civil society and in informal daily interaction. The "micropolitical" counterpart of fordist accumulation, these practices of "governmentality" embodied a distinctive "political rationality." Reducible neither to *raison d'état* nor to universal instrumental reason, the regulatory grammar of fordism operated far beneath the commanding heights. Yet it was equally far removed from "traditional" social regulation by customs and values. Organizing individuals, arraying bodies in space and time, coordinating their forces, transmitting power among them, this mode of governmentality ordered ground-level social relations according to expertly designed logics of control. The upshot was a historically new mode of social regulation – a *fordist* mode suited to nationally bounded societies of mass production and mass consumption.

So far I have sketched the idea of fordist regulation in the abstract. Now I must fill in its qualitative character. Exactly what sort of governmentality is proper to fordism? What constitutes the specificity of its characteristic ordering mechanisms and political rationality? The answers, I suggest, can be found in Foucault's account of disciplinary biopower. But this suggestion raises serious problems. What in Foucauldian discipline is specifically fordist? Moreover, what should we make of the fact that Foucault located many of discipline's defining moments long prior to the twentieth century – in Enlightenment medical reforms, Jeremy Bentham's panopticon, and nineteenth-century uses of population statistics?[3] Finally, how shall we understand the fact that although Foucault never thematized the problem of scale, he nevertheless implicitly situated his analysis of discipline in relation to a historically specific understanding of the national/international nexus?

To begin with the historical problem: it is certainly true that Foucault traced the origins of discipline to the eighteenth and nineteenth centuries. But he also claimed to be writing "the history of the present." Thus, we are justified, I contend, in reading his early material through the prism of genealogy (his word). In that case, the clinic and the prison appear as early and still isolated proving grounds for regulatory practices that became fully developed, operational, and hegemonic only much later, in the twentieth century. On this reading, for which one could cite textual support, the disciplinary society emerged in its own right only after the general diffusion of techniques that had been pioneered much earlier, in scattered discrete institutions.[4] Only then, with the advent of fordism, did discipline become generalized and emblematic of society at large.

Not only is this hypothesis historically plausible, but it also affords some clues to our two other questions: the qualitative character of fordist governmentality and the problem of scale. In particular, it suggests three defining features of that mode of social regulation, now interpreted as Foucauldian discipline: totalization, social concentration within a national frame, and self-regulation. Let me elaborate each in turn, drawing largely on US examples, construed in Foucauldian terms.

First of all, fordist discipline was *totalizing*, aimed at rationalizing all major aspects of social life, including many never before subject to deliberate organization. Animated by a passion for control, Henry Ford's managers sought to rationalize not only factory production but also the family and community life of their workers, on the assumption that work habits began in the home. Likewise, in the 1910s and the 1920s, US reformers began to build municipal, state, and federal regulatory agencies aimed at ensuring public health and safety. The same period saw the proliferation of codified bodies of rationalizing social expertise: manuals of child-rearing, household management ("home economics"), social work (casework), psychotherapy (medicalized and lay-popular), industrial psychology, to name just a few. Later came special age-targeted control agencies (juvenile justice) and body-regimens (sex manuals, nutrition programs, and physical fitness schedules). Apparently, no social arena was off-limits in the campaign to subject everything to rational control. The fordist passion for planning even found expression in mass culture's utopian fantasies, especially the elaborate synchronized chorus lines of Holly-wood films.[5]

If fordist discipline was totalizing, it was nevertheless – and this is its second defining feature – *socially concentrated within a national frame*. As the century unfolded, various previously discrete disciplines converged upon a new societal space within the nation-state. Called "the social" both by Hannah Arendt and by the Foucauldian Jacques Donzelot, this was a dense nexus of overlapping apparatuses where institutions of social control became interconnected.[6] In the social, the fields of industrial relations, social work, criminal justice, public health, corrections, psychotherapy, marriage-counseling, and educa-tion became mutually permeable, each drawing from the same reservoir of rationalizing practices, while elaborating its own variations on the common grammar of governmentality. In some countries, including Foucault's France, this disciplinary heartland was largely the province of the national state; in others, such as the United States, nongovernmental agencies played a larger role, supplementing state apparatuses. In all cases, however, the social was correlated with a national state. Although Foucault did not explicitly thematize the question of scale, his account assumed that disciplinary ordering was nationally bounded.[7] From his perspective, the national-social was fordist regulation's ground zero, the zone of its densest elaboration and the launching pad for its wider diffusion. It was from this zone that fordist discipline radiated outward, imper-ceptibly spreading throughout national society. Yet social concentration did not entail vertical hierarchy, with commands flowing unidirectionally downward from the top of a traditional pyramid. Rather, disciplinary apparatuses subsisted side-by-side in the space of the national-social, their agents cooperating and competing on a par. Their milieu was one of middle-class professionalism, in which practitioners enjoyed considerable discretion, even as their activities were highly rationalized. The result was that disciplinary powers were socially concentrated yet horizontally arrayed within a national frame. Thus, as Fou-cault insisted, fordist discipline was simultaneously systematic and "capillary."

The third major feature of fordist discipline follows from the preceding two: this mode of social ordering worked largely through *individual self-regulation*. This was the original meaning of the phrase "social control," coined in 1907 by the American sociologist Edward Ross, as a democratic alternative to hierarchy and external coercion. As Foucault emphasized, advocates of social control sought to foster self-activating subjects, capable of internal self-governance. Wagering that such subjects would be more rational, cooperative, and productive than those directly subordinated to external authority, fordist reformers devised new organizational forms and management practices. In offices, factories, and social-service agencies, supervisors were urged to listen to workers and clients, solicit their input, and increase their scope of autonomous action. On the supply side, meanwhile, child psychologists, educators, and child-raising experts proposed to reform practices for socializing children. Aiming to nurture future autonomous self-regulating citizens, they urged mothers to feed on demand, fathers to abjure corporal punishment, teachers to foster curiosity and to explain the rationales behind rules. Analogous desiderata informed practices as disparate as marriage counseling and open-ended sentencing of criminals. The overall thrust was to "subjectify" individuals, to encourage linguistification of their internal processes as a means of holding them responsible for those processes, thereby augmenting their capacities for self-policing. Effectively conscripting individuals as agents of social control, while at the same time promoting their autonomy, fordist discipline sought to replace external coercion with internal self-regulation.[8]

In general, then, fordist discipline was totalizing, socially concentrated within a national frame, and oriented to self-regulation. The result was a form of governmentality that far transcended the bounds of the state, even as it remained nationally bounded. Widely diffused throughout national societies, productive as opposed to repressive, rational as opposed to charismatic, it mobilized "useful [if not wholly] docile bodies" in nationally bounded societies of mass production and mass consumption.

Certainly, many criticisms can be raised against this quasi-Foucauldian account of fordist regulation. For one thing, it is overly condemnatory of fordism, neglectful of the latter's progressive and emancipatory aspects. In particular, it is too dismissive of the individualizing, subjectifying moment of social control, too quick to reduce its autonomy-fostering orientation to a normalizing regimentation. Finally, it is embroiled in a performative contradiction, as it depends for its critical power on the very humanist norms, above all autonomy, that it wants simultaneously to unmask. Although I myself have raised such criticisms of Foucault in the past, and although I still consider them pertinent now, I shall not pursue them here. Here, rather, I address a different problem: the relation between discipline and postfordism. In so doing, I intend to problematize what I once called Foucault's "empirical insights," as opposed to his "normative confusions."[9]

From discipline to flexibilization?

The preceding account of fordist discipline assumes at least three empirical propositions that no longer hold true today. It assumes, first, that social regulation is organized nationally, that its object is a national population living in a national society under the auspices of a national state, which in turn manages a national economy. It assumes, second, that social regulation constitutes a non-marketized counterpart to a regime of capital accumulation, that it is concentrated in the zone of "the social," and that its characteristic institutions are the governmental and nongovernmental agencies that comprise the (national) social-welfare state. It assumes, finally, that regulation's logic is subjectifying and individualizing, that in enlisting individuals as agents of self-regulation, it simultaneously fosters their autonomy and subjects them to control, or, rather, it fosters their autonomy as a means to their control.

If these propositions held true in the era of fordism, their status is doubtful today. In the post-'89 era of postfordist globalization, social interactions increasingly transcend the borders of states. As a result, the ordering of social relations is undergoing a major shift in scale, equivalent to *de-nationalization* and *transnationalization*. No longer exclusively a national matter, if indeed it ever was, social ordering now occurs simultaneously at several different levels. In the case of public health, for example, country-based agencies are increasingly expected to harmonize their policies with those at the transnational and international levels. The same is true for policing, banking regulation, labor standards, environmental regulation, and counter-terrorism.[10] Thus, although national ordering is not disappearing, it is in the process of being decentered, as its regulatory mechanisms become articulated (sometimes cooperatively, sometimes competitively) with those at other levels. What is emerging, therefore, is a new type of regulatory structure, a multi-layered system of globalized governmentality, whose full contours have yet to be determined.

At the same time, regulation is also undergoing a process of *de-socialization*. In today's hegemonic neoliberal variant of globalization, massive, unfettered, transnational flows of capital are derailing the Keynesian project of national economic steering. The tendency is to transform the fordist welfare state into a postfordist "competition state," as countries scramble to cut taxes and eliminate "red tape," in hopes of keeping and attracting investment.[11] The resulting "race to the bottom" fuels myriad projects of *de*regulation, as well as efforts to privatize social services, whether by shifting them onto the market or by devolving them onto the family (which means, in effect, onto women). Although the extent of such projects varies from country to country, the overall effect is a global tendency to destructure the zone of "the (national) social," formerly the heartland of fordist discipline. Decreasingly socially concentrated, and increasingly marketized and familialized, postfordist processes of social ordering are less likely to converge on an identifiable zone. Rather, globalization is generating a new landscape of social regulation, more privatized and dispersed than any envisioned by Foucault.

Finally, as fordist discipline wanes in the face of globalization, its orientation to self-regulation tends to dissipate too. As more of the work of socialization is marketized, fordism's labor-intensive individualizing focus tends to drop out. In psychotherapy, for example, the time-intensive talk-oriented approaches favored under fordism are increasingly excluded from insurance coverage and replaced by instant-fix pharmapsychology. In addition, the enfeeblement of Keynesian state steering means more unemployment and less downward redistribution, hence increased inequality and social instability. The resulting vacuum is more likely to be filled by outright repression than by efforts to promote individual autonomy. In the US, accordingly, some observers posit the transformation of the social state into a "prison-industrial complex," where incarceration of male minority youth becomes the favored policy on unemployment.[12] The prisons in question, moreover, have little in common with the humanist panopticons described by Foucault. Their management often subcontracted to for-profit corporations, they are less laboratories of self-reflection than hotbeds of racialized and sexualized violence – of rape, exploitation, corruption, untreated HIV, murderous gangs, and murderous guards. If such prisons epitomize one aspect of postfordism, it is one that no longer works through individual self-governance. Here, rather, we encounter the return of repression, if not the return of the repressed.

In all these respects, postfordist globalization is a far cry from Foucauldian discipline: multi-layered as opposed to nationally bounded, dispersed and marketized as opposed to socially concentrated, increasingly repressive as opposed to self-regulating. With such divergences, it is tempting to conclude that the disciplinary society is simply *dépassé*. One might even be tempted to declare, following Jean Baudrillard, that we should "*oublier Foucault.*"

Globalized governmentality

That, however, would be a mistake. If contemporary society is postfordist and therefore post-disciplinary, it can nevertheless be profitably analyzed from a quasi-Foucauldian point of view. The key is to identify the characteristic ordering mechanisms and political rationality of the emerging new mode of regulation. The result would be a quasi-Foucauldian account of a new form of globalizing governmentality.[13]

As I see it, this project has at least three major parameters. A first crucial task is to conceptualize the transnational character of postfordist regulation. A second task is to theorize its increasing reliance on dispersed and marketized modes of governmentality. A third task is to analyze its distinctive political rationality, including its characteristic objects of intervention, modes of subjectification, and mix of repression and self-regulation. For each task, fortunately, we can draw on some pioneering work that is already available.

The transnational character of contemporary governmentality is the explicit subject of a large body of literature on globalization. Under the heading of "governance without government," many scholars are mapping the contours of a new multi-layered regulatory apparatus, which operates on a transnational scale. In this picture, social ordering is no longer nationally bounded, or correlated with a national state, or centered in any single locus of coordination. Rather, the locus of governmentality is being unbundled, broken up into several distinct functions and assigned to several distinct agencies, which operate at several distinct levels, some global, some regional, some local and subnational. For example, military and security functions are being disaggregated, relocated, and rescaled as a result of "humanitarian interventions," "peacekeeping operations," the "war on terror," and a host of multilateral security arrangements. Likewise, criminal law and policing functions are being unbundled, rebundled, and rescaled, sometimes upward, as in the case of international war crimes tribunals, the International Criminal Court, "universal jurisdiction," and Interpol; but sometimes downward, as in the case of tribal courts and the privatization of prisons. Meanwhile, responsibility for contract law is being rescaled as a result of the emergence of a private transnational regime for resolving business disputes (a revival of the *lex mercatoria*). Economic steering functions are being rescaled upward to regional trading blocs, such as the European Union, NAFTA, and Mercosur, and to formal and informal transnational bodies, such as the World Bank, the International Monetary Fund, and the World Economic Forum; but also downward, to municipal and provincial agencies, increasingly responsible for fostering development, regulating wages and taxes, and providing social welfare. In general, then, we are seeing the emergence of a new multi-leveled structure of governmentality, a complex edifice in which the national state is but one level among others.[14]

This new globalizing mode of regulation brings a considerable dispersion of governmentality. Unlike its fordist predecessor, the postfordist mode of regulation tends to "govern at a distance," through flexible fluctuating networks that transcend structured institutional sites.[15] No longer nation-state-centered, today's social ordering works through the powers and wills of a dispersed collection of entities, including states, supranational organizations, transnational firms, NGOs, professional associations, and individuals. At the country level, for example, QUANGOs assume regulatory functions previously held by the state; with the privatization of prisons, utilities, and schools, electoral accountability is supplanted by negotiations among "partners" on "community" boards.[16] At the international level, likewise, a motley and changing crew of unelected notables convenes annually for loosely institutionalized discussions at Davos, while legal regulation of transnational business gives way to new forms of ad hoc, informal arbitration, whose private and discretionary character insulates them from public scrutiny.[17] The result is a ruling apparatus whose composition is so complex and shifting that the distinguished international-relations theorist Robert F. Cox has named it *"la nebleuse."*[18]

Its shadowy quality notwithstanding, postfordist governmentality evinces some recognizable qualitative traits. This mode of regulation relies far more heavily than its predecessor on marketized ordering mechanisms. In the guise of neoliberalism, it vastly expands the scope of economic rationality, introducing competition into social services, transforming clients into consumers, and subjecting expert professionals to market discipline. In this regime of "de-statized governmentality," substantive welfare policy gives way to formal technologies of economic accountability, as auditors replace service professionals as the frontline disciplinarians.[19] Meanwhile, as vouchers replace public services, and privatized "risk management" replaces social insurance, individuals are made to assume new levels of "responsibility" for their lives. Displacing fordist techniques of "social control," market mechanisms organize large swaths of human activity; even decisions about marriage and childbearing are entangled with market incentives and disincentives.

The result is a new, postfordist mode of subjectification. Neither the Victorian subject of individualizing normalization nor the fordist subject of collective welfare, the new subject of governmentality is the actively responsible agent. A subject of (market) choice and a consumer of services, this individual is obligated to enhance her quality of life through her own decisions.[20] In this new "care of the self," everyone is an expert as regards herself, responsible for managing her own human capital to maximal effect.[21] In this respect the fordist project of self-regulation is continued by other means.

Nevertheless, the postfordist mode of governmentality differs sharply from its predecessor. Fordist regulation implicitly aspired to universality, despite persistent social inequality. In Foucault's account its object of intervention was not only the disciplined individual but the "general welfare" of "the population" as a whole; disciplinary normalization was linked to "biopower," which projected national synchronization and standardization, albeit on the backs of subjugated colonials.[22] In contrast, postfordist governmentality has burst open the national frame, as we have seen. In so doing, moreover, it simultaneously renounces the latter's universalist thrust, without, however, resorting to laissez-faire. Rather, postfordist regulation establishes new forms of (transnational) segmentation. Working largely through population profiling, it separates and tracks individuals for the sake of efficiency and risk prevention. Sorting the capable-and-competitive wheat from the incapable-and-noncompetitive chaff, postfordist welfare policy constructs different life courses for each. The result is a new kind of segmented governmentality: responsibilized self-regulation for some, brute repression for others. In this "dual society," a hypercompetitive, fully networked zone coexists with a marginal sector of excluded low-achievers.[23]

The preceding sketch is only that: a cursory overview of some of the ways in which postfordist governmentality is being elaborated. Much work remains to be done. Let me close by indicating two additional directions for further research.

One intriguing possibility concerns the ordering functions performed by "networks" in postfordism. A ubiquitous buzzword of globalization, the term "network" names both a form of social organization and an infrastructure of communication. The hallmark of networks is their ability to combine rule-governed organization with flexibility, open-endedness, decenteredness, and spatial dispersion. Thus, in business, we have the various transnational chains of firms – suppliers, contractors, jobbers, etc. – that comprise the lean, easily altered structure of niche-oriented "just-in-time" production. Likewise, in the peculiar intersection of politics, religion, and criminality that is so much on our minds today, we have terrorist networks: transnational, decentered, spatially dispersed, seemingly leaderless, and impossible to locate, at least by anything as clunky as a national state, yet capable of stunningly well-organized acts of synchronized massive destruction, enlisting McWorld in the service of jihad, if not forever destabilizing the distinction between them.[24]

Seemingly more rhizomatic and Deleuzian than disciplinary and Foucauldian, networks may nevertheless be emerging as important new vehicles of postfordist governmentality. Critical theorists of globalization would do well to try to analyze them in Foucauldian terms. Above all, we might explore their articulation (both competitive and cooperative) with more familiar types of regulatory agencies.

A second candidate for a quasi-Foucauldian analysis of globalization is the related notion of "flexibilization." Another ubiquitous buzzword of globalization, "flexibilization" names both a mode of social organization and a process of self-constitution. Better: it is a process of self-constitution that correlates with, arises from, and resembles a mode of social organization. The hallmarks of flexibilization are fluidity, provisionality, and a temporal horizon of "no long term." Thus, what networks are to space, flexibilization is to time. So we have the flexible specialization of just-in-time production in the world of business. And we have the "flexible men" (and women) described by Richard Sennett, who frequently change jobs and even careers, relocating at the drop of a hat, whose collegial relations and friendships are trimmed to fit the horizon of "no long term," and whose selfhood does not consist in a single meaningful, coherent, overarching life-narrative.[25] Such flexible selves seem more fragmented and postmodern than do the subjectified, identitarian selves described by Foucault. Yet they may nevertheless be emerging as important new vehicles of self-regulation – at least for the "capable classes." And so critical theorists might subject them too to a quasi-Foucauldian analysis. Above all, they might try to determine whether the project of social control through self-governance and even personal autonomy might outlive fordism in some new guise.

In all such analyses, we should recall that discipline was Foucault's answer to the following question: How does power operate in the absence of the king? Today, of course, his answer is no longer persuasive, but that is not all. More disturbingly, the question itself needs to be reformulated: How does power operate after the decentering of the national frame, which continued to organize social regulation long after the demise of the monarch? In fact, it would be hard to formulate a better guiding question, as we seek to understand new modes of governmentality in the era of neoliberal globalization. In my view, such an effort is the most fitting way by far to honor one of the most original and important thinkers of the previous century.

8

Threats to Humanity in Globalization

Arendtian Reflections on the Twenty-First Century

Hannah Arendt was the great theorist of mid-twentieth-century catastrophe. Writing in the aftermath of the Nazi holocaust, she taught us to conceptualize what was at stake in this darkest of historical moments. Seen through her eyes, the extermination camps represented the most radical negation of the quintessentially human capacity for spontaneity and the distinctively human condition of plurality. Thus for Arendt they had a revelatory quality. By taking to the limit the project of rendering superfluous the human being as such, the Nazi regime crystallized in the sharpest and most extreme way humanity-threatening currents that characterized the epoch more broadly.

Arendt explored these currents elsewhere as well. In Stalinism, for example, she discerned a not wholly dissimilar effort to re-engineer human life on a mass scale. Seeking to totalize a single vision, it, too, obliterated public space and endangered individuality and plurality. But that was not all. Unlike the cold warriors who later appropriated her concept of totalitarianism to stifle criticism of what they called the "free world," Arendt also excavated what we might call some proto- or quasi-totalitarian crystals in the democratic "mass societies" of the 1950s: the eclipse of politics by "social housekeeping" and the colonization of public space by scientistic techniques for manipulating opinion and managing populations. Without in any way glossing over the enormous differences between

Nazism, Stalinism, and democratic mass society, she enter-
tained the heretical thought that the latter, too, harbored
structural threats to the fundamental conditions of human
being. The result was a far-reaching vision of the distinctive
evils of the twentieth century and a diagnosis of humanity's
vulnerability.

Many of the specifics of these analyses are certainly debat-
able. But this is not the level at which I want to engage Arendt's
thought. What interests me, rather, is the larger diagnosis that
underlies them. From Arendt's perspective, the twentieth century's distinctive and characteristic catastrophes arose from the
fateful convergence of two major historical streams. One was
the crisis of the nation-state, which had become unmoored
from the limits of place by the expansive logic of imperialism;
this crisis produced intense national and pan-national chauvinisms, stigmatized and vulnerable minorities, and defenseless
stateless persons, deprived of political membership and thus of
"the right to have rights." The other stream was the intrusion
into politics of a totalizing and fundamentally anti-political way
of seeing, not unlike what James Scott has called "seeing like
a state."[1] Affecting a God's-eye view from the commanding
heights, above and outside the human world, this way of seeing
cast human beings as materiel for deterministic totalizing
schemes. Such seeing did not merely overlook human plurality
and spontaneity; its *raison d'être* was precisely to eliminate
them. When the crisis of the nation-state met the totalizing
view from the commanding heights, the result was a new kind
of evil and threat to humanity.

Arendt's analysis was an exemplary effort to grasp her time
in thought. Focused on the most terrible and disturbing phenomena of the age, she sought to comprehend what was new
and unprecedented in them, hence what could not be reduced
to past horrors. She herself was explicit about this orientation.
Seeking to inhabit the space "between past and future," she
self-consciously cultivated a way of thinking that was both
historicizing and present-focused.

It is this stance that I find most compelling in Arendt's
thought – and most worth emulating in the twenty-first century.
Our time, too, can be illuminated by theorizing that histori-
cizes the present and diagnoses its characteristic dangers in the
hope of forestalling their future realization. Akin in some

respects to the orientation of Michel Foucault, this stance strikes me as not merely relevant but downright indispensable to vital political theorizing in the coming period.[2]

Nevertheless, I do not insist on the historically located quality of Arendt's thought solely in order to validate her general approach. In addition, I want to think more specifically about its relevance to the present. I wish to ask: If Arendt theorized the characteristic catastrophes of the twentieth century, then how does her diagnosis bear on those looming before us in the twenty-first? Do today's dangers to humanity still arise from projects aimed at obliterating spontaneity and plurality? And do those dangers still stem from the same fateful conjunction of the nation-state's crisis with the proclivity for seeing like a state?

I suspect that the answer to each of these questions is yes and no. On the one hand, our present dangers diverge sufficiently from those of the mid-twentieth century to preclude any simple extension of Arendt's analysis. On the other hand, the deeper dynamic she identified can nevertheless clarify those newer threats to humanity that are gathering force today. In general, then, the approach I propose is this: we should neither rashly reject nor slavishly preserve Arendt's analysis. Rather, we should creatively transform Arendtian thinking to account for new modes of negating the human in the twenty-first century.

In what follows, accordingly, I shall try to demonstrate Arendt's continuing relevance while avoiding any hint of worshipful piety. I begin by noting that her diagnosis of the dynamics of disaster still possesses the power to illuminate features of our own time. Certainly, 9/11 and its aftermath can be fruitfully analyzed in terms of the mutual entwinement of the nation-state's crisis and the tendency to "see like a state." On the one hand, the rise of a radically new form of transnational political Islamism responds to the failure of modern secular nationalism in the Middle East and beyond, a failure rooted in old and new forms of imperialism. In addition, Al-Qaeda and its offshoots bear an eerie resemblance to the anti-political "pan" movements that Arendt traced to the destructuration of the nation-state in *The Origins of Totalitarianism*. On the other hand, the Bush government's response to 9/11, above all its disastrous invasion and occupation of Iraq, stands as a textbook example of the anti-political, totalizing view from nowhere. Intent on molding reality to the contours of its will, and on negating the human capacity for spontaneous action, this administration set its course in direct opposition to mobilized world opinion and in flagrant violation of international law. In these respects, its actions encapsulate both the nation-state's crisis and the view from the commanding heights. Locked together in a self-propelling destructive cycle, then, the mutually reinforcing projects of "jihadism" and the "war on terror" recapitulate key aspects of Arendt's diagnosis, even as they also generate new forms of menace to humanity, which she herself could not have imagined.

If these features of the present echo key aspects of Arendt's diagnosis, others go well beyond it. One such "post-Arendtian" development is the halting but unmistakable emergence of an international human rights regime, accompanied by a resurgence of interest in cosmopolitanism. Another is a new appreciation of plurality – not only the national and individual plurality that Arendt theorized, but other forms as well, including those associated with gender, sexuality, and multiculturalism. Still another is the effort to replace the Westphalian idea of sovereignty, undivided, territorially bounded, and state-centered – but now being destabilized by globalization, by new forms of shared political responsibility, which are trans-territorial and multi-leveled.

What shall we make of this twenty-first-century conjunction of Arendtian and post-Arendtian crystals? Might the new strands of cosmopolitanism, pluralism, and postwestphalianism acquire sufficient weight finally to resolve the crisis of the nation-state and to counteract the drive to rule from the commanding heights? Or are the latter tendencies more likely to overpower and co-opt the former? It is a measure of Arendt's ongoing relevance that these questions structure much of today's most interesting political theorizing. Although opinion about them remains sharply divided, many thoughtful observers invoke Arendtian motifs, whether wittingly or unwittingly, as they seek to locate our twenty-first-century present in the space between past and future.

On one side stand those, such as Jürgen Habermas and David Held, who derive hope from the post-Arendtian strands of cosmopolitanism, pluralism, and postwestphalianism. For such

theorists, these developments suggest a way out of the dynamics of disaster that Arendt analyzed. Habermas, for example,
notes that the increased migration associated with globalization
is now transforming the ethical-political self-understanding of
many people. The results include defensive nativist reactions,
on the one hand, and a new interest in difference and hybridity,
on the other. The first, defensive, response evokes the possibility analyzed by Arendt of renewed statelessness and expulsion
from humanity. The second, in contrast, evokes new forms of
living together in plurality that could conceivably put an end
to that dynamic. This second response also suggests that the
nation-state could be *dépassé*. In place of the Herderian assumptions of previous centuries, we now encounter a new awareness
of the social construction of the nation as an "imagined community." With this skepticism toward primordial community
goes a new appreciation of the plurality within every political
community: plurality of national origin, plurality of religion,
plurality of ethnicity, and plurality of language, on the one
hand, and of genders and sexualities, on the other. And this in
turn gives rise to efforts to reconceive political community in
ways that do not require homogeneity. The result is a new
political project aimed at dissolving the hyphen between nation
and state – hence at decoupling political community from
nationality.[3]

This project goes well beyond anything that Arendt envisioned, although it is by no means without problems of its own.
Habermas, for example, proposes to replace ethnonationalism
with "constitutional patriotism." In that case the solidarity of
citizens would no longer rest on any presumed pre-existing
substantial sameness; rather it would emerge from the "communicative mastery of conflicts."[4] On that basis, democratic
constitutional states could now develop new liberal self-
understandings. Sensitive to intra-community differences, they
could formulate their laws in general terms, terms that are
sufficiently neutral to avoid casting immigrants and ethnic
minorities as second-class citizens. Such an approach could also
go some way to protect the rights of non-citizens on their territory. In that case, so the argument goes, the disastrous dynamic
diagnosed by Arendt would come to a halt. Fully included
as citizens, members of minorities would be assured membership in a (de-nationalized) political community, which would

guarantee their right to have rights; and foreigners would enjoy protection of their basic rights. Unlike ethnonationalism, then, constitutional patriotism would halt the production of stateless and superfluous persons.[5]

It is interesting to speculate as to what Arendt would have thought of this proposal. I imagine her response would have been twofold. On the one hand, she would surely have applauded the shift from a polity based on ethnonationalism to one premised on constitutional patriotism, given her own republican enthusiasm for communicatively generated solidarity. On the other hand, she would have also noted that this approach makes minority protection dependent on the majority's continued liberal self-understanding; and that is a fragile basis, as the majority's self-understanding could change. In that case, there could be a regression to ethnonationalism, and the twentieth-century dynamic of statelessness and expulsion from humanity could resume.[6] For Arendt, accordingly, a minority's best safeguard of its right to have rights was a state of its own; in her view, the restoration of human rights seemed possible "only through the restoration or the establishment of national rights."[7] Thus, she was driven to resurrect the nation-state, even though her own analysis had already shown with perfect clarity where that could lead.

Fortunately, however, the resurrection of the nation-state is not the only possible response to the reasonable worry that constitutional patriotism alone may be insufficient to prevent the production of superfluous stateless people. More promising, I think, is the move to the cosmopolitical level, a move that Arendt famously considered utopian. Writing in *The Origins of Totalitarianism* in 1951, she noted: "for the time being, a sphere that is above the nations does not exist."[8] In this formulation, the phrase "for the time being" is particularly striking, as it leaves open the possibility of new developments, such as the emerging human-rights protections that twenty-first-century cosmopolitans find so encouraging. Unlike Arendt, these thinkers envision an actionable international-legal status for individuals that is not mediated through states. For them, accordingly, this emerging form of "world citizenship" represents a backup for constitutional patriotism, which could prevent statelessness and human superfluity in case the latter should fail.[9] Advocating a postwestphalian world order, then, cosmopolitans aim to subordinate state sovereignty to international courts, global human rights law enforcement, and, in the worst cases, humanitarian interventions.[10]

Today, of course, we are still a long way from all that. Under current conditions, moreover, our halting steps in that direction are subject to serious abuse. Humanitarian interventions that may be entirely defensible in the abstract quickly devolve into superpower machinations in pursuit of narrow national interests. Similarly, international war crimes prosecutions, even when entirely appropriate in themselves, are vulnerable to the charge of victors' justice, as the author of *Eichmann in Jerusalem* well understood. Such suspicions are fueled, of course, when the world's sole superpower claims the right to determine unilaterally when humanitarian intervention is called for, while also claiming blanket advance exemption from any possible international prosecution for war crimes.[11]

Such worries have led some observers to see in cosmopolitanism nothing but a mask of empire. Concentrating exclusively on the dark side of the move beyond nation-state sovereignty, these thinkers wager that the sources of catastrophe that Arendt identified retain sufficient power to co-opt the apparently more hopeful developments of our age. Focusing especially on the continuing strength of the totalizing view from the commanding heights, they challenge us to probe the world-historical implications of the collapse of communism. The crucial question, from this perspective, is this: Are we really living in a post-totalitarian world? Does the demise, first, of fascism, then of communism, really mean the end of hyper-totalizing projects that would destroy the public world and render superfluous human being? Or do other such projects lurk in the wings?

Let me suggest that there are three different ways of approaching such questions. The first approach looks for new versions of the kind of classical totalitarianism analyzed by Arendt. The best contemporary example is Paul Berman's controversial book *Terrorism and Liberalism*, which analyzes early twenty-first-century radical political Islamism as a variant of classical totalitarianism, with many similarities to European fascism. Like the latter, claims Berman, Al-Qaeda and its offshoots hark back to an imagined past, are obsessed with identifying internal and external enemies, and seek to institute a totalizing social system, undergirded by absolutist law, that allows no space for privacy or free association.[12]

In its highly provocative character this analysis may remind some of Arendt. But I am convinced that it contravenes the deeper spirit of her thought. Rushing to assimilate a new phenomenon to a familiar past model, Berman misses its genuine novelty. Locating the intellectual sources of Al-Qaeda in European cultural modernity, he neglects to illuminate the social sources of Islamism's appeal. Analogizing the latter to fascism, finally, he disavows any underlying commonalities between "us" and "them." The effect is to replicate precisely the sort of Manichean thinking that Berman himself aims to criticize – and that Arendt wholeheartedly detested.

Fortunately, however, Berman's method is not the only way of examining the possibility of renewed totalitarianism in the twenty-first century. A second approach contemplates the prospect of new, quasi-totalitarian projects of bird's-eye view domination that do not resemble the classical forms. Two examples, from opposite sides of the political spectrum, are John Gray's 1998 book *False Dawn*, on the one hand, and Michael Hardt and Antonio Negri's *Empire*, on the other.

Influenced more by Isaiah Berlin than by Arendt, Gray nevertheless suggests that human spontaneity and plurality are currently endangered by a totalizing project that is every bit as arrogant and freedom-threatening as communism was: the project of imposing a single "free-market society" everywhere, disembedding markets from their social and cultural frameworks and over-riding all national particularities. According to Gray, moreover, this project cannot come about naturally; contrary to its ideological presentation of the free market as "natural," the "free-market society" can only arise through a massive effort of social engineering. For Gray, accordingly, it represents a new, quasi-totalitarian system, centered more on the market than the state, but still totalizing and destructive of plurality.[13]

In contrast, Hardt and Negri discern the contours of a new system of totalizing domination in the emerging regime of global governance that is currently replacing the state-centered Westphalian order. Unsurprisingly, this quasi-totalitarian regime encompasses the governing institutions of the new global economic order, which are insulating transnational corporate capital from democratic political control. More surprisingly, however, it also includes many of the cosmopolitan institutions that theorists like Habermas and Held support, including the emerging human-rights regime. In Hardt and Negri's view, *all* of these new global institutions lack democratic accountability and serve the interests of the global elite. Thus, they, too, project a new quasi-totalitarian system that occupies the view from the commanding heights.[14]

Interestingly, both Gray, on the one hand, and Hardt and Negri, on the other, imply a structure of control very different from Arendtian totalitarianism. In neither case is domination institutionalized directly, by a powerful identifiable center analogous to the Nazi or Stalinist party-state. Rather, it is institutionalized indirectly, by means of a decentralized apparatus: the market, in one case, and the nexus of multiple governance apparatuses, in the other. Thus, the source of the threat is more elusive and harder to pin down than in the cases analyzed by Arendt. Nevertheless, the projected outcome is not wholly dissimilar. Both Gray, on the one hand, and Hardt and Negri, on the other, posit virtually all-encompassing systems of control whose expansive logic would drive out all possible alternatives. Both also posit that the effect is to subjugate human spontaneity to the false necessity of a social determinism, despite the rhetoric of market freedom and cosmopolitan democracy. Thus, both effectively posit the need for a quasi-Arendtian investigation of the deep grammar of new social phenomena in terms of their potential to render human beings superfluous.

Nevertheless, neither account achieves the perspicacity of Arendt's best work, as both are hyperbolic and misleading. Gray is so preoccupied with preserving a plurality of capitalisms that he ends up defending non-democratic alternatives to American hegemony. And while Hardt and Negri fantasize about the spontaneous revolt of a constituting "multitude," they have little appreciation of either the practice of democracy or its institutional conditions.[15] In addition, both books exaggerate the systematicity and totalizing character of twenty-first-century forms of domination. Where they do not simply obscure emancipatory counter-tendencies and contrary and oppositional elements, they interpret these as mere internal ruses of the system.

To avoid such an over-systematic and over-totalized analysis, one might take still another approach to our quasi-Arendtian question: Are we really living in a post-totalitarian world? This third approach would try to identify quasi-totalitarian moments embedded in political projects that are not themselves inherently totalitarian. Alerting us to potential dangers lurking in even apparently favorable social tendencies, it would seek to ascertain the relative weight of positive and negative crystals within them. The point, however, would not be to analyze each such political project discretely, in isolation from the others. Rather, this third approach would seek to uncover the dynamics of their mutual interaction. Seeking to map the overall constellation of the age, it would identify the latter's most compelling alternative projects and the larger force-field in which they compete for hegemony.

At minimum, then, this approach would search out proto-totalitarian crystals in each of the following formations: (1) existing liberal-democratic societies, which are currently being transformed by globalization – especially those, like the United States, whose political culture is proving vulnerable to quasi-totalitarian manipulations; (2) emerging postwestphalian structures of governance, including both the governance structures of the global economy, which currently promote neoliberalism, and the changing contours of international law, which could in principle promote cosmopolitan democracy – without, however, collapsing the differences between them; (3) apparently regressive "pan" movements, which may also contain in mystified form a kernel of legitimate, anti-imperialist grievance, and which include Jewish and Christian political fundamentalisms, as well as their Islamist analogues; and (4) apparently emancipatory transnational movements, such as international feminism, environmentalism, and the anti-neoliberal-globalization movements associated with the World Social Forum, which may contain elite biases and do not always manage to live up to their own democratic aspirations. In each case, the goal of the analysis would be to ascertain the precise mix of proto-totalitarian and anti-totalitarian crystals – hence to encourage us to guard against the first and to foster the second.

The underlying assumption of this approach is twofold. On the one hand, none of these twenty-first-century political formations is totalitarian *per se*. On the other hand, none is wholly devoid of quasi-totalitarian crystals. Thus, these projects are best understood by an approach that forswears use of the noun form "totalitarianism" in favor of such modified adjectival forms as "proto-totalitarian" and "quasi-totalitarian."[16]

This, I suspect, would be the most fitting way to carry forward Arendt's legacy. In this way, we could begin to theorize the dangers of the twenty-first century on a scale roughly comparable to her account of those of the twentieth, without sacrificing complexity or subtlety. Absent such ambitious yet nuanced analyses of present-day threats to humanity, the twenty-first century is still awaiting its Hannah Arendt. Let us hope she arrives soon.

9

The Politics of Framing
An Interview with Nancy Fraser

Kate Nash and Vikki Bell

Vikki Bell: In your current work, would you say that what you're attempting to do is to describe something that's already happening? Or are you trying to lend some support to something that's emergent, or do you see yourself more as trying to bring about change through your work? In my mind, this is the same question as, "What is the role of the (political) theorist?"

Nancy Fraser: The short answer is: all of the above. And I agree that what underlies your question is one's conception of the role of the critical theorist. So everything depends on figuring out how to get the various tasks you outline in the right relation to one another. Let me explain what I have in mind by way of a historical contrast. In the early 1980s, when I was first starting to publish, I still had one foot in the activist milieu associated with the new social movements, especially second-wave feminism. In those days, the relation between theory and practice seemed relatively fluid. It felt natural to address problems that emerged out of political practice and to trust that one's reflections would filter back down to the grassroots, if not directly, then through various intermediaries. Thus, it seemed possible to write for at least two different publics at once: on the one hand, one could address one's fellow academics, criticizing mainstream theoretical paradigms and exposing their ideological distortions and blindspots; on the other hand, one could engage the social movements with which one identified, giving systematic expression to their aspirations and evaluating proposals for realizing them. What united these enterprises was an overarching ethos in which theoretical clarity and political confidence seemed to go hand in hand. There was an unspoken but vividly felt sense that the political objectives were clear and that the road to achieving them was open. Today, however, the situation is different, largely because the overall political landscape is so much darker. Emancipatory movements still exist, to be sure, but their energies tend to be dwarfed by the twin forces of neoliberalism and reactionary chauvinism. In addition, the earlier sense of clarity has given way to a "new obscurity" (to use Habermas's phrase), in which progressive currents lack both a coherent vision of an alternative to the present order and also a plausible scenario as to how such a vision, if one existed, could conceivably be realized. Certainly, there are many reasons for this historical shift, but I will mention just one, which looms large in my current thinking: the new salience of globalization, which is exploding the previously taken-for-granted idea that the bounded territorial state is both the appropriate frame for conceiving questions of justice and the proper arena for waging struggles to achieve it. As that doxa recedes in the face of intensified experiences of transnationalization, many of the assumptions that undergirded earlier projects of critical theorizing and political practice are being called into question – revealed to be indefensible expressions of what Ulrich Beck calls "methodological nationalism." In this context, it becomes harder to sustain a productive relation between theory and practice. As both terms of that relation are destructured, each of them needs to be rethought.

The upshot is that I find myself trying in my current work to do simultaneously all of the things that you mentioned at the outset. One aim is to describe a new grammar of political claims-making, in which what is at issue are not only first-order questions of justice, but also meta-questions about how first-order questions ought to be framed. In attempting to map a new discursive constellation, I find myself stepping back from immediate practical questions and taking the perspective of an observer. Thus, I have proposed to conceive present-day arguments about distribution, recognition, and representation as a species of "abnormal justice" in which the taken-for-granted parameters of "normal justice," such as a shared sense of "who counts," are up for grabs. At the same time, however, I am also trying to clarify the aspirations of those social movements that seem to me to carry our best hopes for emancipatory change. Insofar as I wear this second hat, which is closer to the participant's perspective, I see myself as trying to theorize concepts and formulate arguments that can be of use to those movements. This involves giving an explicit systematic conceptual spin to what some social actors are already doing or saying. An example is my account of *misframing*. That is my term for a type of meta-injustice that arises when first-order questions of justice are framed in a way that wrongly excludes some from consideration – as when the national framing of distributive issues forecloses the claims of the global poor. Although they don't themselves use the term, many globalization activists seem to me to rely implicitly on such an idea. In making their assumption explicit and giving it a name, I am trying to enrich the pool of justifications at their disposal. But that is not all. Even as I describe discursive structures and make explicit implicit claims, I am also offering a *Zeitdiagnose* that serves to criticize counterproductive forms of Left thinking and practice. An example is my diagnosis of the shift in political claims-making from redistribution to recognition, which has proved so disabling for the Left in recent years. When speaking in that register I am drawing my own conclusions about what is to be done. Thus, all three of the objectives you distinguish are conjoined in my current work. Together they entail a complex conception of the role of the critical theorist. Perhaps I could summarize it like this: a situated thinker, with determinate partisan identifications, who nevertheless cultivates the practice of relatively distanced reflection aimed at disclosing, and fostering, possible links between existing social struggles and historically emergent possibilities for emancipation.

Kate Nash: In your *New Left Review* article, "Reframing Justice in a Globalizing World,"[1] you're talking about questions of representation alongside recognition and redistribution; this is a new development in your work. The word "representation" is ambiguous and you seem to be using it in its symbolic sense, talking about "frame", but in some way you're also clearly relating it to democracy. Please could you say a bit more about the relationship between the idea of symbolic representation and representation as accountability to groups in some way?

NF: Great question! By way of background, I should note that the incorporation of political representation as a third dimension of justice constitutes a major revision of my framework, which was originally two-dimensional. During the ten-year period in which I developed the original theory, I often encountered readers who asked, "What about the political?" and my answer was always, "Ah! But don't you see that distribution and recognition *are* political, because both of them concern power asymmetries and structures of subordination? The political is already there, in those economic and cultural dimensions of (in)justice. There is no need to treat it as a separate dimension." In the back of my mind, however, I worried that that answer might not suffice. And so, beginning in the late 1990s, I began to qualify my elaborations of the original theory. If you look at my writings from that period, you will find many formulations like the following: "In my view, justice has at least two dimensions, economic redistribution and cultural recognition. But there is also the possibility of a third, political, dimension, which I cannot develop here."

In those early days, when I first began to worry that I might need to introduce the political as a distinct category, I was thinking of the sorts of issues that preoccupy political scientists: Do all of those who are included in principle in a given political community really have equal voice? Can all participate fully, as peers, in political life? As you know, political scientists typically approach such questions in terms of political decision rules. Studying the effects of different electoral systems on political voice, they weigh the relative merits of, say, proportional representation versus winner-take-all, first-past-the-post systems. What interested me, however, was not such technicalities but the larger question that lies behind them: Can the relations of representation be unjust in and of themselves, apart from the effects of maldistribution and misrecognition on their operation? That question nagged at me because I have always conceived injustice in terms of institutionalized obstacles to parity of participation in social life. In my framework, each type of institutionalized obstacle corresponds to a dimension of (in)justice. So it has always been crucial for me to distinguish different kinds of obstacles to participatory parity. From the beginning it was clear to me that there could exist (and did!) economic and cultural obstacles to parity, which is why I originally conceived justice in terms of those two dimensions. Later, however, I began to ask myself whether political obstacles to parity could exist even in the absence of maldistribution and misrecognition. For example, could an electoral system, operating in a context of relatively fair distribution and reciprocal recognition, leave ideological minorities permanently voiceless? If so, that would be a case in which the relations of representation were *per se* unjust. And in time, I came to believe that such distinctively political injustices *are* in fact possible.

But this was not the decisive consideration that led me to incorporate representation into my framework as the third dimension of justice. Decision rules typically involve first-order political injustices, which arise *within* the established frame of a bounded polity. My primary concern, by contrast, is with meta-level political injustices, which arise as a result of the division of political space *into* bounded polities. An example is the way in which the international system of (supposedly) sovereign states gerrymanders political space at the expense of the global poor. Channeling the latter's claims into the domestic political arenas of relatively powerless, if not wholly failed, states, this system denies them the means to confront the off-shore architects of their dispossession – and thereby shields transnational malefactors from critique and control. It was my interest in such meta-injustices of misframing, which are at the center of present-day struggles over globalization, that decided me in the end to take the plunge and introduce the political dimension of justice into my framework.

Well, all of that is by way of background. Now I must explain why I chose the term *representation* to name this dimension. One motive, I confess, was to preserve the alliteration with redistribution and recognition. Another was to exploit the polysemy of the term, which, as you point out, can mean both symbolic framing and political voice. It is important to me to conceive the political dimension of justice in a way that draws on both of those meanings and discloses the relation between them. The reason is that I conceive this dimension as comprising two levels. On the one hand, I intend representation to encompass those familiar questions about electoral rules that I just described. At this first-order level, representation has the straightforward sense of political voice and democratic accountability. This sense correlates with an equally familiar sense of political injustice, which I have called *ordinary-political misrepresentation*, and which consists in the politically institutionalized denial of participatory parity among those who are already included in principle within a bounded polity. On the other hand, I also intend representation to encompass newly salient questions about the (in)justice of boundaries and frames. At this meta-level, the term calls attention to the patterning of the broader space within which bounded polities are embedded and, so, to the question of who is included, and who excluded, from the circle of those entitled to participate within them. Evoking representation's symbolic meaning, this second level correlates with political injustices of misframing, which arise, as I have said, when the partitioning of political space blocks some who are poor or despised from challenging the forces that oppress them. In this latter idea, of misframing, the two senses of representation converge. When political space is unjustly framed, the result is the denial of political voice to those who are cast outside the universe of those who "count." Thus, representation concerns the intersection of symbolic framing and democratic voice. As the term that names the political dimension of justice, it allows us to grasp the question of the frame as a question of justice.

VB: This next question follows, to an extent, because I also wanted to take up the language of framing, and in a sense to ask a sort of "So what?" question in relation to the question of justice and the frame. It just so happened that as I was thinking up questions for you I was also preparing a seminar on Michel Callon's work, where he's also talking about the frame. Now, he's talking about it as a *technical* issue, so I was thinking suppose you were to concede the frame as a technical issue within politics, so that the frame becomes a necessity. It's about the necessity of excluding in order to govern, so that the framing will, of course, attempt to render some issues non-political, while others are allowed to be raised within it. Now, what's interesting, I thought, about bringing your work alongside this use of the frame in Callon is that it highlights a sense that I had in your work that you think the frame really does work to exclude. His argument is that the frame will produce externalities, which seems a bit different from yours. A factory's economic decisions are made within a frame. So, say a factory produces toxic waste. It may invest in order to do something about that production, or it may not. If it invests in it, it attends to that externality, but if it doesn't, then, you know, it ignores its externalities. Now, I was wondering what you might think of that? Is that a way of thinking about a frame that you would approve of? Because it seems to me that the crucial difference between that way of thinking and the way of thinking – as I understand it – that you're proposing is that it wouldn't be a solution, from Callon's point of view, to widen the frame, or to have a meta-institution. The solution would be much more on the same level as the production of the frame. So it might encourage people, within the frame, to take account of their externalities, rather than having a meta-moment. So it's about how people understand the consequences of what they're doing within the frame.

NF: That's an interesting question. At first glance, the approach you sketch seems to present an alternative to mine, stressing attention to externalities in lieu of reframing. But whether it is really in the end incompatible with mine depends on how one interprets it. Suppose we agree that at least some transnational injustices can be remedied by reforms aimed at holding liable those who produce negative externalities that degrade the lives of others who reside beyond their borders and/or are not their fellow citizens. Then the question arises, does this solution avoid a meta-moment of reframing? I think not. For starters, the notion that one is obligated to avoid harming those beyond one's borders assumes an enlarged, transnational sense of who counts as one's fellow subjects of justice; conceptually, therefore, we have already moved beyond the Westphalian frame. Institutionally, moreover, this solution requires some transnational regulatory and policing powers to enforce the obligation on recalcitrant actors, such as outlaw states and large transnational corporations, some of which are bigger than many states. Also required are transnational courts or arbitration bodies to resolve disputes about standing, liability, and damages and to determine penalties and compensation. If such powers are to be legitimate, finally, they must be accountable to everyone potentially affected.[2] Their design, staffing, and operation must be subject to democratic oversight based on fair transnational mechanisms of representation. Absent such post-westphalian powers and mechanisms of accountability, attempts to deal with unjust transboundary externalities are doomed to fall short – witness the ease with which Union Carbide has minimized its liability for Bhopal. As I understand it, then, Callon's approach *does* require a meta-moment of reframing. And if that is right, then his approach is not incompatible with mine.

In any case, I agree with him that politics, as we have known it historically, always involves a frame in the sense of closure, which means that there is always an inside and an outside – hence, that exclusions arise as a matter of necessity. Thus, I do not imagine we could ever get beyond framing altogether, to a point where absolutely nothing was excluded. Nevertheless, it is not the case that any frame is as good as any other frame, which is one conclusion your question seemed to invite. It won't do, in other words, to say, "Any frame is going to exclude and to produce externalities. Therefore, it doesn't matter which frame we use. Instead of worrying about reframing, we should focus on getting firms and other actors to internalize the externalities they produce." That may sound like a coherent position, but it is normatively and politically inadequate – for at least two reasons. First, given present levels of economic integration and ecological interdependence, we face political problems that cannot be handled by the Westphalian frame – such as the problem of global warming. In such cases, we have no choice but to look for other frames, which will often (though not always) mean bigger frames, including, for some issues, global frames. Second, there is the problem of power. The fact is some interests derive substantial benefit from a world in which others have no venues where they can lodge claims against offshore powers and be taken seriously. And that is an injustice – in part because those "others" are deprived of the basic democratic right to a say in decision-making that profoundly affects them. In these situations, it makes perfect sense to ask: Is there a better frame? Granted, as I noted before, any frame will produce exclusions. But the question arises as to whether these exclusions are *unjust*, and if so, whether there is a way to remedy them. Granted, too, any remedy will produce its own exclusions, which may generate claims for further reframing, if the newer exclusions are seen as unjust. Thus, in the best-case scenario, we should envision an ongoing process of critique, reframing, critique, reframing, and so on. In this scenario, framing disputes appear to be a permanent part of the political landscape and will never be resolved definitely, once and for all. But this means we need spaces and institutions where those questions can be democratically debated and addressed.

KN: Another question about the boundary-setting of political community. I think there's no doubt that you're right that what you call the Westphalian-Keynesian system does produce injustices, and that we have got used to thinking of justice within its terms. One of the really difficult areas to think about outside that frame is welfare, and economic redistribution, and partly because it depended, as I understand it, historically, on a certain exclusionary version of solidarity which was often racialized. The Left has had a lot of difficulty with that in the first place, but now we're talking about developing solidarity from the North to the South, for example, and against these existing and even quite virulently rejuvenated forms of national solidarity. I wonder if you have any kind of thoughts about that?

NF: This question could not be more pressing: assuming we agree that justice requires redistribution across borders, is it possible to envision a form of transnational solidarity that is sufficiently robust to support it? Many people contend that the answer is no. In their view, any "we" is necessarily erected against a corresponding "they." By definition, however, a global "we" could have no corresponding "they." Ergo there can be no global "we." Despite its appearance of irresistible logic, I believe we should resist this line of reasoning, which prematurely forecloses the search for other ways of understanding, and building, solidarity.

   To explain why, let me distinguish three different kinds of supports that can underpin solidarity, either separately or in combination with one another. First, there are what I would call "subjective" supports, such as ethnonational identity, which base solidarity on sensed affinity and posited similarity, themselves constructed in opposition to an excluded "other." This schema corresponds to the exclusionary form of racialized solidarity you mentioned. Second, there are what I would call "objective" supports, such as cognitive awareness of causal interdependence or mutual vulnerability, which can generate solidarity based in shared interest; the solidarity associated with ecological consciousness is an example. Third, there are what I would call "communicative" supports, such as the experience of participating in common public arguments and decision-making structures, which lead to solidarity based in shared political practice; one variant of this third type is the kind of solidarity that Habermas, writing about formally con-stituted bounded polities, has called "constitutional patriotism." If we take into account these additional possibilities, we can restate the question like this: Can some combination of objective and communicative supports underpin an enlarged, transnational solidarity that is sufficiently robust to sustain redistribution across borders? Or, failing that, can such a com-bination be strengthened by the addition of a different kind of subjective support, one that is not ethnonational or unjustly exclusionary?

Interestingly, that last idea has surfaced in the recent argu-ments about European identity. Those arguments have engaged many people, including some, like Habermas, who regard the European Union as a model or a stepping-stone to something bigger. All sides agree that it is not enough to base a European identity on appeals to objective causal interdependence. That would not suffice to demarcate Europe from the rest of the world; nor is it thought capable of generating a sufficiently thick "we" to support transnational redistribution. And many doubt that constitutional patriotism alone could take up the slack, if and when the EU constitution were ratified. So most parties to the debate, including Habermas, seek an additional, subjective support of some kind. But there the agreement ends. Conservatives advocate a European identity based on an enlarged, continental form of cultural nationalism; insisting that what binds Europeans together is a shared ethos of Judeo-Christian values, they would erect the European "we" in oppo-sition to a Muslim "they," which makes the admission of Turkey a non-starter. Meanwhile, liberals and social democrats look instead to negative features of a shared European history, which includes untold wars and several genocides; evoking the idea of "never again," they would counterpose the tolerant, pacific "we" of the European present to the sectarian, bellicose "they" of the European past.

The second view suggests an attractive possibility: a relative thick, subjective alternative to ethnonationalism, which projects the condescension normally reserved for present-day ethnicized others onto one's own past self. Yet the version under discussion here is problematic. Offering a highly selective view of Europe's history, it focuses exclusively on internecine conflicts within the continent. Airbrushing out of the picture all transcontinental aggressions and depredations, it omits consideration of European colonialism and imperialism. If the latter were acknowledged, however, they would point to a much larger, transcontinental "we" that also includes the postcolonial world. So what about that possibility? Could a broader, transcontinental understanding of "never again" supply the necessary subjective support for a relatively thick transnational solidarity that includes, but is not limited to, Europe? Could this notion, based on a critical interpretation of history, provide an alternative to ethnonationalism and add some substantive heft to the thin notions of causal interdependence and communicative patriotism? In theory, yes, but skeptics will note that it is hard to envision the route by which it could be created in practice. The proposal to base solidarity on a global "never again" assumes that the beneficiaries of historical injustice are prepared to take responsibility for it. It appears, therefore, to beg the question, by presupposing the very outcome that it hopes to foster.

So what other strategies for building solidarity are possible? Another approach worth considering is the one that informs the transcontinental activist milieux of the World Social Forum. This conception has some affinities with the objective interest model, on the one hand, and the communicative model, on the other. But it goes beyond thin notions of interdependence and constitutional patriotism to offer a thicker transnational identity, grounded in an us-versus-them opposition. Here the stress is more on the "them" than on the "us," as the latter are interpellated simply as those who share a common enemy. Unlike the case of the Conservatives' Europe, however, that enemy is not identified in ethnocultural terms. Rather it is defined systemically and functionally, as those who occupy the commanding heights of neoliberal globalizing capitalism. This approach is attractive on at least two counts: first, its systemic character avoids any hint of racial-ethnic demonization; and, second, it correctly identifies one, if not *the*, major source of transnational injustice. For such reasons, this formula resonates with the many disparate constituencies that make up the WSF, including trade unionists and indigenous peoples, international feminists and landless peasants, environmentalists and undocumented immigrants – constituencies that are otherwise pitted against one another. The result is a communicatively generated, interest-based solidarity that derives its affective force from a historical narrative of predation, various in its local particulars, but linked to a global system.

What undergirds WSF solidarity, then, is a combination of several different supports: first, an explicit renunciation of ethnocultural sectarianism and an express validation of cultural plurality; second, a shared context and practice of political communication (a "forum") that generates a communicatively based solidarity reminiscent of constitutional patriotism, but not focused on a bounded polity; third, a loose-knit organizational model that allays the constituents' fears of coercive hegemonization; and, fourth, an overarching interpretive horizon that allows participants to situate their struggles within the frame of neoliberal globalizing capitalism and to posit a common enemy. In general, then, and despite all its defects, the WSF suggests a model of solidarity that combines some of the strengths and avoids some of the weaknesses of other models. Without wanting to idealize a flawed real-world institution, I believe that this model of solidarity holds some promise for addressing the tough questions of transnational welfare and redistribution that you have raised.

KN: The next question also concerns frames, but it comes largely from political theory rather than activism. The question is: How can framing itself be made democratic? How is it possible to democratically contest the frame within which the political community, which is doing the contesting, is situated? How can the political community of the all affected, as you put it, be formed out of a political community which is not already that of those who are all affected?

NF: This kind of contestation has both conceptual and institutional preconditions. Conceptually, it rests on the capacity for reflexivity, the ability to jump to another level and reflect about one's first-order practice. That capacity is built into the sociolinguistic human life form generally and into the practice of politics specifically. One way to understand politics is as a kind of meta-practice, which seeks to order first-order social practice through intentional collective action. Reflexivity is also a hallmark of political radicalism, which is distinguished from other orientations by its willingness to step back from apparently discrete issues and to problematize the deep structures that underlie them. The capacity to interrogate the frame, to make it an object of critique and political action, is yet another instance of reflexivity, and a radical one at that. In this case, we take first-order politics as the object of our reflection. Not content simply to treat problems in the form in which they are given within the established frame, we make the frame itself the focus of attention and potential reconstruction. The result is a form of meta-politics, in which the exclusions of ordinary political practice are exposed and contested. In the *New Left Review* essay that you mentioned earlier, I called this meta-contestation *the politics of framing*.

But the politics of framing also has institutional presuppositions. What makes this politics possible, in a practical way, is the growing gap between the two tracks of politics – one informal and located in civil society, the other formal and institutionalized in the state. According to the Westphalian political imaginary, these two tracks are supposed to be aligned: national civil society is supposed to map neatly onto the national state, which is in turn supposed to be held accountable to the national public sphere. In reality, however, they don't line up. Despite Herculean state-led efforts to make the Westphalian vision a reality, the two tracks of the political were never perfectly isomorphic, even in the heyday of social democracy. Today, moreover, the gaps between civil society processes of contestation and state-centered processes of legislation and administration are especially dramatic. Many of us participate in several different civil society arenas and public spheres, some of which are national, to be sure, but others of which are local, regional, transnational, and global. In this situation of non-isomorphism, non-state-centered public spheres become spaces for contesting state-centered frames. It is precisely from such postwestphalian public spheres, which trespass the boundaries of territorial states, that claims against misframing are now being launched. This is not to deny that these spaces, too, are structured by power asymmetries that marginalize some voices vis-à-vis others. But that disparity, too, can be reflectively addressed by meta-contestation about the unjust dynamics of existing contestation.

KN: Elsewhere in your work you've made a pretty compelling argument for strong counterpublic spheres. My question is: How does that translate, if you're talking about jumping up a level, for example, in terms of reflexivity? How do we envisage a strong counterpublic, without a world state, and without a global civil society?

NF: This question goes to the heart of my current work. I am trying to understand how counterpublic spheres could conceivably play an emancipatory, democratizing role under current conditions. This problem arises because, as I just said, public spheres and sovereign public powers do not line up. Although I just cast that fact in a positive light, as the enabling condition for contesting misframing, it also has a negative side: when public spheres don't align with states, it is hard to imagine how the opinion generated within them could be either normatively legitimate or politically efficacious. Let me explain.

From the standpoint of critical theory, public spheres fulfill their emancipatory, democratizing function when the public opinion formed within them is both legitimate and efficacious. In this formulation, *legitimate* means formed through fair and inclusive processes of communication, while *efficacious* means capable of influencing the use of public power and of holding public officials accountable. Both ideas were relatively clear when viewed through the Westphalian lens. From that perspective, legitimacy would be achieved if and only if national public spheres became genuinely inclusive of all citizens and enabled all of them to participate as peers in communicative processes of public opinion formation. Analogously, efficacy would be realized if and only if national public opinion attained sufficient political force to subject the actions of national state officials to citizen control. The result was a reasonably clear picture of what was at stake in deploying the concept of the public sphere in critical theorizing.

In the case of transnational publicity, however, the stakes are by no means clear. What could it mean to posit the *legitimacy* of transnational public opinion, when the interlocutors are not fellow citizens with equal participation rights and a common status as political equals? And what could it mean to speak of the *efficacy* of transnational public opinion, when it is not addressed to a sovereign state that is capable in principle of implementing the interlocutors' will and solving their problems? Absent plausible answers to these questions, all our talk of transnational public spheres remains merely descriptive, lacking a conceptual grounding in critical theory.

In a recent essay,[3] I have tried to reconstruct the notions of legitimacy and efficacy in a form that is suitable to current conditions. Without rehearsing that argument here, let me simply note that the nonalignment of states with public spheres introduces difficulties of two different kinds. One problem arises when transnationalization of the formal institutional track of politics outstrips that of the civil society track, leading to a *deficit of democratic legitimacy*. This is the case today with the European Union, where existing transnational administrative and legislative bodies are not matched by a European public sphere that could hold them acccountable. At the global level, in contrast, the reverse is true. There, existing transnational publics are not matched by comparable administrative and legislative powers, which leads to the second problem: a *deficit of political efficacy*. We witnessed a dramatic example of this latter sort of deficit in the worldwide anti-war demonstrations of February 15, 2003, which mobilized an enormous body of transnational public opinion against the impending US invasion of Iraq. Although this outpouring of opinion could not have been more forceful or clear, it lacked an addressee capable of restraining George W. Bush, and so, in a sense, remained powerless.

What these examples suggest to me is that critical theorists must address the problem at both ends. Overcoming the legitimacy deficit appears to require the creation of enlarged transnational public spheres in which all affected can participate as peers. Overcoming the efficacy deficit seems to require the creation of new transnational public powers, which can implement democratically formed transnational popular will. Yet if the result were a perfect alignment of counterpublics with state-like powers, we would have re-created the Westphalian imaginary on a larger scale and possibly closed the gaps where critical reflexivity flourishes. In that case, perhaps what is needed is something else, some new, *postwestphalian* configuration of multiple public spheres and public powers. But critical theorists are only beginning to formulate this problem. We are far from having convincing answers.

VB: I want to ask a final question which returns to the idea of misframing. It seems that your work has a sort of optimism about it. There is an optimism that this troublesome little question "Is this frame fair?" or "Are we representative?" *will be* debated, or that it really *could be* debated in institutions in a meaningful way. One of our MA students wrote a fantastic essay this year about export processing zones. And reading your work on global injustice I was thinking: well, supposing you – or the people affected – went to a country, say, in Southern Africa, and said, "This export processing zone that you've set up here, you know, it's treating these citizens unfairly," because the labour laws are suspended, or the companies are given special provision in relation to the laws of the land, and so on. The government's argument would be, "Well, yes, but we're doing it for the future good of this nation" or "We're doing it so that we can attract investment into the country, so that we will, ultimately, become part of global capitalism." So the justifications are not without logic. So I suppose the question is: Where does your optimism come from that, you know, we can debate these in a way that reaches beyond a laying out of different logics?

NF: What you've described is a classic collective action problem. Suppose we are talking about South Africa, whose government is certainly not the worst in the world. Given the presumption of its good intentions, on the one hand, and the magnitude of the injustices it is trying to redress, on the other, the justifications you cite sound eminently reasonable. The argument runs: "This is the way the game is organized, and we have no choice but to play the game. Given the way things are, export processing zones represent our best shot – to attract industry and create jobs, to accumulate capital for ongoing development projects." And it's true, if we treat the rules of the game as unalterable constants, then this strategy makes good sense. But is this really the only possibility? Suppose workers in nineteenth-century England had said, "Well, you know, we have no choice but to play the existing game and to try to get the best deal we can within it." If everyone had said that, there would have been no Labour Movement, no eight-hour day, no welfare state, and so on. History is constantly generating such collective action problems. In these situations, people must decide whether to accept the given architecture and to function within it – in which case, they will act as you have described. But if, on the other hand, they come to believe that others will join them in a struggle to change the architecture, then other, better possibilities open up. It is true, of course, that they could lose, in which case things could turn out even worse. Because there are no guarantees, people contemplating such struggles must try to figure out whether they are strong and numerous enough to risk trying to change the game, instead of playing it as it lies.

I'm not sure whether this way of thinking is cause for optimism. The fact is that I can't ever remember such a dark period in my lifetime. So I'm not optimistic now, certainly not compared to the 1960s and '70s. But I am aware that history is punctuated by moments in which people overcome these collective action problems, when they rewrite the rules and change the game. This has happened in the past and will doubtless happen again. Of course, the result will not be perfect justice, but some differently imperfect arrangement. The social-democratic welfare state was an achievement, although it was premised on unjust exclusions, both internal and external. Now we, who are aware, with the advantage of hindsight, of those exclusions, have a chance to redress them by changing the rules of the game yet again.

This is another crucial job for the critical theorist: to reflect on the historical situation one inhabits, to ask oneself: What do the times "demand"? What are the challenges, the opportunities, the perils? And I must say that, based on my recent teaching experiences, I do feel there is something new in the air today. Are we on the brink of a new explosion of emancipatory radicalism, one comparable to 1968? Probably not. But I find that my current undergraduates are quite different from their predecessors of five to ten years ago. Today's students have little patience for identity politics and are passionately interested in capitalism. So while I can't exactly say I'm optimistic, I am invigorated by the prospect of engaging a new set of challenges. And I see my job – coming back to your first question again – as trying to articulate what these are. This means trying to develop, along with others – because it's not an individual job – terminology and concepts that can clarify the perils and prospects of the present age. If I were able to formulate some arguments or create some conceptual resources that turned out to be of use in emancipatory social struggles, I would feel that the time I spend doing critical theory was time well spent.

Notes

Chapter 2   Reframing Justice in a Globalizing World

This chapter is a revised and expanded version of my second Spinoza Lecture, delivered at the University of Amsterdam, December 2, 2004. The lecture was drafted during my tenure there as Spinoza Professor in spring 2004 and revised during my subsequent fellowship year at the Wissenschaftskolleg zu Berlin, 2004–5. My warmest thanks to both institutions for their generous support of this work. Special thanks to Yolande Jansen and Hilla Dayan for selfless and good-natured assistance in a time of great need and to James Bohman for expert bibliographical advice. Thanks, also, to Amy Allen, Seyla Benhabib, Bert van den Brink, Alessandro Ferrara, Rainer Forst, Stefan Gosepath, John Judis, Ted Koditschek, Maria Pia Lara, David Peritz, Ann Laura Stoler, and Eli Zaretsky for thoughtful comments on earlier drafts. Thanks, finally, to Kristin Gissberg and Keith Haysom for expert research assistance.

1   The phrase "Keynesian-Westphalian frame" is meant to signal the national-territorial underpinnings of justice disputes in the heyday of the postwar democratic welfare state, roughly 1945 to the 1970s. The term "Westphalian" refers to the Treaty of 1648, which established some key features of the modern international state system. The precise contributions of the Treaty are a subject of scholarly debate, as is the "Westphalian System" more broadly. However, I am concerned neither with the actual achievements of the Treaty nor with the centuries-long process by which the system it inaugurated evolved. Rather, I invoke "Westphalia" as a political imaginary that mapped the world as

a system of mutually recognizing sovereign territorial states. My claim is that this imaginary informed the postwar framing of debates about justice in the First World, even as the beginnings of a postwestphalian human-rights regime emerged. For the distinction between Westphalia as "event," as "idea/ideal," as "process of evolution," and as "normative scoresheet," see Richard Falk, "Revisiting Westphalia, Discovering Post-Westphalia," *Journal of Ethics* 6, 4 (2002): 311–52.

2 It might be assumed that, from the perspective of the Third World, Westphalian premises would have appeared patently counterfactual. Yet it is worth recalling that the great majority of anti-colonialists sought to achieve independent Westphalian states of their own. Only a small minority consistently championed justice within a global framework – for reasons that are entirely understandable.

3 The literature on this point is vast. See, for example: Linda Basch, Nina Glick Schiller, and Christina Szanton Blanc, *Nations Unbound: Transnational Projects, Postcolonial Predicaments, and De-territorialized Nation-States* (New York: Gordon and Breach, 1994); Stephen Castles and Alastair Davidson, *Citizenship and Migration: Globalization and the Politics of Belonging* (London: Routledge, 2000), pp. 1–25, 156–83; *Globalization and Social Movements: Culture, Power and the Transnational Public Sphere*, ed. John A. Guidry, Michael D. Kennedy, and Mayer N. Zald (Ann Arbor: University of Michigan Press, 2001); David Held, "Cosmopolitanism: Ideas, Realities and Deficits," in *Governing Globalization: Power, Authority, and Global Governance*, ed. David Held and Anthony McGrew (Cambridge: Polity, 2002), pp. 305–25; Mary Kaldor, *New and Old Wars: Organized Violence in a Global Era* (Cambridge: Polity, 1999); Margaret E. Keck and Kathryn Sikkink, *Activists beyond Borders: Advocacy Networks in International Politics* (Ithaca, NY: Cornell University Press, 1998); *Restructuring World Politics: Transnational Social Movements, Networks, and Norms*, ed. Sanjeev Khagram, James V. Riker, and Kathryn Sikkink (Minneapolis: University of Minnesota Press, 2002); Aihwa Ong, *Flexible Citizenship: The Cultural Logics of Transnationality* (Durham, NC: Duke University Press, 1999); and Mark W. Zacher, "The Decaying Pillars of the Westphalian Temple," in *Governance without Government*, ed. James N. Rosenau and Ernst-Otto Czempiel (Cambridge: Cambridge University Press, 1992), pp. 58–101.

4 Dale Hathaway, *Allies Across the Border: Mexico's "Authentic Labor Front" and Global Solidarity* (Cambridge, MA: South End Press, 2000); Kim Moody, *Workers in a Lean World: Unions in*

the International Economy (London: Verso Books, 1997); and Ronaldo Munck and Peter Waterman, *Labour Worldwide in the Era of Globalization: Alternative Union Models in the New World Order* (New York: Palgrave Macmillan, 1999).

5   Dan La Botz, *Democracy in Mexico: Peasant Rebellion and Political Reform* (Cambridge, MA: South End Press, 1995); June Nash, *Mayan Visions: The Quest for Autonomy in an Age of Globalization* (London: Routledge, 2001); and Ronald Niezen, *The Origins of Indigenism: Human Rights and the Politics of Identity* (Berkeley: University of California Press, 2003).

6   Robert O'Brien, Anne Marie Goetz, Jan Art Scholte, and Marc Williams, *Contesting Global Governance Multilateral Economic Institutions and Global Social Movements* (Cambridge: Cambridge University Press, 2000).

7   Brooke A. Ackerly, *Political Theory and Feminist Social Criticism* (Cambridge: Cambridge University Press, 2000); *The Challenge of Local Feminisms: Women's Movements in Global Perspective*, ed. Amrita Basru (Boulder, CO: Westview Press, 1995); and *Human Rights of Women: National and International Perspectives*, ed. Rebecca J. Cook (Philadelphia: University of Pennsylvania Press, 1994).

8   Avtar Brah, *Cartographies of Diaspora: Contesting Identities* (London: Routledge, 1997), pp. 178–210; Georges Eugene Fouron and Nina Glick Schiller, *Georges Woke Up Laughing: Long-Distance Nationalism and the Search for Home* (Durham, NC: Duke University Press, 2001); and Yasemin Soysal, *Limits of Citizenship: Migrants and Postnational Membership in Europe* (Chicago: University of Chicago Press, 1995).

9   Andrew Clapham, "Issues of Complexity, Complicity and Complementarity: From the Nuremberg Trials to the Dawn of the New International Criminal Court," in *From Nuremberg to The Hague: The Future of International Criminal Justice*, ed. Philippe Sands (Cambridge: Cambridge University Press, 2003), pp. 233–81; Holly Cullen and Karen Morrow, "International Civil Society in International Law: The Growth of NGO Participation," *Non-State Actors & International Law* 1, 1 (2001): 7–39; Paul Gordon Lauren, *The Evolution of International Human Rights: Visions Seen* (Philadelphia: University of Pennsylvania Press, 2003); and Rik Panganiban, "The NGO Coalition for an International Criminal Court," *UN Chronicle* 34, 4 (1997): 36–9.

10   I discuss the elision of the problem of the frame in mainstream theories of justice in chapter 3 of this volume, "Two Dogmas of Egalitarianism."

11   Nancy Fraser, *Justice Interruptus: Critical Reflections on the "Post-socialist" Condition* (London: Routledge, 1997).

12   This "status model" of recognition represents an alternative to the standard "identity model." For a critique of the latter and a defense of the former, see my "Rethinking Recognition," *New Left Review* 3 (May/June 2000): 107–20.

13   For the full argument, see my "Social Justice in the Age of Identity Politics: Redistribution, Recognition and Participation," in Nancy Fraser and Axel Honneth, *Redistribution or Recognition? A Political-Philosophical Exchange*, trans. Joel Golb, James Ingram, and Christiane Wilke (London: Verso, 2003), pp. 7–110.

14   The neglect of the third, political, dimension is especially glaring in the case of theorists of justice who subscribe to liberal or communitarian philosophical premises. In contrast, deliberative democrats, agonistic democrats, and republicans have sought to theorize the political. But most of these theorists have had relatively little to say about the relation between democracy and justice; and none has conceptualized the political as one of three dimensions of justice.

15   Classic works on representation have dealt largely with what I am calling the decision-rule aspect, while ignoring the membership aspect. See, for example, Hanna Fenichel Pitkin, *The Concept of Representation* (Berkeley: University of California Press, 1967) and Bernard Manin, *The Principles of Representative Government* (New York: Cambridge University Press, 1997).

16   Lani Guinier, *The Tyranny of the Majority* (New York: Free Press, 1994); Robert Ritchie and Steven Hill, "The Case for Proportional Representation," in *Whose Vote Counts?* ed. Robert Ritchie and Steven Hill (Boston: Beacon Press, 2001), pp. 1–33.

17   Tricia Gray, "Electoral Gender Quotas: Lessons from Argentina and Chile," *Bulletin of Latin American Research* 21, 1 (2003): 52–78; Mala Htun, "Is Gender Like Ethnicity? The Political Representation of Identity Groups," *Perspectives on Politics* 2, 3 (2004), 439–58; Anne Phillips, *The Politics of Presence* (Oxford: Clarendon Press, 1995); and Shirin M. Rai, "Political Representation, Democratic Institutions and Women's Empowerment: The Quota Debate in India," in *Rethinking Empowerment: Gender and Development in a Global/Local World*, ed. Jane L. Parpart, Shirin M. Rai, and Kathleen Staudt (New York: Routledge, 2002), pp. 133–45.

18   Hannah Arendt, *The Origins of Totalitarianism*, new edition with added prefaces (New York: Harcourt Brace Jovanovich, 1973), pp. 269–84. "Political death" is my phrase, not Arendt's.

19   Among the best accounts of the normative force of these strug-
     gles are Will Kymlicka, *Multicultural Citizenship: A Liberal
     Theory of Minority Rights* (London: Oxford University Press,
     1995) and Melissa Williams, *Voice, Trust, and Memory: Margin-
     alized Groups and the Failings of Liberal Representation* (Prince-
     ton: Princeton University Press, 1998).

20   See, in particular, Rainer Forst, "Towards a Critical Theory of
     Transnational Justice," in *Global Justice*, ed. Thomas Pogge
     (Oxford: Blackwell, 2001), pp. 169–87, and "Justice, Morality
     and Power in the Global Context," in *Real World Justice*, ed.
     Andreas Follesdal and Thomas Pogge (Dordrecht: Springer,
     2005), pp. 27–36; Thomas Pogge, "The Influence of the Global
     Order on the Prospects for Genuine Democracy in the Develop-
     ing Countries," *Ratio Juris* 14, 3 (2001): 326–43, and "Economic
     Justice and National Borders," *Revision* 22 (1999): 27–34.

21   Alfred C. Aman, Jr., "Globalization, Democracy and the Need
     for a New Administrative Law," *Indiana Journal of Global Legal
     Studies* 10, 1 (2003): 125–55; James K. Boyce, "Democratizing
     Global Economic Governance," *Development and Change* 35, 3
     (2004): 593–9; Robert W. Cox, "A Perspective on Globaliza-
     tion," in *Globalization: Critical Reflections*, ed. James H. Mittel-
     man (Boulder, CO: Lynne Rienner, 1996), pp. 21–30, and
     "Democracy in Hard Times: Economic Globalization and the
     Limits to Liberal Democracy," in *The Transformation of Democ-
     racy?* ed. Anthony McGrew (Cambridge: Polity, 1997), pp.
     49–72; Stephen Gill, "New Constitutionalism, Democratisation
     and Global Political Economy," *Pacifica Review* 10, 1 (February
     1998): 23–38; Eric Helleiner, "From Bretton Woods to Global
     Finance: A World Turned Upside Down," in *Political Economy
     and the Changing Global Order*, ed. Richard Stubbs and Geof-
     frey R. D. Underhill (New York: St Martin's Press, 1994), pp.
     163–75; David Schneiderman, "Investment Rules and the Rule
     of Law," *Constellations* 8, 4 (2001): 521–37; and Servaes Storm
     and J. Mohan Rao, "Market-Led Globalization and World
     Democracy: Can the Twain Ever Meet?" *Development and
     Change* 35, 5 (2004): 567–81.

22   James Bohman, "International Regimes and Democratic Gover-
     nance," *International Affairs* 75, 3 (1999): 499–513; John Dryzek,
     "Transnational Democracy," *Journal of Political Philosophy* 7, 1
     (1999): 30–51; David Held, "Regulating Globalization?" *Inter-
     national Journal of Sociology* 15, 2 (2000): 394–408, *Democracy
     and the Global Order: From the Modern State to Cosmopolitan
     Governance* (Cambridge: Polity, 1995), pp. 99–140, "The Trans-
     formation of Political Community: Rethinking Democracy in

the Context of Globalization," in *Democracy's Edges*, ed. Ian Shapiro and Cassiano Hacker-Cordón (Cambridge: Cambridge University Press, 1999), pp. 84–111, "Cosmopolitanism: Globalization Tamed?" *Review of International Studies* 29, 4 (2003): 465–80, and "Democratic Accountability and Political Effectiveness from a Cosmopolitan Perspective," *Government and Opposition* 39, 2 (2004): 364–91.

23 I do not mean to suggest that the political is the master dimension of justice, more fundamental than the economic and the cultural. Rather, the three dimensions stand in relations of mutual entwinement and reciprocal influence. Just as the ability to make claims for distribution and recognition depends on relations of representation, so the ability to exercise one's political voice depends on the relations of class and status. In other words, the capacity to influence public debate and authoritative decision-making depends not only on formal decision rules, but also on power relations rooted in the economic structure and the status order, a fact that is insufficiently stressed in most theories of deliberative democracy. Thus, maldistribution and misrecognition conspire to subvert the principle of equal political voice for every citizen, even in polities that claim to be democratic. But of course the converse is also true. Those who suffer from misrepresentation are vulnerable to injustices of status and class. Lacking political voice, they are unable to articulate and defend their interests with respect to distribution and recognition, which in turn exacerbates their misrepresentation. In such cases, the result is a vicious circle in which the three orders of injustice reinforce one another, denying some people the chance to participate on a par with others in social life. As these three dimensions are intertwined, efforts to overcome injustice cannot, except in rare cases, address themselves to just one of them. Rather, struggles against maldistribution and misrecognition cannot succeed unless they are joined with struggles against misrepresentation – and vice versa. Where one puts the emphasis, of course, is both a tactical and a strategic decision. Given the current salience of injustices of misframing, my own preference is for the slogan, "No redistribution or recognition without representation." But even so, the politics of representation appears as one among three interconnected fronts in the struggle for social justice in a globalizing world.

24 In distinguishing "affirmative" from "transformative" approaches, I am adapting terminology I have used in the past with respect to redistribution and recognition. See, *inter alia*, my "From Redistribution to Recognition? Dilemmas of Justice in a 'Postsocialist'

Age," *New Left Review* 212 (1995): 68–93, and "Social Justice in the Age of Identity Politics."

25 For the state-territorial principle, see Thomas Baldwin, "The Territorial State," in *Jurisprudence: Cambridge Essays*, ed. Hyman Gross and Ross Harrison (Oxford: Clarendon Press, 1992), pp. 207–30. For doubts about the state-territorial principle (among other principles), see Frederick Whelan, "Democratic Theory and the Boundary Problem," in *Nomos XXV: Liberal Democracy*, ed. J. Roland Pennock and John W. Chapman (New York and London: New York University Press, 1983), pp. 13–47. For accounts of the pathos inherent in affirmative struggles against misframing, see: Partha Chatterjee, *Nationalist Thought and the Colonial World* (Minneapolis: University of Minnesota Press, 1993); Frantz Fanon, "On National Culture," in Fanon, *The Wretched of the Earth* (New York: Grove, 1963), pp. 165–99; and Tom Nairn, "The Modern Janus," in Nairn, *The Break-Up of Britain: Crisis and Neo-Nationalism* (London: New Left Books, 1977), pp. 329–63. For the gender dimension of such struggles, see: Deniz Kandiyoti, "Identity and Its Discontents: Women and the Nation," in *Colonial Discourse and Post-Colonial Theory: A Reader*, ed. Patrick Williams and Laura Chrisman (New York: Columbia University Press, 1994), pp. 376–91; Anne McClintock, "Family Feuds: Gender, Nation and the Family," *Feminist Review* 44 (1993): 61–80; and Nira Yuval-Davis, *Gender and Nation* (London: Sage Publications, 1997).

26 I borrow this terminology from Manuel Castells, *The Rise of the Network Society* (Oxford: Blackwell, 1996), pp. 440–60.

27 I owe the idea of a post-territorial "mode of political differentiation" to John Ruggie. See his immensely suggestive essay, "Territoriality and Beyond: Problematizing Modernity in International Relations," *International Organization* 47 (1993): 139–74.

28 Thinking develops in time, often in unanticipated ways. The present chapter, which dates from 2004–5, reflects my view at that time that the all-affected principle was the most promising candidate on offer for a postwestphalian mode of frame-setting, even though I also register important worries about that principle in note 29, just below. Soon thereafter, however, those worries came to seem insurmountable. In chapter 4, therefore, which was completed in 2007, I reject the "all-affected" principle in favor of another possibility, not considered here. The new approach, still undergoing development in my ongoing work, refers disputes about the frame instead to the "all-subjected principle." Introduced in the chapter on "Abnormal Justice," the shift from affectedness to subjection reflects my continuing

effort to probe the deep internal connection between the concepts of justice and democracy. Instead of erasing it by *post hoc* revision, I have chosen to display the shift here as a mark of difficulty, a sign that the challenges this issue poses are grave indeed.

29 Everything depends on finding a suitable interpretation of the all-affected principle. The key issue is how to narrow the idea of "affectedness" to the point where it becomes an operationalizable standard for assessing the justice of various frames. The difficulty arises thanks to the so-called "butterfly effect," which holds that everyone is affected by everything. To avoid that *reductio ad absurdum*, one needs a qualitative normative standard that identifies levels and kinds of effectivity that are sufficient to confer moral standing. One proposal, suggested by Carol Gould, is to limit such standing to those whose human rights are violated by a given practice or institution. Another, suggested by David Held, is to accord standing to those whose life expectancy and life-chances are significantly affected. My own view is that the all-affected principle is open to a plurality of reasonable interpretations. As a result, its interpretation cannot be determined monologically, by philosophical fiat. Rather, philosophical analyses of affectedness should be understood as contributions to a broader public debate about the principle's meaning. The same is true for empirical social-scientific accounts of who is affected by given institutions or policies. In general, the all-affected principle must be interpreted dialogically, through the give-and-take of argument in democratic deliberation. That said, however, one thing is clear. Injustices of misframing can be avoided only if moral standing is not limited to those who are already accredited as official members of a given institution or as authorized participants in a given practice. To avoid such injustices, standing must also be accorded to those non-members and non-participants significantly affected by the institution or practice at issue. Thus sub-Saharan Africans who have been involuntarily disconnected from the global economy count as subjects of justice in relation to it, even if they do not actually participate in it. For the human-rights interpretation, see Carol Gould, *Globalizing Democracy and Human Rights* (Cambridge: Cambridge University Press, 2004); for the life-expectancy and life-chances interpretation, David Held, *Global Covenant: The Social Democratic Alternative to the Washington Consensus* (Cambridge: Polity, 2004), pp. 99ff.; and for the dialogical approach, chapters 3 ("Two Dogmas of Egalitarianism") and 4 ("Abnormal Justice") of this volume.

30 For the time being, efforts to democratize the process of frame-setting are confined to contestation in transnational civil society. Indispensable as this level is, it cannot succeed so long as there exist no formal institutions that can translate transnational public opinion into binding, enforceable decisions. In general, then, the civil-society track of transnational democratic politics needs to be complemented by a formal-institutional track. See chapters 4 ("Abnormal Justice"), 5 ("Transnationalizing the Public Sphere"), and 9 ("The Politics of Framing") of this volume.

31 The phrase comes from Ian Shapiro, *Democratic Justice* (New Haven: Yale University Press, 1999). But the idea can also be found in Seyla Benhabib, *The Rights of Others* (Cambridge: Cambridge University Press, 2004); Rainer Forst, *Contexts of Justice* (Berkeley: University of California Press, 2002); and Jürgen Habermas, *Between Facts and Norms: Contributions to a Discourse Theory of Law and Democracy*, trans. William Rehg (Cambridge, MA: MIT Press, 1996).

32 None of the theorists cited in the previous note has attempted to apply the "democratic justice" approach to the problem of the frame. The thinker who has come closest to this is Rainer Forst, but even he does not envisage democratic processes of frame-setting.

Chapter 3   Two Dogmas of Egalitarianism

1 The allusion is to Willard Van Orman Quine's famous essay, "Two Dogmas of Empiricism," in W. V. O. Quine, *From a Logical Point of View: 9 Logico-Philosophical Essays* (Cambridge, MA: Harvard University Press, 1953), pp. 20–46.

2 Amartya Sen, "Equality of What?" in *Liberty, Equality, and Law*, ed. Sterling M. McMurrin (Salt Lake City: University of Utah Press, 1987), pp. 137–62.

3 The literature on this debate is enormous. Helpful overviews include Elizabeth Anderson, "What is the Point of Equality?" *Ethics* 109 (1999): 287–337 and G. A. Cohen, "On the Currency of Egalitarian Justice," *Ethics* 99 (1989): 906–44.

4 See the contributions to Charles Taylor, *Multiculturalism: Examining the Politics of Recognition*, ed. Amy Gutmann (Princeton: Princeton University Press, 1994). Also see my debate with Axel Honneth: Nancy Fraser and Axel Honneth, *Redistribution or Recognition? A Political-Philosophical Exchange*, trans. Joel Golb, James Ingram, and Christiane Wilke (London: Verso, 2003).

5 Deborah Satz, "Equality of What among Whom? Thoughts on Cosmopolitanism, Statism and Nationalism," in *Global Justice*,

ed. Ian Shapiro and Lea Brilmayer (New York: New York University Press, 1999), pp. 67–85; and Iris Marion Young, "Equality of Whom? Social Groups and Judgments of Injustice," *Journal of Political Philosophy* 9, 1 (2001): 1–18.

6   Two early and important exceptions were Charles R. Beitz, *Political Theory and International Relations* (Princeton: Princeton University Press, first edition, 1979; second edition, 1999) and Henry Shue, *Basic Rights* (Princeton: Princeton University Press, 1980).

7   Martha C. Nussbaum with Respondents, *For Love of Country? Debating the Limits of Patriotism*, ed. Joshua Cohen (Boston: Beacon Press, 1996); and Peter Singer, *One World: The Ethics of Globalization*, second edition (New Haven: Yale University Press, 2004).

8   Craig Calhoun, "The Class Consciousness of Frequent Travelers: Toward a Critique of Actually Existing Cosmopolitanism," *South Atlantic Quarterly* 101, 4 (2002): 869–98; Susan L. Hurley, "Rationality, Democracy and Leaky Boundaries: Vertical vs. Horizontal Modularity," *Journal of Political Philosophy* 7, 2 (1999): 126–46; Onora O'Neill, *Bounds of Justice* (Cambridge: Cambridge University Press, 2000), pp. 115–202; and Kok-Chor Tan, *Justice without Borders: Cosmopolitanism, Nationalism, and Patriotism* (Cambridge: Cambridge University Press, 2004).

9   David Miller, *On Nationality* (Oxford: Oxford University Press, 1995), "The Ethical Significance of Nationality," *Ethics* 98 (1988): 647–62, and "The Limits of Cosmopolitan Justice," in *International Society: Diverse Ethical Perspectives*, ed. David Maple and Terry Nardin (Princeton: Princeton University Press, 1998), pp. 164–83; and Michael Walzer, *Spheres of Justice: A Defense of Pluralism and Equality* (New York: Basic Books, 1984), esp. pp. 31–63.

10   John Rawls, *The Law of Peoples*, new edition (Cambridge, MA: Harvard University Press, 2001), and "The Law of Peoples," in *On Human Rights: The Oxford Amnesty Lectures*, ed. Stephen Shute and Susan Hurley (New York: Basic Books: 1994), pp. 41–84. Hereafter all citations are to the 2001 edition of the book.

11   On the one hand, Rawls excluded social and economic rights from the class of "urgent" human rights that international society was obliged to protect; thus, he denied impoverished individuals in the Third World standing to make claims for distributive justice across state borders. On the other hand, Rawls also limited the economic obligations of prosperous "well-ordered peoples" toward impoverished "peoples" in "burdened societies"

to a non-egalitarian "duty of assistance"; thus, he denied the latter societies, *qua* corporate political communities, any basis for making transborder egalitarian claims as a matter of justice. The result was a double exclusion: both *qua* individuals and *qua* corporate political communities, the global poor were excluded by territorial borders from any "who" of distributive justice that included the rich.

12 Charles Jones, *Global Justice: Defending Cosmopolitanism* (Oxford: Oxford University Press, 1999); and Martha Nussbaum, "Beyond the Social Contract: Capabilities and Global Justice," *Oxford Development Studies* 32, 1 (2004): 1–15.

13 Wilfried Hinsch, "Global Distributive Justice," *Metaphilosophy* 32, 1/2 (2001): 58–78; Andrew Hurrell, "Global Inequality and International Institutions," *Metaphilosophy* 32, 1/2 (2001): 34–57.

14 Charles R. Beitz, "Rawls's *Law of Peoples*," *Ethics* 110, 4 (2000): 670–8; Charles Jones, "Global Liberalism: Political or Comprehensive?" *University of Toronto Law Journal* 54, 2 (2004): 227–48; Thaddeus Metz, "Open Perfectionism and Global Justice," *Theoria: A Journal of Social & Political Theory* 114 (2004): 96–125; Richard W. Miller, "Cosmopolitanism and Its Limits," *Theoria: A Journal of Social & Political Theory* 114 (2004): 38–43; and Paul Voice, "Global Justice and the Challenge of Radical Pluralism," *Theoria: A Journal of Social & Political Theory* 114 (2004): 15–37.

15 Among the key differences are these: The cosmopolitans endorse a single global original position in which the parties represent individuals whose primary concern is the equal autonomy of individuals. The liberal-nationalists endorse a two-step procedure, in which principles of international justice are selected in a second run of the original position, by parties representing previously constituted "well-ordered peoples," whose primary concern is the justice of their own domestic societies. And the egalitarian-internationalists endorse a procedure that combines elements of both those designs. For the purposes of the present inquiry, however, these disagreements are less important than the one addressed here, which concerns what exactly the parties are held to know about the nature and workings of contemporary society.

16 Rawls, *The Law of Peoples*, pp. 29–30.

17 Chris Brown, "International Social Justice," in *Social Justice: From Hume to Walzer*, ed. David Boucher and Paul Kelly (London: Routledge, 1998), pp. 102–19; Simon Caney, "Cosmopolitanism and *The Law of Peoples*," *Journal of Political*

Philosophy 10, 1 (2002): 95–123, esp. 114–18; Andrew Kuper, "Rawlsian Global Justice: Beyond *The Law of Peoples* to a Cosmopolitan Law of Persons," *Political Theory* 28, 5 (2000): 640–74, esp. 645–8; and Leif Wenar, "Contractualism and Global Economic Justice," *Metaphilosophy* 32, 1/2 (2001): 79–94.

18 Beitz, "Rawls's *Law of Peoples*"; and Thomas Pogge, "An Egalitarian Law of Peoples," *Philosophy and Public Affairs* 23, 5 (2000): 195–224, esp. 197–9.

19 Rawls, *The Law of Peoples*, pp. 111–20.

20 Beitz, "Rawls's *Law of Peoples*"; Pogge, "An Egalitarian Law of Peoples."

21 Brown, "International Social Justice"; Caney, "Cosmopolitanism and *The Law of Peoples*"; Kuper, "Rawlsian Global Justice"; and Wenar, "Contractualism and Global Economic Justice."

22 In the first case, the empirical postulate of a global basic structure is held to justify the choice of the global cosmopolitan frame. In the second case, the contrary empirical postulate of a world composed of highly self-sufficient societies, each autonomously regulated by its own domestic basic structure, is held to justify the choice of the Keynesian-Westphalian frame. In the third case, finally, the empirical postulate of a two-tiered basic structure, comprising domestic and international elements, is held to justify the choice of a split-level frame with two different tiers of distributive obligations. What decides the "who," in other words, is the relative causal weight of social structures at the national, international, and global levels. It is each philosopher's understanding of that issue that determines his or her view of the concept that all consider the proper focus for reflection on distributive justice: "the basic structure." For the internationalists and cosmopolitans, the centrality of the causal issue is explicit; associating the basic structure with an objective system of interdependence, they maintain that all that is needed to secure a postwestphalian "who" is to demonstrate the transterritorial causal efficacy of the world economy. What may be less evident, however, is that the causal question is also decisive for the liberal-nationalists. Granted, they equate the basic structure with the "constitutional essentials" of a politically organized "scheme of cooperation," a view that is not ostensibly causal; and granted, too, they draw the ostensibly non-causal inference that, absent a global or international polity, there exists no basis for a postwestphalian "who." But when pushed to explain *why* the political community should constitute the unit of distributive justice, the liberal-nationalists invoke a causal rationale. For them, that structure is "basic" because it, more than anything

else, determines individuals' chances to live good lives. This causal postulate is as central for Rawls, who privileges the constitutional essentials of a bounded political community, as it is for his critics, who ascribe greater efficacy to the objective system mechanisms of global capitalism. I am grateful to Seyla Benhabib for raising this issue. For her views, see Seyla Benhabib, "*The Law of Peoples*, Distributive Justice, and Migrations," *Fordham Law Review* 72, 5 (2004): 1761–87.

23 Rawls, *The Law of Peoples*, pp. 105–13.

24 Beitz, "Rawls's *Law of Peoples*"; Allen Buchanan, "Rawls's *Law of Peoples*: Rules for a Vanished Westphalian World," *Ethics* 110, 4 (2000): 697–721; Caney, "Cosmopolitanism and the Law of Peoples"; and Kuper, "Rawlsian Global Justice."

25 An exception is Thomas Pogge, who has developed a sophisticated conceptual argument against "explanatory nationalism." See Pogge, "The Influence of the Global Order on the Prospects for Genuine Democracy in the Developing Countries," *Ratio-Juris* 14, 3 (2001): 326–43, and *World Poverty and Human Rights: Cosmopolitan Responsibilities and Reforms* (Cambridge: Polity, 2002), esp. chapter 5.

26 Usually, philosophers in this tradition tacitly assume a hermeneutical approach to the "how." Thus, Charles Taylor (*Multiculturalism*) assumes that the proper way to determine the "who" is by explicating the collective self-understandings of the peoples in question; but he neglects to weigh the merits of this assumption against the alternatives. Another, more promising tack is that of Rainer Forst, which also derives from recognition-theoretic premises. In *Contexts of Justice* (Berkeley: University of California Press, 2002), esp. pp. 230–41, Forst usefully distinguishes between four different contexts of justice, which correspond to four different types of justification, and in effect to four different normative "who's": moral, legal, political, and ethical. But he neglects to tell us how we are to resolve disputes as to which of these contexts applies when. Here, too, therefore, a sophisticated account, which insightfully differentiates among various "who's," fails to grapple seriously with the "how."

27 The reference is to Thomas Kuhn, *The Structure of Scientific Revolutions*, third edition (Chicago: University of Chicago Press, 1996).

28 David Held, Anthony McGrew, David Goldblatt, and Jonathan Perraton, *Global Transformations: Politics, Economics and Culture* (Cambridge: Polity, 1999); and Paul Hirst and Graham Thompson, *Globalization in Question: The International Economy and*

the Possibilities of Governance (Oxford: Blackwell Publishers, 1996).

29 John Rawls, *A Theory of Justice* (Cambridge, MA: Harvard University Press, 1999), p. 7.

30 Like the previous chapter, this one was written in 2004–5 and reflects my attraction then to the all-affected principle. Here, however, my doubts receive a more insistent, explicit formulation – in the form of criticisms of the principle's standard, "normal-scientific," interpretation. The guiding assumption is that we might remedy those defects by developing a different, "critical-democratic," interpretation of affectedness. Later, however, by 2006–7, the reconstructive difficulties seemed too large and the possibility of an alternative dawned. In the next chapter, therefore, I take a different tack, proposing not to reconstruct, but rather to jettison, the all-affected principle. Pondering problems of "Abnormal Justice" in chapter 4, I elaborate the alternative "all-subjected principle," which represents my current view. Here, too, however, as in the previous chapter, I have elected to eschew *post hoc* revision, leaving the present essay in its original form, to document my evolving thinking and to mark the issue as one I continue to grapple with.

31 I am grateful to David Peritz for enlightening discussions of this issue. I benefited greatly from the opportunity to read two chapters of his unpublished manuscript: "A Diversity of Diversities: Liberalism's Implicit Social Theories," paper prepared for presentation at the 53rd Annual Political Studies Association Conference, University of Leicester, April 15–17, 2003, Panel 6–11, Copyright © [PSA], and "The Complexities of Complexity: Habermas and the Hazards of Relying Directly on Social Theory," paper prepared for discussion at the Critical Theory Roundtable, October 2001, San Francisco.

32 I am grateful to Bert van den Brink for very helpful discussions of this issue.

33 For the distinction between weak and strong publics, see my "Rethinking the Public Sphere: A Contribution to the Critique of Actually Existing Democracy," in *Habermas and the Public Sphere*, ed. Craig Calhoun (Cambridge, MA: MIT Press, 1991), pp. 109–42; reprinted in Fraser, *Justice Interruptus: Critical Reflections on the "Postsocialist" Condition* (London: Routledge, 1997). See also Jürgen Habermas, *Between Facts and Norms: Contributions to a Discourse Theory of Law and Democracy*, trans. William Rehg (Cambridge, MA: MIT Press, 1996), pp. 307ff. See, finally, chapter 5 of this volume, "Transnationalizing the Public Sphere."

34 Daniele Archibugi, "A Critical Analysis of the Self-Determination of Peoples: A Cosmopolitan Perspective," *Constellations* 10, 4 (2003): 488–505.

35 For an argument that political frames cannot be determined democratically, see Frederick Whelan, "Democratic Theory and the Boundary Problem," in *Nomos XXV: Liberal Democracy*, ed. J. Roland Pennock and John W. Chapman (New York and London: New York University Press, 1983), pp. 13–47. For other treatments of the democratic paradox, see William Connolly, *Identity/Difference: Democratic Negotiations of Political Paradox* (Minneapolis: University of Minnesota Press, 2002) and Chantal Mouffe, "Democracy, Power and the 'Political'," in *Democracy and Difference: Contesting the Boundaries of the Political*, ed. Seyla Benhabib (Princeton: Princeton University Press, 1996), pp. 245–56.

36 For an example of the sort of institutional creativity I have in mind, which successfully finesses the democratic paradox, see Thomas Pogge's fascinating essay, "How to Create Supra-National Institutions Democratically: Some Reflections on the European Union's Democratic Deficit," *Journal of Political Philosophy* 5 (1997): 163–82.

37 Thanks to Bert van den Brink (personal communication) for suggesting this expression.

38 Some political theorists appear to have in mind something like this idea of a virtuous spiral starting from "good-enough deliberation." One promising proposal, suggested by Rainer Forst, is to institutionalize a "basic justification procedure" within which arguments about global justice can be mooted, and which can itself be reconstructed on increasingly egalitarian and just terms, as a result of reforms that emerge from, and are validated through, such arguments. So far as I know, Forst has not (yet) envisioned the possibility of applying his idea of a basic justification procedure at the meta-level to disputes about the frame, when not just the "what" but also the "who" is up for grabs; but I see no reason why this could not be done. See Forst, *Contexts of Justice*. A similar idea appears to inform Jürgen Habermas's proposal to institutionalize basic rights that point toward the fair value of political liberty, while also assuming that the content of those rights will be unfolded and enriched over time, as a result of ongoing (quasi-)democratic contestation. See Habermas, *Between Facts and Norms*.

39 I am grateful to Alessandro Ferrara for illuminating discussions of this issue. For his views, see Alessandro Ferrara, "Two Notions of Humanity and the Judgment Argument for Human Rights," *Political Theory* 31, 3 (June 2003): 392–420.

Chapter 4   Abnormal Justice

1 One aspect of my debt to Richard Rorty will be obvious here: my appropriation of his distinction between normal and abnormal discourse. What may be less evident is the larger inspiration he provided. By his example, Rorty emboldened an entire generation of American philosophers to refuse the intimidation of professional analytic philosophy, which had seemed so overwhelming, and crippling, in graduate school. It was from *Philosophy and the Mirror of Nature* that I gleaned the courage to chart my own path in philosophy, to write in my own voice about what I consider truly important. I cannot thank him enough for that. For insightful responses that helped me refine the argument of this chapter, I am indebted to Horst Bredekamp, Vincent Descombes, Rainer Forst, Robert Goodin, Kimberly Hutchings, Will Kymlicka, Maria Pia Lara, Jane Mansbridge, Faviola Rivera-Castro, Gabriel Rockhill, Nancy Rosenblum, Ann Laura Stoler, Philippe van Parijs, Eli Zaretsky, and W. J. T. Mitchell and the *Critical Inquiry* editorial collective.

2 Thomas S. Kuhn, *The Structure of Scientific Revolutions*, third edition (Chicago: University of Chicago Press, 1996).

3 If one were to be strictly faithful to Kuhn, one would speak here of "revolutionary justice." But given that expression's associations, I prefer to take my cue from Richard Rorty and speak instead of "abnormal justice." Rorty distinguishes "normal" from "abnormal" discourse in *Philosophy and the Mirror of Nature* (Princeton: Princeton University Press, 1981) and in *Contingency, Irony, and Solidarity* (Cambridge: Cambridge University Press, 1989).

4 For a fascinating discussion of US "importation" of "foreign law," see Judith Resnik, "Law's Migration: American Exceptionalism, Silent Dialogues, and Federalism's Multiple Ports of Entry," *The Yale Law Journal* 115, 7 (May 2006): 1546–70.

5 John G. Ruggie, "Territoriality and Beyond: Problematizing Modernity in International Relations," *International Organization* 47 (1993): 139–74.

6 Hannah Arendt, *The Origins of Totalitarianism*, new edition with added prefaces (New York: Harcourt Brace Jovanovich, 1973).

7 Disagreements about social ontology often translate into disagreement about the social cleavages that harbor injustice. Thus, where one side sees class injustice, another sees gender injustice, while still another sees injustice that tracks ethnic or religious fault-lines.

8   In many cases, disagreement about the scope of concern translates into disagreement about the scope of address, that is, about the public in and before which a claim for justice is rightfully debated. Thus, it is typical of abnormal contexts that one party addresses its claims to a territorially bounded public, while others address publics that are regional, transnational, or global.

9   Procedural disagreements often translate into disputes over representation or political voice. Where one party would restrict representation in dispute resolution bodies to states, others countenance representation for NGOs, and still others envision cosmopolitan-democratic schemes that directly represent individuals *qua* "world-citizens."

10   This frame also tended to marginalize claims pertaining to social fault-lines other than class, including claims concerning gender, sexuality, religion, and race or ethnicity.

11   Some readers have suggested that colonized people never accepted the legitimacy of the Westphalian frame, hence that this frame was never truly normalized. In my view, however, the great majority of anti-colonialists in the post-World War II era sought to achieve independent Westphalian states of their own. In contrast, only a small minority consistently championed justice within a global frame – for reasons that are entirely understandable. My claim, then, is that, far from contesting the Westphalian frame *per se*, anti-imperialist forces generally sought rather to realize it in a genuinely universal, even-handed way. Thanks to Ann Laura Stoler for forcefully raising this issue, although she will not be satisfied with my answer.

12   The Westphalian frame also partitioned public debates about justice along state lines. Channeling justice claims into the domestic public spheres of territorial states, it discouraged transnational public debate on matters of justice.

13   I discuss *misframing* in greater detail below and in chapter 2.

14   Two examples, from opposite ends of the philosophical spectrum, are Ronald Dworkin and Axel Honneth. Dworkin maintains that all injustices reduce in the end to resource maldistribution, while Honneth holds that all are at bottom variants of misrecognition. For Dworkin's view, see his "What is Equality? Part 2: Equality of Resources," *Philosophy and Public Affairs* 10, 4 (Fall 1981): 283–345. For a critique, see Elizabeth S. Anderson, "What is the Point of Equality?" *Ethics* 109, 2 (Jan. 1999): 287–337. For Honneth's view, see his "Redistribution as Recognition: A Response to Nancy Fraser," in Nancy Fraser and Axel Honneth, *Redistribution or Recognition? A Political-Philosophical Exchange,*

trans. Joel Golb, James Ingram, and Christiane Wilke (London: Verso, 2003), pp. 110–98. For a critique, see my "Distorted Beyond All Recognition: A Rejoinder to Axel Honneth," in ibid., pp. 198–237.

15 For a fuller elaboration and defense of this view, see my "Social Justice in the Age of Identity Politics," in Fraser and Honneth, *Redistribution or Recognition?*

16 For an account of second-wave feminism along these lines, see Richard Rorty, "Feminism and Pragmatism," *Michigan Quarterly Review* 30, 2 (1991): 231–58.

17 The "test" I am proposing has two aspects, one moral-philosophical, the other social-theoretical. From the perspective of moral philosophy, the question is: Does the proposed new interpretation of the "what" of justice identify a genuine injustice, which violates a morally valid norm? From the perspective of social theory, the question is: Does the proposed new interpretation disclose a hitherto neglected type of institutionalized obstacle to parity of participation, one that is rooted in a previously neglected dimension of social ordering?

18 As the previous note suggests, implicit in this discussion is another, social-theoretical rationale for a three-dimensional view of the "what." Modern societies encompass three distinct dimensions of social ordering: economic structure, status order, and political constitution. None of these can be reduced to the others, and each can give rise to injustice. For a fuller discussion, see my "Social Justice in the Age of Identity Politics."

19 I have elaborated and defended this principle in my "Social Justice in the Age of Identity Politics."

20 For the "status model" of recognition, see my "Rethinking Recognition," *New Left Review* 3 (May/June 2000): 107–20.

21 The incorporation of political representation as a third dimension of justice constitutes a major revision of my framework, which was originally two-dimensional. For an account of this dimension, and my reasons for adding it, see chapters 2 ("Reframing Justice in a Globalizing World") and 9 ("The Politics of Framing") of this volume. See also my "Identity, Exclusion, and Critique: A Response to Four Critics," *European Journal of Political Theory* 6, 3 (2007): 305–38.

22 In the first case, the problem arises from the economic structure of society, which corresponds to the economic dimension of justice. In the second case, the problem is the status order, which corresponds to the cultural dimension. In the third case, the problem is the constitution of the political system, which corresponds to the political dimension of justice.

23   One might well ask, why parity of participation, as opposed to
     rival principles of commensuration? Without pretending to
     present a full defense here, let me note only that this notion has
     an elective affinity with the problematic of abnormal justice.
     When the basic parameters of justice are contested, we lack
     authoritative standards for assessing the merits of justice claims.
     Effectively thrown back on procedural criteria, we have no
     alternative but to envision scenarios in which all the parties can
     engage one another on fair terms. In such cases, we must ask:
     Do all concerned have equal chances to participate fully, *as
     peers*? Or are some excluded or marginalized as a consequence
     of unjust social arrangements, which institutionalize structural
     impediments to participation? Thus, the principle of participa-
     tory parity directs us to interrogate social arrangements, to
     uncover, and criticize, entrenched obstacles to fair engagement.
     As a commensurating principle, moreover, it serves as a standard
     for evaluating justice claims in all three dimensions. For each
     dimension, only those claims that promote parity of participa-
     tion are morally justified. Whether the issue concerns distribu-
     tion, recognition, or representation, those who claim to suffer
     injustice should show, first, that current arrangements prevent
     them from participating as peers in social life; and, second, that
     the remedies they propose would diminish disparities. More-
     over, the parity standard applies transcategorially, across the
     different dimensions of justice: one can use it, for example, to
     assess the impact of proposed economic reforms on social status,
     or vice versa. Likewise, the parity standard applies recursively,
     across different axes of subordination: one can use it, for example,
     to assess the effects on gender relations of proposed forms of
     ethno-cultural recognition, or vice versa. For a fuller account of
     such complexities, see my "Social Justice in the Age of Identity
     Politics."

24   For discussions of such issues, see Lani Guinier, *The Tyranny of
     the Majority* (New York: Free Press 1994); Mala Htun "Is Gender
     like Ethnicity? The Political Representation of Identity Groups,"
     Perspectives on Politics 2, 3 (2004): 439–58; Will Kymlicka,
     Multicultural Citizenship: A Liberal Theory of Minority Rights
     (London: Oxford University Press, 1995); Shirin M. Rai, "Politi-
     cal Representation, Democratic Institutions and Women's
     Empowerment: The Quota Debate in India," in *Rethinking
     Empowerment: Gender and Development in a Global/Local World*,
     ed. Jane L. Parpart, Shirin M. Rai, and Kathleen A. Staudt (New
     York: Routledge, 2002), pp. 133–45; Robert Ritchie and Steven
     Hill, "The Case for Proportional Representation," in *Whose Vote*

Counts? ed. Robert Ritchie and Steven Hill (Boston: Beacon Press, 2001), pp. 1–33; and Melissa Williams, *Voice, Trust, and Memory: Marginalized Groups and the Failings of Liberal Representation* (Princeton: Princeton University Press, 1998).

25 See chapter 2, note 20.

26 Richard L. Harris and Melinda J. Seid, *Critical Perspectives on Globalization and Neoliberalism in the Developing Countries* (Boston: Leiden, 2000); and Ankie M. M. Hoogvelt, *Globalization and the Postcolonial World: The Political Economy of Development* (Baltimore: Johns Hopkins University Press, 2001). See also chapter 2, notes 21 and 22.

27 For the citizenship variant of the membership principle, see Will Kymlicka, "Territorial Boundaries. A Liberal-Egalitarian Perspective," in *Boundaries and Justice: Diverse Ethical Perspectives,* ed. David Miller and Sohail H. Hashmi (Princeton University Press, 2001), pp. 249–75; and Thomas Nagel, "The Problem of Global Justice," *Philosophy & Public Affairs* 33 (2005): 113–47. For the nationality variant, see David Miller, *On Nationality* (Oxford: Oxford University Press, 1995), esp. chapter 3. For an account that, oriented to "peoples," lies somewhere between citizenship and nationality, see John Rawls, *The Law of Peoples,* new edition (Cambridge, MA: Harvard University Press, 2001).

28 Proponents of this approach include Martha Nussbaum, "Patriotism and Cosmopolitanism," in Martha C. Nussbaum with Respondents, *For Love of Country? Debating the Limits of Patriotism,* ed. Joshua Cohen (Boston: Beacon Press, 1996), pp. 3–21.

29 Proponents of this approach include Thomas W. Pogge, *World Poverty and Human Rights: Cosmopolitan Responsibilities and Reforms* (Cambridge: Polity, 2002); Peter Singer, *One World: The Ethics of Globalization,* second edition (New Haven: Yale University Press, 2004); and Iris Marion Young, "Responsibility and Global Justice: A Social Connection Model," *Social Philosophy and Policy* 23, 1 (2006): 102–30. Until recently, I myself considered the all-affected principle the most promising candidate on offer for a "postwestphalian principle" of frame-setting, even though I criticized its standard scientistic interpretation and its "butterfly-effect" indeterminacy, as explained below. Now, however, I believe that these difficulties are so serious that the better course of wisdom is to abandon the all-affected principle in favor of the alternative presented here. For my earlier views, see chapters 2 ("Reframing Justice in a Globalizing World") and 3 ("Two Dogmas of Egalitarianism") of this volume.

30 The expression "all-subjected principle" is my own, but the idea
can be found in Joshua Cohen and Charles Sabel, "*Extra Republicam Nulla Justitia?*" *Philosophy & Public Affairs* 34 (2006):
147–75; and in Rainer Forst, "Justice, Morality and Power in the
Global Context," in *Real World Justice*, ed. Andreas Follesdal
and Thomas Pogge (Dordrecht: Springer, 2005), pp. 27–36.

31 James Ferguson, "Global Disconnect: Abjection and the
Aftermath of Modernism," in Ferguson, *Expectations of Modernity: Myths and Meanings of Urban Life on the Zambian
Copperbelt* (Berkeley: University of California Press, 1999), pp.
234–54.

32 See chapter 3 ("Two Dogmas of Egalitarianism") of this volume.

33 A similar argument is found in Amartya Sen, *Development as
Freedom* (New York: Anchor Books, 1999).

34 For one influential variant of populism, see Michael Hardt and
Antonio Negri, *Empire* (Cambridge, MA: Harvard University
Press, 2000). For another, less romantic, variant, see recent work
by James Bohman, who appears to hold that public-sphere contestation alone can resolve conflicts over the "who," hence that
no cosmopolitan political institutions are needed for that
purpose. A similar view is endorsed by Seyla Benhabib, who is
in other respects far from populist, but who also appears to put
the full onus of resolving disputes about the "who" on "democratic iterations" conducted in civil society. For Bohman's views,
see his "From *Demos* to *Demoi*: Democracy across Borders," *Ratio
Juris* 18, 3 (2005): 293–314; and "The Democratic Minimum: Is
Democracy a Means to Global Justice?" *Ethics and International
Affairs* 19, 1 (2004): 101–16. For Benhabib's view, see her Tanner
Lectures in *Another Cosmopolitanism: Hospitality, Sovereignty,
and Democratic Iterations*, ed. Robert Post (Oxford: Oxford University Press, 2006).

35 For a communications-theoretic account of the two-track model,
see Jürgen Habermas, *Between Facts and Norms: Contributions
to a Discourse Theory of Law and Democracy*, trans. William Rehg
(Cambridge, MA: MIT Press, 1996). For a critique of the tacit
Westphalian framing of that account, see chapter 5 ("Transnationalizing the Public Sphere") of this volume.

36 Thanks to the many interlocutors who raised this question,
especially Nancy Rosenblum, whose characteristically forceful
and crisp formulation made the issue impossible to evade.

37 My current interest in scrambling the distinction between normal
and abnormal discourse is prefigured in my exchanges with
Richard Rorty. In a 1988 essay (Nancy Fraser, "Solidarity or

Singularity? Richard Rorty between Romanticism and Technocracy," *Praxis International* 8, 3 (1988): 257–72), I noted Rorty's tendency to align abnormal discourse with "private irony" and normal discourse with "public solidarity"; and I proposed that radical social criticism upset those dichotomies insofar as it was both abnormal and solidaristic. Later, in his 1991 Tanner Lecture ("Feminism and Pragmatism"), Rorty provocatively transgressed his original alignment by reading radical second-wave feminism as both abnormal and publicly relevant. In my response (Nancy Fraser, "From Irony to Prophecy to Politics: A Response to Richard Rorty," *Michigan Quarterly Review* 30, 2 (1991): 259–66), I applauded that move, even as I faulted Rorty's account for individualizing and aestheticizing the process of linguistic innovation in feminism and for neglecting the latter's collective, democratic character. That argument now appears, in retrospect, to presage my present proposal to unsettle the distinction between normal and abnormal discourse.

38 Clearly, this preference for reflexive justice also distinguishes my position from proponents of abnormal discourse, paradigmatically Jean-François Lyotard, *The Differend: Phrases in Dispute*, trans. Georges Van Den Abbeele (Minneapolis: University of Minnesota Press, 1988). Thanks to Vincent Descombes for the comparison to Lyotard.

39 Classic critiques of discourse ethics from the standpoint of agonism include Jean-François Lyotard, *The Postmodern Condition: A Report on Knowledge*, trans. Geoff Bennington and Brian Massumi (Minneapolis: University of Minnesota Press, 1984) and Chantal Mouffe, "Deliberative Democracy or Agonistic Pluralism?" *Social Research* 66, 3 (1999): 745–58. Classic versions of the discourse-ethical critique of agonism include Jürgen Habermas, *The Philosophical Discourse of Modernity: Twelve Lectures*, trans. Frederick Lawrence (Cambridge, MA: MIT Press, 1987) and Seyla Benhabib, "Epistemologies of Postmodernism: A Rejoinder to Jean-François Lyotard," *New German Critique* 22 (1984): 103–26. For a recent round of the debate, see the exchange between Seyla Benhabib and Bonnie Honig in Benhabib, *Another Cosmopolitanism*.

40 For classic accounts of hegemony, see Antonio Gramsci, *Prison Notebooks*, ed. Joseph A. Buttigieg, trans. Joseph A. Buttigieg and Antonio Callari (New York: Columbia University Press, 1991) and Ernesto Laclau and Chantal Mouffe, *Hegemony and Socialist Strategy: Towards a Radical Democratic Politics* (London: Verso, 1985).

41 For accounts that stress the exclusionary aspects of discursive formations, albeit without reference to the term "hegemony," see Pierre Bourdieu, *Language and Symbolic Power*, ed. John B. Thompson, trans. Gino Raymond and Matthew Adamson (Cambridge, MA: Harvard University Press, 1991); Judith Butler, *Excitable Speech: A Politics of the Performative* (New York: Routledge, 1997); and Michel Foucault, *Essential Works of Foucault, 1954–1988*, ed. Paul Rabinow (New York: New Press, 1997).

42 Richard Rorty, *Philosophy and Social Hope* (New York: Penguin Books, 1999).

Chapter 5 Transnationalizing the Public Sphere: On the Legitimacy and Efficacy of Public Opinion in a Postwestphalian World

1 See, for example, John R. Bowen, "Beyond Migration: Islam as a Transnational Public Space," *Journal of Ethnic & Migration Studies* 30, 5 (2004): 879–94; *Globalizations and Social Movements: Culture, Power, and the Transnational Public Sphere*, ed. John A. Guidry, Michael D. Kennedy, and Mayer N. Zald (Ann Arbor: University of Michigan Press, 2000); Warwick Mules, "Media Publics and the Transnational Public Sphere," *Critical Arts Journal* 12, 1/2 (1998): 24–44; Thomas Olesen, "Transnational Publics: New Spaces of Social Movement Activism and the Problem of Global Long-Sightedness," *Current Sociology* 53, 3 (2005): 419–40; Rudolf Stichweh, "The Genesis of a Global Public Sphere," *Development* 46, 1 (2003): 26–9; Khachig Tololyan, "Rethinking Diaspora(s): Stateless Power in the Transnational Moment, *Diaspora* 5, 1 (1996): 3–36; Ingrid Volkmer, "The Global Network Society and the Global Public Sphere," *Development* 46, 1 (2003): 9–16; and Pnina Werbner, "Theorising Complex Diasporas: Purity and Hybridity in the South Asian Public Sphere in Britain," *Journal of Ethnic & Migration Studies* 30, 5 (2004): 895–911.

2 See, above all, Jürgen Habermas, *Structural Transformation of the Public Sphere*, trans. Thomas Burger (Cambridge, MA: MIT Press, 1989), esp. pp. 51–6, 140 and 222ff.; and *Between Facts and Norms: Contributions to a Discourse Theory of Law and Democracy*, trans. William Rehg (Cambridge, MA: MIT Press, 1996), esp. pp. 359–79. Hereafter I shall refer to these texts as *STPS* and *BFN*, respectively.

3 For an explanation of my use of the term "Westphalian," see chapter 2, note 1.

4 *STPS*, pp. 14–26 and 79–88; see also *BFN*, pp. 135–8, 141–4, 352, 366–7 and 433–6.

5 *STPS*, pp. 20–4, 51–7, 62–73, 83–8, 141ff.; see also *BFN*, pp. 365–6, 381–7.

6 *STPS*, pp. 14–20, esp. p. 17; see also *BFN*, pp. 344–51, esp. pp. 349–50.

7 *STPS*, pp. 58, 60–70; see also *BFN*, pp. 373–4 and 376–7.

8 *STPS*, pp. 24–39, esp. 36–7, 55–6, 60–3; see also *BFN*, pp. 360–2, 369–70, 375–7.

9 *STPS*, pp. 41–3, 48–51; see also *BFN*, pp. 373–4. The phrase "print capitalism" is not Habermas's, but Benedict Anderson's. See his *Imagined Communities: Reflections on the Origin and Spread of Nationalism*, second edition (London: Verso, 1991).

10 Anderson, *Imagined Communities*.

11 Jürgen Habermas, "The European Nation-State: On the Past and Future of Sovereignty and Citizenship," *Public Culture* 10, 2 (1998): 397–416.

12 Ibid.

13 The Black Public Sphere Collective, *The Black Public Sphere* (Chicago: University of Chicago Press, 1995); Evelyn Brooks-Higginbotham, *Righteous Discontent: The Women's Movement in the Black Baptist Church, 1880–1920* (Cambridge, MA: Harvard University Press, 1993); Geoff Eley, "Nations, Publics, and Political Cultures: Placing Habermas in the Nineteenth Century," in *Habermas and the Public Sphere*, ed. Craig Calhoun (Cambridge, MA: MIT Press, 1995), pp. 289–350; Nilufer Gole, "The Gendered Nature of the Public Sphere," *Public Culture* 10, 1 (1997): 61–80; Michael Rabinder James, "Tribal Sovereignty and the Intercultural Public Sphere," *Philosophy & Social Criticism* 25, 5 (1999): 57–86; Joan Landes, *Women and the Public Sphere in the Age of the French Revolution* (Ithaca, NY: Cornell University Press, 1988); Jane Rendall, "Women and the Public Sphere," *Gender & History* 11, 3 (1999): 475–89; Mary P. Ryan, *Women in Public: Between Banners and Ballots, 1825–1880* (Baltimore: Johns Hopkins University Press, 1990); and "Gender and Public Access: Women's Politics in Nineteenth-Century America," in *Habermas and the Public Sphere*, ed. Calhoun, pp. 259–89; Yasemin Nuhoglu Soysal, "Changing Parameters of Citizenship and Claims-Making: Organized Islam in European Public Spheres," *Theory and Society* 26 (1997): 509–27; Michael Warner, *Publics and Counterpublics* (New York: Zone Books, 2002); and Iris Marion Young, "Impartiality and the Civic Public: Some Implications of Feminist Critiques of Moral and Political Theory," in *Feminism as Critique*, ed. Seyla Benhabib and

Drucilla Cornell (Minneapolis: University of Minnesota Press, 1987), pp. 56–76.

14   An early form of this critique can be found in Niklas Luhman, "Öffentliche Meinung," *Politische Vierteljahresschrift* 11 (1970): 2–28. See also Stanley Aronowitz, "Is a Democracy Possible? The Decline of the Public in the American Debate," in *The Phantom Public Sphere*, ed. Bruce Robbins (Minneapolis: University of Minnesota Press, 1993), pp. 75–92; Nicholas Garnham "The Media and the Public Sphere," in *Habermas and the Public Sphere*, ed. Calhoun, pp. 359–76; Jürgen Gerhards and Friedhelm Neidhardt, *Strukturen und Funktionen Moderner Öffentlichkeit* (Berlin: Fragestellungen und Ansätze, 1990); and Michael Warner, "The Mass Public and the Mass Subject," in *The Phantom Public Sphere*, ed. Robbins, pp. 234–56.

15   Nancy Fraser, "Rethinking the Public Sphere: A Contribution to the Critique of Actually Existing Democracy," in *Habermas and the Public Sphere*, ed. Calhoun, pp. 109–42, esp. pp. 117–29. See also Nancy Fraser, "Sex, Lies, and the Public Sphere: Some Reflections on the Confirmation of Clarence Thomas," *Critical Inquiry* 18 (1992): 595–612.

16   Fraser, "Rethinking the Public Sphere," esp. pp. 129–32.

17   *BFN*, pp. 420–3.

18   Ibid., pp. 360–3.

19   According to William E. Scheuerman, for example, Habermas oscillates inconsistently between two antithetical stances: on the one hand, a "realistic," resigned, objectively conservative view that accepts the grave legitimacy and efficacy deficits of public opinion in really existing democratic states; on the other, a radical-democratic view that is still committed to overcoming them. I suspect that Scheuerman may well be right. Nevertheless, for purposes of the present argument, I shall stipulate that Habermas convincingly negotiates the tension "between fact and norm" in the democratic state. William E. Scheuerman, "Between Radicalism and Resignation: Democratic Theory in Habermas' *Between Facts and Norms*," in *Habermas: A Critical Reader*, ed. Peter Dews (Oxford: Blackwell, 1999), pp. 153–78.

20   *BFN*, pp. 465–6 and 500.

21   *Political Space: Frontiers of Change and Governance in a Globalizing World*, ed. Yale H. Ferguson and Barry Jones (Albany: State University of New York Press, 2002); David Held, *Democracy and the Global Order: From the Modern State to Cosmopolitical Governance* (Cambridge: Polity, 1995); David Held, Anthony McGrew, David Goldblatt, and Jonathan Perraton, *Global Transformations: Politics, Economics and Culture*

(Cambridge: Polity, 1999); Saskia Sassen, *Globalization and Its Discontents* (New York: Free Press, 1998); and *Territory, Authority, Rights: From Medieval to Global Assemblages* (Princeton: Princeton University Press, 2006).

22 *Constructing World Culture: International Nongovernmental Organizations since 1875*, ed. John Boli and John Thomas (Stanford: Stanford University Press, 1999); and Margaret E. Keck and Kathryn Sikkink, *Activists beyond Borders: Advocacy Networks in International Politics* (Ithaca, NY: Cornell University Press, 1998).

23 Some scholars do raise these questions. For genuinely critical treatments, see James Bohman, "The Globalization of the Public Sphere: Cosmopolitan Publicity and the Problem of Cultural Pluralism," *Philosophy and Social Criticism* 24, 2–3 (1998): 199–216; and "The Public Spheres of the World Citizen," in *Perpetual Peace: Essays on Kant's Cosmopolitan Ideal*, ed. James Bohman and Matthias Lutz-Bachmann (Cambridge, MA: MIT Press, 1997); and Maria Pia Lara, "Globalizing Women's Rights: Building a Public Sphere," in *Recognition, Responsibility, and Rights: Feminist Ethics and Social Theory. Feminist Reconstructions*, ed. Robin N. Fiore and Hilde Lindemann Nelson (Totowa, NJ: Rowman & Littlefield, 2003), pp. 181–93.

24 *Global Transformations*; James N. Rosenau, Held et al., "Governance and Democracy in a Globalizing World," in *Re-imagining Political Community: Studies in Cosmopolitan Democracy*, ed. Daniel Archibugi and David Held (Stanford: Stanford University Press, 1999), pp. 28–58, and *Along the Domestic–Foreign Frontier: Exploring Governance in a Turbulent World* (Cambridge: Cambridge University Press, 1997); William E. Scheuerman, "Economic Globalization and the Rule of Law," *Constellations* 6, 1 (1999): 3–25; David Schneiderman, "Investment Rules and the Rule of Law," *Constellations* 8, 4 (2001): 521–37; Anne-Marie Slaughter, *A New World Order* (Princeton: Princeton University Press, 2005); Susan Strange, *The Retreat of the State: The Diffusion of Power in the World Economy* (Cambridge: Cambridge University Press, 1996); and Mark W. Zacher, "The Decaying Pillars of the Westphalian Temple," in *Governance without Government*, ed. James N. Rosenau and Ernst-Otto Czempiel (Cambridge: Cambridge University Press, 1992), pp. 58–101.

25 Michael Hardt and Antonio Negri, *Empire* (Cambridge, MA: Harvard University Press, 2000); Raul C. Pangalangan, "Territorial Sovereignty: Command, Title, and Expanding the Claims of the Commons," in *Boundaries and Justice: Diverse Ethical*

Perspectives, ed. David Miller and Sohail H. Hashmi (Princeton: Princeton University Press, 2001), pp. 164–82; Saskia Sassen, *Losing Control? Sovereignty in an Age of Globalization* (New York: Columbia University Press, 1995); and Strange, *The Retreat of the State*.

26 *Citizenship Today: Global Perspectives and Practices*, ed. T. Alexander Aleynikoff and Douglas Klusmeyer (Washington, DC: Carnegie Endowment for Peace, 2001); *Theorizing Citizenship*, ed. Ronald Beiner (Albany: State University of New York Press, 1995); Seyla Benhabib, *The Rights of Others: Aliens, Residents, and Citizens* (Cambridge: Cambridge University Press, 2004) and "Transformations of Citizenship: The Case of Contemporary Europe," *Government and Opposition: An International Journal of Comparative Politics* 37, 4 (2002): 439–65; Charles Husband, "The Right to be Understood: Conceiving the Multi-ethnic Public Sphere," *Innovation: The European Journal of Social Sciences* 9, 2 (1996): 205–15; and Andrew Linklater, "Citizenship and Sovereignty in the Post-Westphalian European State" and Ulrich Preuss, "Citizenship in the European Union: A Paradigm for Transnational Democracy?" both in *Re-imagining Political Community*, ed. Archibugi and Held, pp. 113–38 and 138–52, respectively.

27 Craig Calhoun, "Imagining Solidarity: Cosmopolitanism, Constitutional Patriotism, and the Public Sphere," *Public Culture* 14, 1 (2002): 147–71.

28 Phil Cerny, "Paradoxes of the Competition State: The Dynamics of Political Globalization," *Government and Opposition* 32, 2 (1997): 251–74; Randall Germain, "Globalising Accountability within the International Organisation of Credit: Financial Governance and the Public Sphere," *Global Society: Journal of Interdisciplinary International Relations* 18, 3 (2004): 217–42; Held et al., *Global Transformations*; Eric Helleiner, "From Bretton Woods to Global Finance: A World Turned Upside Down," in *Political Economy and the Changing Global Order*, ed. Richard Stubbs and Geoffrey R. D. Underhill (New York: St Martin's Press, 1994), pp. 163–75; Jonathan Perraton, David Goldblatt, David Held, and Anthony McGrew, "The Globalisation of Economic Activity," *New Political Economy* 2, 2 (1997): 257–77; Gunter G. Schulze, *The Political Economy of Capital Controls* (Cambridge: Cambridge University Press, 2000); *Global Change and Transformation: Economic Essays in Honor of Karsten Laursen*, ed. Lauge Stetting, Knud Erik Svendsen and Edde Yndgaard (Copenhagen: Handelshojskolens Forlag, 1999); and Joseph E. Stiglitz, *Globalization and Its Discontents* (New York: Norton, 2003).

29 Bart Cammaerts and Leo van Audenhove, "Online Political Debate, Unbounded Citizenship, and the Problematic Nature of a Transnational Public Sphere," *Political Communication* 22, 2 (2005): 179–96; Peter Dahlgren, "The Internet, Public Spheres, and Political Communication: Dispersion and Deliberation," *Political Communication* 22, 2 (2005): 147–62; Held et al., *Global Transformations*; Robert W. McChesney, *Rich Media, Poor Democracy: Communications Politics in Dubious Times* (Chicago: University of Illinois Press, 1999) and "Global Media, Neoliberalism, and Imperialism," *Monthly Review* 50, 10 (2001): 1–19; Zizi Papacharissi, "The Virtual Sphere: The Internet as a Public Sphere," *New Media & Society* 4, 1 (2002): 9–36; and George Yudice, *The Expediency of Culture: Uses of Culture in the Global Era* (Durham, NC: Duke University Press, 2004).

30 Jean-Bernard Adrey, "Minority Language Rights before and after the 2004 EU Enlargement: The Copenhagen Criteria in the Baltic States," *Journal of Multilingual & Multicultural Development* 26, 5 (2005): 453–68; Neville Alexander, "Language Policy, Symbolic Power and the Democratic Responsibility of the Post-Apartheid University," *Pretexts: Literary & Cultural Studies* 12, 2 (2003): 179–90; Matthias König, "Cultural Diversity and Language Policy," *International Social Science Journal* 51, 161 (1999): 401–8; Alan Patten, "Political Theory and Language Policy," *Political Theory* 29, 5 (2001): 691–715; Robert Phillipson, *English-Only Europe? Challenging Language Policy* (New York: Routledge, 2003); Omid A. Payrow Shabani, "Language Policy and Diverse Societies: Constitutional Patriotism and Minority Language Rights," *Constellations* 11, 2 (2004): 193–216. Philippe van Parijs, "The Ground Floor of the World: On the Socio-economic Consequences of Linguistic Globalization," *International Political Science Review* 21, 2 (2000): 217–33; and Kenton T. Wilkinson, "Language Difference and Communication Policy in the Information Age," *Information Society* 20, 3 (2004): 217–29.

31 Arjun Appadurai, *Modernity at Large: Cultural Dimensions of Globalization* (Minneapolis: University of Minnesota Press, 1996); Kevin Michael DeLuca and Jennifer Peeples, "From Public Sphere to Public Screen: Democracy, Activism, and the 'Violence' of Seattle," *Critical Studies in Media Communication* 19, 2 (2002): 125–51; Ulf Hannerz, *Transnational Connections: Culture, People, Places* (New York: Routledge, 1996); Fredric Jameson, *The Cultural Turn* (London: Verso, 1998); P. David Marshall, *New Media Cultures* (New York: Oxford University Press, 2004); and George Yudice, *The Expediency of Culture*.

32 Anderson, *Imagined Communities.*

33 Habermas has himself remarked many of the developments cited above that problematize the Westphalian presuppositions of public-sphere theory. See his essay, "The Postnational Constellation and the Future of Democracy," in Jürgen Habermas, *The Postnational Constellation: Political Essays,* trans. and ed. Max Pensky (Cambridge, MA: MIT Press, 2001), pp. 58–113.

34 Certainly, these conditions are highly idealized and never fully met in practice. But it is precisely their idealized character that ensured the *critical* force of public-sphere theory. By appealing to the standard of inclusive communication among peers, the theory was able to criticize existing, power-skewed processes of publicity. By exposing unjustified exclusions and disparities, the theory was able to motivate its addressees to try to overcome them.

35 Thomas W. Pogge, *World Poverty and Human Rights: Cosmopolitan Responsibilities and Reforms* (Cambridge: Polity, 2002), especially the sections on "The Causal Role of Global Institutions in the Persistence of Severe Poverty," pp. 112–16, and "Explanatory Nationalism: The Deep Significance of National Borders," pp. 139–44.

36 Here I have modified the text. In its original publication as an article, this chapter endorsed the affectedness standard embedded in Habermas's discourse principle. For reasons explained in chapter 4 ("Abnormal Justice"), I propose in future work to develop a modified form of the discourse principle, centered on the idea that what turns a collection of people into fellow members of a public is their joint subjection to a governance structure that sets the ground rules for their interaction.

Chapter 6   Mapping the Feminist Imagination: From Redistribution to Recognition to Representation

This chapter originated as a keynote lecture delivered at the conference on "Gender Equality and Social Change," Cambridge University, March 2004. A later version was delivered at the conference on "Gender in Motion," University of Basel, March 2005. Thanks to Juliet Mitchell, Andrea Maihofer, and the participants at those conferences who discussed these ideas with me. Thanks, too, to Nancy Naples; although she does not share all of my views, our conversations influenced my thinking greatly, as is clear from our joint project:

"To Interpret the World and to Change It: An Interview with Nancy Fraser," by Nancy Fraser and Nancy A. Naples, *Signs: Journal of Women in Culture and Society* 29, 4 (Summer 2004): 1103–24. I am also grateful to Keith Haysom for efficient and cheerful research assistance and to Veronika Rall, whose German translation ("Frauen, denkt ökonomisch!" in *Die Tageszeitung* 7633 [April 7, 2005], pp. 4–5) so greatly improved on the original that I incorporated some of her phrasings here. Thanks, finally, to the Wissenschaftskolleg zu Berlin, which provided financial support, intellectual stimulation, and an ideal working environment.

1 See, for example, bell hooks, *Feminist Theory: From Margin to Center*, second edition (Boston: South End Press, 1981); Ruth Rosen, *The World Split Open: How the Modern Women's Movement Changed America* (New York: Penguin, 2001); and Benita Roth, *Separate Roads to Feminism: Black, Chicana, and White Feminist Movements in America's Second Wave* (Cambridge: Cambridge University Press, 2004).

2 Eric Hobsbawm, *The Age of Extremes: A History of the World, 1914–1991* (London: Abacus, 1995), pp. 320–41, 461–518.

3 *New Social Movements: From Ideology to Identity*, ed. Hank Johnston, Enrique Larana, and Joseph R. Gusfield (Philadelphia: Temple University Press, 1994); *Nomads of the Present: Social Movements and Individual Needs in Contemporary Society*, ed. Alberto Melucci, John Keane, and Paul Mier (Philadelphia: Temple University Press, 1989); and Alain Touraine, *Return of the Actor: Social Theory in Postindustrial Society* (Minneapolis: University of Minnesota Press, 1988).

4 Alice Echols, *Daring to Be Bad: Radical Feminism in America, 1967–75* (Minneapolis: University of Minnesota Press, 1990); Sara Evans, *Personal Politics: The Roots of Women's Liberation in the Civil Rights Movement and the New Left* (New York: Vintage, 1980); and Myra Marx Ferree and Beth B. Hess, *Controversy and Coalition: The Feminist Movement across Three Decades of Change* (New York: Routledge, 1995).

5 For some examples of this ambivalence, see the essays collected in *Women, the State and Welfare: Historical and Theoretical Perspectives*, ed. Linda Gordon (Madison: University of Wisconsin Press, 1990), including my own contribution, Nancy Fraser, "Struggle over Needs: Outline of a Socialist-Feminist Critical Theory of Late-Capitalist Political Culture," pp. 205–31.

6 Nancy Fraser, *Justice Interruptus: Critical Reflections on the "Postsocialist" Condition* (London: Routledge, 1997).

7   Nancy Fraser, "Multiculturalism, Antiessentialism, and Radical Democracy: A Genealogy of the Current Impasse in Feminist Theory, in Fraser, *Justice Interruptus*, pp. 173–89.

8   Nancy Fraser, "Social Justice in the Age of Identity Politics: Redistribution, Recognition and Participation," in Fraser and Axel Honneth, *Redistribution or Recognition? A Political-Philosophical Exchange*, trans. Joel Golb, James Ingram, and Christiane Wilke (London: Verso, 2003), pp. 7–110.

9   Frank Rich, "How Kerry Became a Girlie Man," *The New York Times* 153, 52963 (September 5, 2004), section 2, p. 1.

10   For related (albeit gender-insensitive) analyses, see Thomas Frank, "What's the Matter with Liberals?" *The New York Review of Books* 52, 8 (May 12, 2005), p. 46; and Richard Sennett, "The Age of Anxiety," *Guardian Saturday*, October 23, 2004, p. 34, available on-line at: *http://books.guardian.co.uk/print/0,3858,5044940–110738,00.html* (last accessed March 17, 2008).

11   Ibid.

12   For accounts of rightwing Christian women, see Sally Gallagher, *Evangelical Identity and Gendered Family Life* (New Brunswick, NJ: Rutgers University Press, 2003); R. Marie Griffith, *God's Daughters: Evangelical Women and the Power of Submission* (Berkeley: University of California Press, 1997); and Julie Ingersoll, *Evangelical Christian Women: War Stories in the Gender Battles* (New York: New York University Press, 2003). Also useful are two early accounts: the chapter on "Fundamentalist Sex: Hitting Below the Bible Belt" in Barbara Ehrenreich, Elizabeth Hess, and Gloria Jacobs, *Re-making Love: The Feminization of Sex* (New York: Anchor Books, 1987); and Judith Stacey, "Sexism by a Subtler Name? Postindustrial Conditions and Postfeminist Consciousness in the Silicon Valley," *Socialist Review* 96 (1987): 7–28.

13   The historic contest between Barack Obama and Hillary Clinton for the Democratic Party nomination in the 2008 US Presidential election precipitated a new political split among US women. Whereas Obama garnered support from academic feminists, college-educated women, younger women, and African-American women, Clinton's strongest backers were older white-ethnic working-class women with lower incomes and less education. The key sociological faultlines were class, education, "race"-ethnicity, and age. Equally important, however, was the fissure between feminist ideological commitment, on the one hand, and female gender identification, on the other. Whereas ideological feminists tended overwhelmingly to support Obama, Clinton forged a surprisingly intense experiential bond with older, poorer, rural and small town women with no

previous history of feminist involvement. Beleaguered in their own lives, they identified with a woman perceived both as perpetually embattled – humiliated by her husband's chronic philandering, vilified by the Right, rejected by young, affluent "liberal elitists" – and also as tough and gritty, a survivor and a fighter. Importantly, too, Clinton cultivated a macho persona, both with respect to policy (promising at one point to "obliterate" Iran) and with respect to conduct (waging a take-no-prisoners, "kitchen-sink," attack-mode campaign, even stooping to play "the race card"), while Obama projected a softer, androgynous posture (advocating international dialogue in place of saber-rattling and domestic comity in place of partisan hostility). Finally, the ideological feminist support for Obama reflected a serious, decades-long grappling with the vexed intersection of gender and race in US history; in contrast, Clinton's campaign showed no compunction in exploiting, indeed repeating, a traumatic history of race-versus-gender schism, stretching from the Reconstruction-era split over Negro manhood suffrage to the O. J. Simpson trial. The contrast between Obama's post-racial, post-partisan cosmopolitanism and Clinton's populist, hawkish nationalism bespoke a further divide: between those women who can imagine themselves thriving in a new, "postnational" knowledge-based world, on the one hand, and those who can only see that world as a threat to their well-being and status, on the other. The challenge of uniting those two groups in a reinvigorated feminist coalition is among the most pressing we face in the coming period – and not only in the United States.

14   Brooke A. Ackerly and Susan Moller Okin, "Feminist Social Criticism and the International Movement for Women's Rights as Human Rights," in *Democracy's Edges*, ed. Ian Shapiro and Casiano Hacker-Cordón (Cambridge: Cambridge University Press, 2002), pp. 134–62; and Donna Dickenson, "Counting Women In: Globalization, Democratization, and the Women's Movement," in *The Transformation of Democracy? Globalization and Territorial Democracy*, ed. Anthony McGrew (Cambridge: Polity, 1997), pp. 97–120. For two assessments of the gender politics of the broader anti-corporate globalization movement, see Judy Rebick, "Lip Service: The Anti-Globalization Movement on Gender Politics," *Herizons* 16, 2 (2002): 24–6; and Virginia Vargas, "Feminism, Globalization and the Global Justice and Solidarity Movement," *Cultural Studies* 17, 6 (2003): 905–20.

15   See chapter 2 of this volume ("Reframing Justice in a Globalizing World").

16   Ibid.

Chapter 7   From Discipline to Flexibilization?
Rereading Foucault in the Shadow of Globalization

1   See, for example, the essays in *Foucault: A Critical Reader*, ed.
    David Couzens Hoy (Oxford: Blackwell, 1986); and *Critique
    and Power: Recasting the Foucault/Habermas Debate*, ed. Michael
    Kelly (Cambridge, MA: MIT Press, 1994).
2   See especially Michel Foucault, *Power/Knowledge: Selected Inter-
    views and Other Writings, 1972–1977*, ed. Colin Gordon (New
    York: Pantheon, 1980); and *Language, Counter-Memory, Prac-
    tice: Selected Essays and Other Writings*, ed. Donald F. Bouchard
    (Ithaca, NY: Cornell University Press, 1977).
3   Michel Foucault, *The Birth of the Clinic: An Archaeology of Medical
    Perception*, trans. A. M. Sheridan Smith (New York: Pantheon,
    1973); *Discipline and Punish: The Birth of the Prison*, trans. Alan
    Sheridan (New York: Pantheon, 1977); and "Governmentality,"
    in *The Foucault Effect: Studies in Governmentality*, ed. Graham
    Burchell, Colin Gordon, and Peter Miller (Chicago: University
    of Chicago Press, 1991), pp. 87–105.
4   Foucault, *Discipline and Punish*.
5   Eli Zaretsky, *Secrets of the Soul: A Social and Cultural History of
    Psychoanalysis* (New York: Knopf, 2004).
6   Hannah Arendt, *The Human Condition* (Chicago: University
    of Chicago Press, 1958); and Jacques Donzelot, *The Policing
    of Families*, trans. Robert Hurley (New York: Pantheon, 1979).
7   This assumption was effectively excavated, and criticized, by
    Ann Laura Stoler, who restored the unthematized colonial back-
    ground of Foucault's accounts of discipline and biopower. See
    her *Race and the Education of Desire* (Chapel Hill, NC: Duke
    University Press, 1995).
8   Zaretsky, *Secrets of the Soul*.
9   Nancy Fraser, "Foucault on Modern Power: Empirical Insights
    and Normative Confusions," *Praxis International* 1, 3 (October
    1981): 272–87.
10 Susan Strange, *The Retreat of the State: The Diffusion of Power in the
    World Economy* (Cambridge: Cambridge University Press, 1996).
11 Phil Cerny, "Paradoxes of the Competition State: The Dynamics
    of Political Globalization," *Government and Opposition* 32, 2
    (1997): 251–74.
12 Loïc Wacquant, "From Slavery to Mass Incarceration," *New Left
    Review* 13 (Jan.–Feb. 2002): 41–60.
13 Some interpreters contend that before his death Foucault himself
    had already conceptualized this project. On their readings, his
    notions of biopower and governmentality represent elements of

a postfordist mode of regulation. In my reading, however, these notions belong rather to fordism, as they produce "welfare," "population," and "security" as objects of national state intervention. For me, accordingly, the main work of theorizing postfordist governmentality remains to be done.

14 Manuel Castells, "A Powerless State?" in Castells, *The Power of Identity* (Oxford: Blackwell, 1996); Cerny, "Paradoxes of the Competition State"; Stephen Gill, "New Constitutionalism, Democratisation and Global Political Economy," *Pacifica Review* 10, 1 (February 1998): 23–38; Jürgen Habermas, "The Postnational Constellation and the Future of Democracy," in *The Postnational Constellation: Political Essays*, trans. and ed. Max Pensky (Cambridge, MA: MIT Press, 2001), pp. 58–113; Michael Hardt and Antonio Negri, *Empire* (Cambridge, MA: Harvard University Press, 2000); David Held, "Democracy and the New International Order," in *Cosmopolitan Democracy: An Agenda for a New World Order*, ed. Daniele Archibugi and David Held (Cambridge: Polity, 1995), pp. 96–120; James Rosenau, "Governance and Democracy in a Globalizing World," in *Re-imagining Political Community: Studies in Cosmopolitan Democracy*, ed. Daniel Archibugi and David Held (Stanford: Stanford University Press, 1999), pp. 28–58; Saskia Sassen, "The State and the New Geography of Power," in Sassen, *Losing Control? Sovereignty in an Age of Globalization* (New York: Columbia University Press, 1995), pp. 1–33; Strange, *The Retreat of the State*; and Wolfgang Streeck, "Public Power beyond the Nation-State: The Case of the European Community," in *States against Markets: The Limits of Globalization*, ed. Robert Boyer and Daniel Drache (New York: Routledge, 1996), pp. 299–316.

15 Hardt and Negri, *Empire*.

16 Nikolas Rose, "Governing Advanced Liberal Democracies," in Peter Miller and Nikolas Rose, *Governing the Present: Administering Economic, Social and Personal Life* (Cambridge: Polity, 2008), pp. 199–218.

17 William E. Scheuerman, "Economic Globalization and the Rule of Law," *Constellations* 6, 1 (1999): 3–25; and David Schneiderman, "Investment Rules and the Rule of Law," *Constellations* 8, 4 (2001): 521–37.

18 Robert W. Cox, "A Perspective on Globalization," in *Globalization: Critical Reflections*, ed. James H. Mittelman (Boulder, CO: Lynne Rienner, 1996), pp. 21–30, and "Democracy in Hard Times: Economic Globalization and the Limits to Liberal Democracy," in *The Transformation of Democracy?* ed. Anthony McGrew (Cambridge: Polity, 1997), pp. 49–75.

19 Rose, "Governing Advanced Liberal Democracies."
20 Ibid.
21 Colin Gordon, "Governmental Rationality: An Introduction," in *The Foucault Effect: Studies in Governmentality*, ed. Graham Burchell, Colin Gordon, and Peter Miller (Chicago: University of Chicago Press, 1991), pp. 1–51.
22 For the unthematized colonial background of Foucault's accounts of discipline and biopower, see Stoler, *Race and the Education of Desire*.
23 Robert Castel, "From Dangerousness to Risk," in *The Foucault Effect*, ed. Burchell et al., pp. 281–98.
24 Benjamin R. Barber, *Jihad vs McWorld: Terrorism's Challenge to Democracy* (New York: Ballantine Books, 1996); Manuel Castells, *The Rise of the Network Society* (Oxford: Blackwell, 1996); and Hardt and Negri, *Empire*.
25 Richard Sennett, *The Corrosion of Character: The Personal Consequences of Work in the New Capitalism* (New York: Norton, 1998).

Chapter 8   Threats to Humanity in Globalization: Arendtian Reflections on the Twenty-First Century

1 James Scott, *Seeing Like a State: How Certain Schemes to Improve the Human Condition Have Failed* (New Haven: Yale University Press, 1998).
2 For a parallel treatment of Foucault's relevance to the twenty-first century, see chapter 7 of this volume, "From Discipline to Flexibilization? Rereading Foucault in the Shadow of Globalization."
3 Jürgen Habermas, "Struggles for Recognition in the Democratic Constitutional State," in *Multiculturalism*, ed. Amy Gutmann, trans. Shierry Weber Nicholsen (Princeton, NJ: Princeton University Press, 1994), pp. 107–65, "The European Nation-State: On the Past and Future of Sovereignty and Citizenship," in *The Inclusion of the Other*, ed. Ciaran Cronin and Pablo de Grieff, trans. Ciaran Cronin (Cambridge, MA: MIT Press, 1999), pp. 105–28, and "The Postnational Constellation and the Future of Democracy," in *The Postnational Constellation*, trans. Max Pensky (Cambridge, MA: MIT Press, 2001), pp. 58–113.
4 Jürgen Habermas, *Between Facts and Norms: Contributions to a Discourse Theory of Law and Democracy*, trans. William Rehg (Cambridge, MA: MIT Press, 1996), p. 308.
5 Habermas, "Struggles for Recognition in the Democratic Constitutional State" and "The European Nation-State."

6   Christiane Wilke, "Habermas, the Alien, and the Escape to Cosmopolitanism," unpublished ms.

7   Hannah Arendt, *The Origins of Totalitarianism,* new edition with added prefaces (New York: Harcourt Brace Jovanovich, 1973), p. 299.

8   Ibid., p. 298.

9   Jürgen Habermas, "Kant's Idea of Perpetual Peace, with the Benefit of 200 Years' Hindsight," in *Perpetual Peace: Essays on Kant's Cosmopolitan Ideal,* ed. James Bohman and Matthias Lutz-Bachmann (Cambridge, MA: MIT Press, 1997), p. 304, and "The Postnational Constellation and the Future of Democracy," pp. 105ff.; and Wilke, "Habermas, the Alien, and the Escape to Cosmopolitanism."

10 Jürgen Habermas, "Bestiality and Humanity: A War on the Border between Legality and Morality," *Constellations: An International Journal of Critical and Democratic Theory* 6, 3 (1999): 263–72, and "Dispute on the Past and Future of International Law: Transition from a National to a Postnational Constellation," unpublished ms, presented at World Congress of Philosophy, Istanbul, August 2003.

11 Allen Buchanan, "From Nuremberg to Kosovo: The Morality of Illegal International Legal Reform," *Ethics* 111, 4 (2001): 673–705; Habermas, "Bestiality and Humanity" and "Dispute on the Past and Future of International Law"; Michael Ignatieff, *Human Rights as Politics and Idolatry* (Princeton: Princeton University Press, 2001), pp. 3–100; and David Rieff, *Slaughterhouse: Bosnia and the Failure of the West* (New York: Simon & Schuster, 1995).

12 Paul Berman, *Terrorism and Liberalism* (New York: Norton, 2003). For a related but less developed argument, see Christopher Hitchens, "Of Sin, the Left and Islamic Fascism," *The Nation,* September 24, 2001.

13 John Gray, *False Dawn: The Delusions of Global Capitalism* (New York: New Press, 1998).

14 Michael Hardt and Antonio Negri, *Empire* (Cambridge, MA: Harvard University Press, 2000).

15 Maeve Cooke, "The Immanence of 'Empire': Reflections on Social Change for the Better in a Globalizing World," in *The Politics of Recognition: Explorations of Difference and Justice,* ed. Baukje Prins and Judith Vega (Amsterdam: Dutch University Press, forthcoming); and Andreas Kalyvas, "Feet of Clay? Reflections on Hardt's and Negri's *Empire,*" *Constellations: An International Journal of Critical and Democratic Theory* 10, 2 (2003): 264–79.

16 I owe this point to Richard J. Bernstein.

Chapter 9   The Politics of Framing:
An Interview with Nancy Fraser

1   Reprinted as chapter 2 of this volume.
2   This interview, as in some earlier chapters, refers occasionally to the all-affected principle, to which I subscribed at the time, in March 2006. For an account of my current view, centered instead on the "all-subjected principle," see chapter 4, "Abnormal Justice," in this volume.
3   "Transnationalizing the Public Sphere," reprinted as chapter 5 of this volume.

References

Brooke A. Ackerly, *Political Theory and Feminist Social Criticism*, Cambridge: Cambridge University Press, 2000

Brooke A. Ackerly and Susan Moller Okin, "Feminist Social Criticism and the International Movement for Women's Rights as Human Rights," in *Democracy's Edges*, ed. Ian Shapiro and Casiano Hacker-Cordón, Cambridge: Cambridge University Press, 2002, pp. 134–62

Jean-Bernard Adrey, "Minority Language Rights before and after the 2004 EU Enlargement: The Copenhagen Criteria in the Baltic States," *Journal of Multilingual & Multicultural Development* 26, 5 (2005): 453–68

Neville Alexander, "Language Policy, Symbolic Power and the Democratic Responsibility of the Post-Apartheid University," *Pretexts: Literary & Cultural Studies* 12, 2 (2003): 179–90

T. Alexander Aleynikoff and Douglas Klusmeyer, eds., *Citizenship Today: Global Perspectives and Practices*, Washington, DC: Carnegie Endowment for Peace, 2001

Alfred C. Aman, Jr., "Globalization, Democracy and the Need for a New Administrative Law," *Indiana Journal of Global Legal Studies* 10, 1 (2003): 125–55

Benedict Anderson, *Imagined Communities: Reflections on the Origin and Spread of Nationalism*, second edition, London: Verso, 1991

Elizabeth Anderson, "What is the Point of Equality?" *Ethics* 109 (1999): 287–337

Arjun Appadurai, *Modernity at Large: Cultural Dimensions of Globalization*, Minneapolis: University of Minnesota Press, 1996

Daniele Archibugi, "A Critical Analysis of the Self-Determination of Peoples: A Cosmopolitan Perspective," *Constellations* 10, 4 (2003): 488–505

Hannah Arendt, *The Human Condition*, Chicago: University of Chicago Press, 1958

Hannah Arendt, *The Origins of Totalitarianism*, new edition with added prefaces, New York: Harcourt Brace Jovanovich, 1973

Stanley Aronowitz, "Is a Democracy Possible? The Decline of the Public in the American Debate," in *The Phantom Public Sphere*, ed. Bruce Robbins, Minneapolis: University of Minnesota Press, 1993, pp. 75–92

Thomas Baldwin, "The Territorial State," in *Jurisprudence: Cambridge Essays*, ed. Hyman Gross and Ross Harrison, Oxford: Clarendon Press, 1992, pp. 207–30

Benjamin R. Barber, *Jihad vs McWorld: Terrorism's Challenge to Democracy*, New York: Ballantine Books, 1996

Linda Basch, Nina Glick Schiller, and Christina Szanton Blanc, *Nations Unbound: Transnational Projects, Postcolonial Predicaments, and De-territorialized Nation-States*, New York: Gordon and Breach, 1994

Amrita Basru, ed., *The Challenge of Local Feminisms: Women's Movements in Global Perspective*, Boulder, CO: Westview Press, 1995

Ronald Beiner, ed., *Theorizing Citizenship*, Albany: State University of New York Press, 1995

Charles R. Beitz, *Political Theory and International Relations*, Princeton: Princeton University Press, first edition, 1979; second edition, 1999

Charles R. Beitz, "Rawls's *Law of Peoples*," *Ethics*, 110, 4 (2000): 670–8

Seyla Benhabib, *Another Cosmopolitanism: Hospitality, Sovereignty, and Democratic Iterations*, ed. Robert Post, Oxford: Oxford University Press, 2006

Seyla Benhabib, "Epistemologies of Postmodernism: A Rejoinder to Jean-François Lyotard," *New German Critique* 22 (1984): 103–26

Seyla Benhabib, "*The Law of Peoples*, Distributive Justice, and Migrations," *Fordham Law Review* 72, 5 (2004): 1761–87

Seyla Benhabib, *The Rights of Others*, Cambridge: Cambridge University Press, 2004

Seyla Benhabib, "Transformations of Citizenship: The Case of Contemporary Europe," *Government and Opposition: An International Journal of Comparative Politics* 37, 4 (2002): 439–65

Paul Berman, *Terrorism and Liberalism*, New York: Norton, 2003

Black Public Sphere Collective, *The Black Public Sphere*, Chicago: University of Chicago Press, 1995

James Bohman, "The Democratic Minimum: Is Democracy a Means to Global Justice?" *Ethics and International Affairs* 19, 1 (2004): 101–16

James Bohman, "From *Demos* to *Demoi*: Democracy across Borders," *Ratio Juris* 18, 3 (2005): 293–314

James Bohman, "The Globalization of the Public Sphere: Cosmopolitan Publicity and the Problem of Cultural Pluralism," *Philosophy and Social Criticism* 24, 2–3 (1998): 199–216

James Bohman, "International Regimes and Democratic Governance," *International Affairs* 75, 3 (1999): 499–513

James Bohman, "The Public Spheres of the World Citizen," in *Perpetual Peace: Essays on Kant's Cosmopolitan Ideal*, ed. James Bohman and Matthias Lutz-Bachmann, Cambridge, MA: MIT Press, 1997

John Boli and John Thomas, eds., *Constructing World Culture: International Nongovernmental Organizations since 1875*, Stanford: Stanford University Press, 1999

Pierre Bourdieu, *Language and Symbolic Power*, ed. John B. Thompson, trans. Gino Raymond and Matthew Adamson, Cambridge, MA: Harvard University Press, 1991

John R. Bowen, "Beyond Migration: Islam as a Transnational Public Space," *Journal of Ethnic & Migration Studies* 30, 5 (2004): 879–94

James K. Boyce, "Democratizing Global Economic Governance," *Development and Change* 35, 3 (2004): 593–9

Avtar Brah, *Cartographies of Diaspora: Contesting Identities*, London: Routledge, 1997

Evelyn Brooks-Higginbotham, *Righteous Discontent: The Women's Movement in the Black Baptist Church, 1880–1920*, Cambridge, MA: Harvard University Press, 1993

Chris Brown, "International Social Justice," in *Social Justice: From Hume to Walzer*, ed. David Boucher and Paul Kelly, London: Routledge, 1998, pp. 102–19

Allen Buchanan, "From Nuremberg to Kosovo: The Morality of Illegal International Legal Reform," *Ethics* 111, 4 (2001): 673–705

Allen Buchanan, "Rawls's *Law of Peoples*: Rules for a Vanished Westphalian World," *Ethics* 110, 4 (2000): 697–721

Judith Butler, *Excitable Speech: A Politics of the Performative*, New York: Routledge, 1997

Craig Calhoun, "The Class Consciousness of Frequent Travelers: Toward a Critique of Actually Existing Cosmopolitanism," *South Atlantic Quarterly* 101, 4 (2002): 869–98

Craig Calhoun, "Imagining Solidarity: Cosmopolitanism, Constitutional Patriotism, and the Public Sphere," *Public Culture* 14, 1 (2002): 147–71

Bart Cammaerts and Leo van Audenhove, "Online Political Debate, Unbounded Citizenship, and the Problematic Nature of a Transnational Public Sphere," *Political Communication* 22, 2 (2005): 179–96

Simon Caney, "Cosmopolitanism and *The Law of Peoples*," *Journal of Political Philosophy* 10, 1 (2002): 95–123

Robert Castel, "From Dangerousness to Risk," in *The Foucault Effect: Studies in Governmentality*, ed. Graham Burchell, Colin Gordon, and Peter Miller, Chicago: University of Chicago Press, pp. 281–98

Manuel Castells, *The Power of Identity*, Oxford: Blackwell, 1996

Manuel Castells, *The Rise of the Network Society*, Oxford: Blackwell, 1996

Stephen Castles and Alastair Davidson, *Citizenship and Migration: Globalization and the Politics of Belonging*, London: Routledge, 2000

Phil Cerny, "Paradoxes of the Competition State: The Dynamics of Political Globalization," *Government and Opposition* 32, 2 (1997): 251–74

Partha Chatterjee, *Nationalist Thought and the Colonial World*, Minneapolis: University of Minnesota Press, 1993

Andrew Clapham, "Issues of Complexity, Complicity and Complementarity: From the Nuremberg Trials to the Dawn of the New International Criminal Court," in *From Nuremberg to The Hague: The Future of International Criminal Justice*, ed. Philippe Sands, Cambridge: Cambridge University Press, 2003, pp. 233–81

G. A. Cohen, "On the Currency of Egalitarian Justice," *Ethics* 99 (1989): 906–44

Joshua Cohen and Charles Sabel, "*Extra Republicam Nulla Justitia?*" *Philosophy & Public Affairs* 34 (2006): 147–75

William Connolly, *Identity/Difference: Democratic Negotiations of Political Paradox*, Minneapolis: University of Minnesota Press, 2002

Rebecca J. Cook, ed., *Human Rights of Women: National and International Perspectives*, Philadelphia: University of Pennsylvania Press, 1994

Maeve Cooke, "The Immanence of 'Empire': Reflections on Social Change for the Better in a Globalizing World," in *The Politics of Recognition: Explorations of Difference and Justice*, ed. Baukje Prins and Judith Vega, Amsterdam: Dutch University Press, forthcoming

Robert W. Cox, "Democracy in Hard Times: Economic Globalization and the Limits to Liberal Democracy," in *The Transformation of Democracy?* ed. Anthony McGrew, Cambridge: Polity, 1997, pp. 49–72

Robert W. Cox, "A Perspective on Globalization," in *Globalization: Critical Reflections*, ed. James H. Mittelman, Boulder, CO: Lynne Rienner, 1996, pp. 21–30

Holly Cullen and Karen Morrow, "International Civil Society in International Law: The Growth of NGO Participation," *Non-State Actors & International Law* 1, 1 (2001): 7–39

Peter Dahlgren, "The Internet, Public Spheres, and Political Communication: Dispersion and Deliberation," *Political Communication* 22, 2 (2005): 147–62

Kevin Michael DeLuca and Jennifer Peeples, "From Public Sphere to Public Screen: Democracy, Activism, and the 'Violence' of Seattle," *Critical Studies in Media Communication* 19, 2 (2002): 125–51

Donna Dickenson, "Counting Women In: Globalization, Democratization, and the Women's Movement," in *The Transformation of Democracy? Globalization and Territorial Democracy*, ed. Anthony McGrew, Cambridge: Polity, 1997, pp. 97–120

Jacques Donzelot, *The Policing of Families*, trans. Robert Hurley, New York: Pantheon, 1979

John Dryzek, "Transnational Democracy," *Journal of Political Philosophy* 7, 1 (1999): 30–51

Ronald Dworkin, "What is Equality? Part 2: Equality of Resources," *Philosophy and Public Affairs* 10, 4 (Fall 1981): 283–345

Alice Echols, *Daring to Be Bad: Radical Feminism in America, 1967–75*, Minneapolis: University of Minnesota Press, 1990

Barbara Ehrenreich, Elizabeth Hess, and Gloria Jacobs, *Remaking Love: The Feminization of Sex*, New York: Anchor Books, 1987

Geoff Eley, "Nations, Publics, and Political Cultures: Placing Habermas in the Nineteenth Century," in *Habermas and the Public Sphere*, ed. Craig Calhoun, Cambridge, MA: MIT Press, 1995, pp. 289–350

Sara Evans, *Personal Politics: The Roots of Women's Liberation in the Civil Rights Movement and the New Left*, New York: Vintage, 1980

Richard Falk, "Revisiting Westphalia, Discovering Post-Westphalia," *Journal of Ethics* 6, 4 (2002): 311–52

Frantz Fanon, "On National Culture," in Fanon, *The Wretched of the Earth*, New York: Grove, 1963, pp. 165–99

James Ferguson, "Global Disconnect: Abjection and the Aftermath of Modernism," in Ferguson, *Expectations of Modernity: Myths and Meanings of Urban Life on the Zambian Copperbelt*, Berkeley: University of California Press, 1999, pp. 234–54

Yale H. Ferguson and Barry Jones, eds., *Political Space: Frontiers of Change and Governance in a Globalizing World*, Albany: State University of New York Press, 2002

Alessandro Ferrara, "Two Notions of Humanity and the Judgment Argument for Human Rights," *Political Theory* 31, 3 (June 2003): 392–420

Myra Marx Ferree and Beth B. Hess, *Controversy and Coalition: The Feminist Movement across Three Decades of Change*, New York: Routledge, 1995

Rainer Forst, *Contexts of Justice*, Berkeley: University of California Press, 2002

Rainer Forst, "Justice, Morality and Power in the Global Context," in *Real World Justice*, ed. Andreas Follesdal and Thomas Pogge, Dordrecht: Springer, 2005, pp. 27–36

Rainer Forst, "Towards a Critical Theory of Transnational Justice," in *Global Justice*, ed. Thomas Pogge, Oxford: Blackwell, 2001, pp. 169–87

Michel Foucault, *The Birth of the Clinic: An Archaeology of Medical Perception*, trans. A. M. Sheridan Smith, New York: Pantheon, 1973

Michel Foucault, *Discipline and Punish: The Birth of the Prison*, trans. Alan Sheridan, New York: Pantheon, 1977

Michel Foucault, *Essential Works of Foucault, 1954–1988*, ed. Paul Rabinow, New York: New Press, 1997

Michel Foucault, "Governmentality," in *The Foucault Effect: Studies in Governmentality*, ed. Graham Burchell, Colin Gordon, and Peter Miller, Chicago: University of Chicago Press, 1991, pp. 87–105

Michel Foucault, *Language, Counter-Memory, Practice: Selected Essays and Other Writings*, ed. Donald F. Bouchard, Ithaca, NY: Cornell University Press, 1977

Michel Foucault, *Power/Knowledge: Selected Interviews and Other Writings, 1972–1977*, ed. Colin Gordon, New York: Pantheon, 1980

Georges Eugene Fouron and Nina Glick Schiller, *Georges Woke Up Laughing: Long Distance Nationalism and the Search for Home*, Durham, NC: Duke University Press, 2001

Thomas Frank, "What's the Matter with Liberals?" *The New York Review of Books* 52, 8 (May 12, 2005), p. 46

Nancy Fraser, "Foucault on Modern Power: Empirical Insights and Normative Confusions," *Praxis International* 1, 3 (October 1981): 272–87; reprinted in Fraser, *Unruly Practices: Power, Discourse and Gender in Contemporary Social Theory*, Cambridge: Polity and Minneapolis: University of Minnesota Press, 1989, pp. 17–34

Nancy Fraser, "From Irony to Prophecy to Politics: A Response to Richard Rorty," *Michigan Quarterly Review* 30, 2 (1991): 259–66

Nancy Fraser, "From Redistribution to Recognition? Dilemmas of Justice in a 'Postsocialist' Age," *New Left Review* 212 (1995): 68–93; reprinted in Fraser, *Justice Interruptus: Critical Reflections on the "Postsocialist" Condition*, London: Routledge, 1997, pp. 11–40

Nancy Fraser, "Identity, Exclusion, and Critique: A Response to Four Critics," *European Journal of Political Theory* 6, 3 (2007): 305–38

Nancy Fraser, *Justice Interruptus: Critical Reflections on the "Postsocialist" Condition*, London: Routledge, 1997

Nancy Fraser, "Rethinking Recognition," *New Left Review* 3 (May/June 2000): 107–20

Nancy Fraser, "Rethinking the Public Sphere: A Contribution to the Critique of Actually Existing Democracy," in *Habermas and the Public Sphere*, ed. Craig Calhoun, Cambridge, MA: MIT Press, 1991, pp. 109–42; reprinted in Fraser, *Justice Interruptus: Critical Reflections on the "Postsocialist" Condition*, London: Routledge, 1997

Nancy Fraser, "Sex, Lies, and the Public Sphere: Some Reflections on the Confirmation of Clarence Thomas," *Critical Inquiry* 18 (1992): 595–612

Nancy Fraser, "Solidarity or Singularity? Richard Rorty between Romanticism and Technocracy," *Praxis International* 8, 3 (1988): 257–72; reprinted in Fraser, *Unruly Practices: Power, Discourse and Gender in Contemporary Social Theory*, Cambridge: Polity and Minneapolis: University of Minnesota Press, 1989, pp. 93–110

Nancy Fraser, "Struggle over Needs: Outline of a Socialist-Feminist Critical Theory of Late-Capitalist Political Culture," in *Women, the State and Welfare: Historical and Theoretical Perspectives*, ed. Linda Gordon, Madison: University of Wisconsin Press, 1990, pp. 205–31; reprinted in Fraser, *Unruly Practices: Power, Discourse and Gender in Contemporary Social Theory*, Cambridge: Polity and Minneapolis: University of Minnesota Press, 1989, pp. 161–87

Nancy Fraser, *Unruly Practices: Power, Discourse and Gender in Contemporary Social Theory*, Cambridge: Polity and Minneapolis: University of Minnesota Press, 1989

Nancy Fraser and Axel Honneth, *Redistribution or Recognition? A Political-Philosophical Exchange*, trans. Joel Golb, James Ingram, and Christiane Wilke, London: Verso, 2003

Nancy Fraser and Nancy A. Naples, "To Interpret the World and to Change It: An Interview with Nancy Fraser," *Signs: Journal of Women in Culture and Society* 29, 4 (Summer 2004): 1103–24

Sally Gallagher, *Evangelical Identity and Gendered Family Life*, New Brunswick, NJ: Rutgers University Press, 2003

Nicholas Garnham "The Media and the Public Sphere," in *Habermas and the Public Sphere*, ed. Craig Calhoun, Cambridge, MA: MIT Press, pp. 359–76

Jürgen Gerhards and Friedhelm Neidhardt, *Strukturen und Funktionen Moderner Öffentlichkeit*, Berlin: Fragestellungen und Ansätze, 1990

Randall Germain, "Globalising Accountability within the International Organisation of Credit: Financial Governance and the

Public Sphere," *Global Society: Journal of Interdisciplinary International Relations* 18, 3 (2004): 217–42

Stephen Gill, "New Constitutionalism, Democratisation and Global Political Economy," *Pacifica Review* 10, 1 (February 1998): 23–38

Nilufer Gole, "The Gendered Nature of the Public Sphere," *Public Culture* 10, 1 (1997): 61–80

Colin Gordon, "Governmental Rationality: An Introduction," in *The Foucault Effect: Studies in Governmentality*, ed. Graham Burchell, Colin Gordon, and Peter Miller, Chicago: University of Chicago Press, 1999, pp. 1–51

Linda Gordon, ed., *Women, the State and Welfare: Historical and Theoretical Perspectives*, Madison: University of Wisconsin Press, 1990

Carol Gould, *Globalizing Democracy and Human Rights*, Cambridge: Cambridge University Press, 2004

Antonio Gramsci, *Prison Notebooks*, ed. Joseph A. Buttigieg, trans. Joseph A. Buttigieg and Antonio Callari, New York: Columbia University Press, 1991

John Gray, *False Dawn: The Delusions of Global Capitalism*, New York: New Press, 1998

Tricia Gray, "Electoral Gender Quotas: Lessons from Argentina and Chile," *Bulletin of Latin American Research* 21, 1 (2003): 52–78

R. Griffith Marie, *God's Daughters: Evangelical Women and the Power of Submission*, Berkeley: University of California Press, 1997

John A. Guidry, Michael D. Kennedy, and Mayer N. Zald, eds, *Globalization and Social Movements: Culture, Power and the Transnational Public Sphere*, Ann Arbor: University of Michigan Press, 2001

Lani Guinier, *The Tyranny of the Majority*, New York: Free Press, 1994

Jürgen Habermas, "Bestiality and Humanity: A War on the Border between Legality and Morality," *Constellations: An International Journal of Critical and Democratic Theory* 6, 3 (1999): 263–72

Jürgen Habermas, *Between Facts and Norms: Contributions to a Discourse Theory of Law and Democracy*, trans. William Rehg, Cambridge, MA: MIT Press, 1996

Jürgen Habermas, "Dispute on the Past and Future of International Law: Transition from a National to a Postnational Constellation," unpublished ms, presented at World Congress of Philosophy, Istanbul, August 2003

Jürgen Habermas, "The European Nation-State: On the Past and Future of Sovereignty and Citizenship," in *The Inclusion of the Other*, ed. Ciaran Cronin and Pablo de Grieff, trans. Ciaran Cronin, Cambridge, MA: MIT Press, 1999, pp. 105–28, originally appeared in *Public Culture* 10, 2 (1998): 397–416

Jürgen Habermas, "Kant's Idea of Perpetual Peace, with the Benefit of 200 Years' Hindsight," in *Perpetual Peace: Essays on Kant's Cosmopolitan Ideal*, ed. James Bohman and Matthias Lutz-Bachmann, Cambridge, MA: MIT Press, 1997, pp. 113–55

Jürgen Habermas, *The Philosophical Discourse of Modernity: Twelve Lectures*, trans. Frederick Lawrence, Cambridge, MA: MIT Press, 1987

Jürgen Habermas, "The Postnational Constellation and the Future of Democracy," in *The Postnational Constellation: Political Essays*, trans. and ed. Max Pensky, Cambridge, MA: MIT Press, 2001, pp. 58–113

Jürgen Habermas, *Structural Transformation of the Public Sphere*, trans. Thomas Burger, Cambridge, MA: MIT Press, 1989

Jürgen Habermas, "Struggles for Recognition in the Democratic Constitutional State," in *Multiculturalism*, ed. Amy Gutmann, trans. Shierry Weber Nicholsen, Princeton, NJ: Princeton University Press, 1994, pp. 107–65

Ulf Hannerz, *Transnational Connections: Culture, People, Places*, New York: Routledge, 1996

Michael Hardt and Antonio Negri, *Empire*, Cambridge, MA: Harvard University Press, 2000

Richard L. Harris and Melinda J. Seid, *Critical Perspectives on Globalization and Neoliberalism in the Developing Countries*, Boston: Leiden, 2000

Dale Hathaway, *Allies across the Border: Mexico's "Authentic Labor Front" and Global Solidarity*, Cambridge, MA: South End Press, 2000

David Held, "Cosmopolitanism: Globalization Tamed?" *Review of International Studies* 29, 4 (2003), 465–80

David Held, "Cosmopolitanism: Ideas, Realities and Deficits," in *Governing Globalization: Power, Authority, and Global Governance*, ed. David Held and Anthony McGrew, Cambridge: Polity, 2002, pp. 305–25

David Held, *Democracy and the Global Order: From the Modern State to Cosmopolitan Governance*, Cambridge: Polity, 1995

David Held, "Democracy and the New International Order," in *Cosmopolitan Democracy: An Agenda for a New World Order*, ed. Daniele Archibugi and David Held, Cambridge: Polity, 1995, pp. 96–120

David Held, "Democratic Accountability and Political Effectiveness from a Cosmopolitan Perspective," *Government and Opposition* 39, 2 (2004): 364–91

David Held, *Global Covenant: The Social Democratic Alternative to the Washington Consensus*, Cambridge: Polity, 2004

David Held, "Regulating Globalization?" *International Journal of Sociology* 15, 2 (2000): 394–408

David Held, "The Transformation of Political Community: Rethinking Democracy in the Context of Globalization," in *Democracy's Edges*, ed. Ian Shapiro and Cassiano Hacker-Cordón, Cambridge: Cambridge University Press, 1999, pp. 84–111

David Held, Anthony McGrew, David Goldblatt, and Jonathan Perraton, *Global Transformations: Politics, Economics and Culture*, Cambridge: Polity, 1999

Eric Helleiner, "From Bretton Woods to Global Finance: A World Turned Upside Down," in *Political Economy and the Changing Global Order*, ed. Richard Stubbs and Geoffrey R. D. Underhill, New York: St Martin's Press, 1994, pp. 163–75

Wilfried Hinsch, "Global Distributive Justice," *Metaphilosophy* 32, 1/2 (2001): 58–78

Paul Hirst and Graham Thompson, *Globalization in Question: The International Economy and the Possibilities of Governance*, Oxford: Blackwell Publishers, 1996

Christopher Hitchens, "Of Sin, the Left and Islamic Fascism," *The Nation*, September 24, 2001

Eric Hobsbawm, *The Age of Extremes: A History of the World, 1914–1991*, London: Abacus, 1995

Axel Honneth, "Redistribution as Recognition: A Response to Nancy Fraser," in Nancy Fraser and Axel Honneth, *Redistribution or Recognition? A Political-Philosophical Exchange*, trans. Joel Golb, James Ingram, and Christiane Wilke, London: Verso, 2003, pp. 110–98

Ankie M. M. Hoogvelt, *Globalization and the Postcolonial World: The Political Economy of Development*, Baltimore: Johns Hopkins University Press, 2001

bell hooks, *Feminist Theory: From Margin to Center*, second edition, Boston: South End Press, 1981

David Couzens Hoy, ed., *Foucault: A Critical Reader*, Oxford: Blackwell, 1986

Mala Htun, "Is Gender Like Ethnicity? The Political Representation of Identity Groups," *Perspectives on Politics* 2, 3 (2004), 439–58

Susan L. Hurley, "Rationality, Democracy and Leaky Boundaries: Vertical vs. Horizontal Modularity," *Journal of Political Philosophy* 7, 2 (1999): 126–46

Andrew Hurrell, "Global Inequality and International Institutions," *Metaphilosophy* 32, 1/2 (2001): 34–57

Charles Husband, "The Right to be Understood: Conceiving the Multi-ethnic Public Sphere," *Innovation: The European Journal of Social Sciences* 9, 2 (1996): 205–15

Michael Ignatieff, *Human Rights as Politics and Idolatry*, Princeton: Princeton University Press, 2001

Julie Ingersoll, *Evangelical Christian Women: War Stories in the Gender Battles*, New York: New York University Press, 2003

Michael Rabinder James, "Tribal Sovereignty and the Intercultural Public Sphere," *Philosophy & Social Criticism* 25, 5 (1999): 57–86

Fredric Jameson, *The Cultural Turn*, London: Verso, 1998

Hank Johnston, Enrique Larana, and Joseph R. Gusfield, eds., *New Social Movements: From Ideology to Identity*, Philadelphia: Temple University Press, 1994

Charles Jones, *Global Justice: Defending Cosmopolitanism*, Oxford: Oxford University Press, 1999

Charles Jones, "Global Liberalism: Political or Comprehensive?" *University of Toronto Law Journal* 54, 2 (2004): 227–48

Mary Kaldor, *New and Old Wars: Organized Violence in a Global Era*, Cambridge: Polity, 1999

Andreas Kalyvas, "Feet of Clay? Reflections on Hardt's and Negri's *Empire*," *Constellations: An International Journal of Critical and Democratic Theory* 10, 2 (2003): 264–79

Deniz Kandiyoti, "Identity and Its Discontents: Women and the Nation," in *Colonial Discourse and Post-Colonial Theory: A Reader*, ed. Patrick Williams and Laura Chrisman, New York: Columbia University Press, 1994, pp. 376–91

Margaret E. Keck and Kathryn Sikkink, *Activists beyond Borders: Advocacy Networks in International Politics*, Ithaca, NY: Cornell University Press, 1998

Michael Kelly, ed., *Critique and Power: Recasting the Foucault/Habermas Debate*, Cambridge, MA: MIT Press, 1994

Sanjeev Khagram, James V. Riker, and Kathryn Sikkink, eds., *Restructuring World Politics: Transnational Social Movements, Networks, and Norms*, Minneapolis: University of Minnesota Press, 2002

Matthias König, "Cultural Diversity and Language Policy," *International Social Science Journal* 51, 161 (1999): 401–8

Thomas Kuhn, *The Structure of Scientific Revolutions*, third edition, Chicago: University of Chicago Press, 1996

Andrew Kuper, "Rawlsian Global Justice: Beyond *The Law of Peoples* to a Cosmopolitan Law of Persons," *Political Theory* 28, 5 (2000): 640–74

Will Kymlicka, *Multicultural Citizenship: A Liberal Theory of Minority Rights*, London: Oxford University Press, 1995

Will Kymlicka, "Territorial Boundaries. A Liberal-Egalitarian Perspective," in *Boundaries and Justice: Diverse Ethical Perspectives*, ed.

David Miller and Sohail H. Hashmi, Princeton, NJ: Princeton University Press, 2001, pp. 249–75

Dan La Botz, *Democracy in Mexico: Peasant Rebellion and Political Reform*, Cambridge, MA: South End Press, 1995

Ernesto Laclau and Chantal Mouffe, *Hegemony and Socialist Strategy: Towards a Radical Democratic Politics*, London: Verso, 1985

Joan Landes, *Women and the Public Sphere in the Age of the French Revolution*, Ithaca, NY: Cornell University Press, 1988

Maria Pia Lara, "Globalizing Women's Rights: Building a Public Sphere," in *Recognition, Responsibility, and Rights: Feminist Ethics and Social Theory. Feminist Reconstructions*, ed. Robin N. Fiore and Hilde Lindemann Nelson, Totowa, NJ: Rowman & Littlefield, 2003, pp. 181–93

Paul Gordon Lauren, *The Evolution of International Human Rights: Visions Seen*, Philadelphia: University of Pennsylvania Press, 2003

Andrew Linklater, "Citizenship and Sovereignty in the Post-Westphalian European State," in Linklater *Critical Theory and World Politics*, London: Routledge, pp. 113–38

Niklas Luhman, "Öffentliche Meinung," *Politische Vierteljahresschrift* 11 (1970): 2–28

Jean-François Lyotard, *The Differend: Phrases in Dispute*, trans. Georges Van Den Abbeele, Minneapolis: University of Minnesota Press, 1988

Jean-François Lyotard, *The Postmodern Condition: A Report on Knowledge*, trans. Geoff Bennington and Brian Massumi, Minneapolis: University of Minnesota Press, 1984

Robert W. McChesney, "Global Media, Neoliberalism, and Imperialism," *Monthly Review* 50, 10 (2001): 1–19

Robert W. McChesney, *Rich Media, Poor Democracy: Communications Politics in Dubious Times*, Chicago: University of Illinois Press, 1999

Anne McClintock, "Family Feuds: Gender, Nation and the Family," *Feminist Review* 44 (1993): 61–80

Bernard Manin, *The Principles of Representative Government*, New York: Cambridge University Press, 1997

P. David Marshall, *New Media Cultures*, New York: Oxford University Press, 2004

Alberto Melucci, John Keane, and Paul Mier, eds., *Nomads of the Present: Social Movements and Individual Needs in Contemporary Society*, Philadelphia: Temple University Press, 1989

Thaddeus Metz, "Open Perfectionism and Global Justice," *Theoria: A Journal of Social & Political Theory* 114 (2004): 96–125

David Miller, "The Ethical Significance of Nationality," *Ethics* 98 (1988): 647–62

David Miller, "The Limits of Cosmopolitan Justice," in *International Society: Diverse Ethical Perspectives*, ed. David Maple and Terry Nardin, Princeton: Princeton University Press, 1998, pp. 164–83

David Miller, *On Nationality*, Oxford: Oxford University Press, 1995

Richard W. Miller, "Cosmopolitanism and Its Limits," *Theoria: A Journal of Social & Political Theory* 114 (2004): 38–43

Kim Moody, *Workers in a Lean World: Unions in the International Economy*, London: Verso Books, 1997

Chantal Mouffe, "Deliberative Democracy or Agonistic Pluralism?" *Social Research* 66, 3 (1999): 745–58

Chantal Mouffe, "Democracy, Power and the 'Political'," in *Democracy and Difference: Contesting the Boundaries of the Political*, ed. Seyla Benhabib, Princeton: Princeton University Press, 1996, pp. 245–56

Warwick Mules, "Media Publics and the Transnational Public Sphere," *Critical Arts Journal* 12, 1/2 (1998): 24–44

Ronaldo Munck and Peter Waterman, *Labour Worldwide in the Era of Globalization: Alternative Union Models in the New World Order*, New York: Palgrave Macmillan, 1999

Thomas Nagel, "The Problem of Global Justice," *Philosophy & Public Affairs* 33 (2005): 113–47

Tom Nairn, "The Modern Janus," in Nairn, *The Break-Up of Britain: Crisis and Neo-Nationalism*, London: New Left Books, 1977, pp. 329–63

June Nash, *Mayan Visions: The Quest for Autonomy in an Age of Globalization*, London: Routledge, 2001

Ronald Niezen, *The Origins of Indigenism: Human Rights and the Politics of Identity*, Berkeley: University of California Press, 2003

Martha Nussbaum, "Beyond the Social Contract: Capabilities and Global Justice," *Oxford Development Studies* 32, 1 (2004): 1–15

Martha Nussbaum with Respondents, *For Love of Country? Debating the Limits of Patriotism*, ed. Joshua Cohen, Boston: Beacon Press, 1996

Robert O'Brien, Anne Marie Goetz, Jan Art Scholte, and Marc Williams, *Contesting Global Governance: Multilateral Economic Institutions and Global Social Movements*, Cambridge: Cambridge University Press, 2000

Thomas Olesen, "Transnational Publics: New Spaces of Social Movement Activism and the Problem of Global Long-Sightedness," *Current Sociology* 53, 3 (2005): 419–40

Onora O'Neill, *Bounds of Justice*, Cambridge: Cambridge University Press, 2000

Aihwa Ong, *Flexible Citizenship: The Cultural Logics of Transnationality*, Durham, NC: Duke University Press, 1999

Raul C. Pangalangan, "Territorial Sovereignty: Command, Title, and Expanding the Claims of the Commons," in *Boundaries and Justice: Diverse Ethical Perspectives*, ed. David Miller and Sohail H. Hashmi, Princeton: Princeton University Press, 2001, pp. 164–82

Rik Panganiban, "The NGO Coalition for an International Criminal Court," *UN Chronicle* 34, 4 (1997): 36–9

Zizi Papacharissi, "The Virtual Sphere: The Internet as a Public Sphere," *New Media & Society* 4, 1 (2002): 9–36

Alan Patten, "Political Theory and Language Policy," *Political Theory* 29, 5 (2001): 691–715

David Peritz, "The Complexities of Complexity: Habermas and the Hazards of Relying Directly on Social Theory," paper prepared for discussion at the Critical Theory Roundtable, October 2001, San Francisco

David Peritz, "A Diversity of Diversities: Liberalism's Implicit Social Theories," paper prepared for presentation at the 53rd Annual Political Studies Association Conference, University of Leicester, April 15–17, 2003, Panel 6-11

Jonathan Perraton, David Goldblatt, David Held, and Anthony McGrew, "The Globalisation of Economic Activity," *New Political Economy* 2, 2 (1997): 257–77

Anne Phillips, *The Politics of Presence*, Oxford: Clarendon Press, 1995

Robert Phillipson, *English-Only Europe? Challenging Language Policy*, New York: Routledge, 2003

Hanna Fenichel Pitkin, *The Concept of Representation*, Berkeley: University of California Press, 1967

Thomas Pogge, "Economic Justice and National Borders," *Revision* 22 (1999): 27–34

Thomas Pogge, "An Egalitarian Law of Peoples," *Philosophy and Public Affairs* 23, 5 (2000): 195–224

Thomas Pogge, "How to Create Supra-National Institutions Democratically: Some Reflections on the European Union's Democratic Deficit," *Journal of Political Philosophy*, 5 (1997): 163–82

Thomas Pogge, "The Influence of the Global Order on the Prospects for Genuine Democracy in the Developing Countries," *Ratio Juris* 14, 3 (2001): 326–43

Thomas Pogge, *World Poverty and Human Rights: Cosmopolitan Responsibilities and Reforms*, Cambridge: Polity, 2002

Ulrich Preuss, "Citizenship in the European Union: A Paradigm for Transnational Democracy?" in *Re-imagining Political Community: Studies in Cosmopolitan Democracy*, ed. Daniele Archibugi and

David Held, Stanford: Stanford University Press, 1999, pp. 138–52

W. V. O. Quine, *From a Logical Point of View: 9 Logico-Philosophical Essays*, Cambridge, MA: Harvard University Press, 1953

Shirin M. Rai, "Political Representation, Democratic Institutions and Women's Empowerment: The Quota Debate in India," in *Rethinking Empowerment: Gender and Development in a Global/Local World*, ed. Jane L. Parpart, Shirin M. Rai, and Kathleen Staudt, New York: Routledge, 2002, pp. 133–45

John Rawls, *The Law of Peoples*, new edition, Cambridge, MA: Harvard University Press, 2001

John Rawls, "The Law of Peoples," in *On Human Rights: The Oxford Amnesty Lectures*, ed. Stephen Shute and Susan Hurley, New York: Basic Books: 1994, pp. 41–83

John Rawls, *A Theory of Justice*, Cambridge, MA: Harvard University Press, 1999

Judy Rebick, "Lip Service: The Anti-Globalization Movement on Gender Politics," *Herizons* 16, 2 (2002): 24–6

Jane Rendall, "Women and the Public Sphere," *Gender & History* 11, 3 (1999): 475–89

Judith Resnik, "Law's Migration: American Exceptionalism, Silent Dialogues, and Federalism's Multiple Ports of Entry," *The Yale Law Journal* 115, 7 (May 2006): 1546–70

Frank Rich, "How Kerry Became a Girlie Man," *The New York Times* 153, 52963, September 5, 2004, section 2, p. 1

David Rieff, *Slaughterhouse: Bosnia and the Failure of the West*, New York: Simon & Schuster, 1995

Robert Ritchie and Steven Hill, "The Case for Proportional Representation," in *Whose Vote Counts?* ed. Robert Ritchie and Steven Hill, Boston: Beacon Press, 2001, pp. 1–33

Richard Rorty, *Contingency, Irony, and Solidarity*, Cambridge: Cambridge University Press, 1989

Richard Rorty, "Feminism and Pragmatism," *Michigan Quarterly Review* 30, 2 (1991): 231–58

Richard Rorty, *Philosophy and Social Hope*, New York: Penguin Books, 1999

Richard Rorty, *Philosophy and the Mirror of Nature*, Princeton: Princeton University Press, 1981

Nikolas Rose, "Governing Advanced Liberal Democracies," in Peter Miller and Nikolas Rose, *Governing the Present: Administering Economic, Social and Personal Life*, Cambridge: Polity, 2008, pp. 199–218

Ruth Rosen, *The World Split Open: How the Modern Women's Movement Changed America*, New York: Penguin, 2001

James N. Rosenau, *Along the Domestic–Foreign Frontier: Exploring Governance in a Turbulent World*, Cambridge: Cambridge University Press, 1997

James N. Rosenau, "Governance and Democracy in a Globalizing World," in *Re-imagining Political Community: Studies in Cosmopolitan Democracy*, ed. Daniele Archibugi and David Held, Stanford: Stanford University Press, 1999, pp. 28–58

Benita Roth, *Separate Roads to Feminism: Black, Chicana, and White Feminist Movements in America's Second Wave*, Cambridge: Cambridge University Press, 2004

John Ruggie, "Territoriality and Beyond: Problematizing Modernity in International Relations," *International Organization* 47 (1993): 139–74

Mary P. Ryan, "Gender and Public Access: Women's Politics in Nineteenth-Century America," in *Habermas and the Public Sphere*, ed. Craig Calhoun, Cambridge, MA: MIT Press, pp. 259–89

Mary P. Ryan, *Women in Public: Between Banners and Ballots, 1825–1880*, Baltimore: Johns Hopkins University Press, 1990

Saskia Sassen, *Globalization and Its Discontents*, New York: Free Press, 1998

Saskia Sassen, *Losing Control? Sovereignty in an Age of Globalization*, New York: Columbia University Press, 1995

Saskia Sassen, *Territory, Authority, Rights: From Medieval to Global Assemblages*, Princeton: Princeton University Press, 2006

Deborah Satz, "Equality of What among Whom? Thoughts on Cosmopolitanism, Statism and Nationalism," in *Global Justice*, ed. Ian Shapiro and Lea Brilmayer, New York: New York University Press, 1999, pp. 67–85

William E. Scheuerman, "Between Radicalism and Resignation: Democratic Theory in Habermas' *Between Facts and Norms*," in *Habermas: A Critical Reader*, ed. Peter Dews, Oxford: Blackwell, 1999, pp. 153–78

William E. Scheuerman, "Economic Globalization and the Rule of Law," *Constellations* 6, 1 (1999): 3–25

David Schneiderman, "Investment Rules and the Rule of Law," *Constellations* 8, 4 (2001): 521–37

Gunter G. Schulze, *The Political Economy of Capital Controls*, Cambridge: Cambridge University Press, 2000

James Scott, *Seeing Like a State: How Certain Schemes to Improve the Human Condition Have Failed*, New Haven: Yale University Press, 1998

Amartya Sen, *Development as Freedom*, New York: Anchor Books, 1999

Amartya Sen, "Equality of What?" in *Liberty, Equality, and Law*, ed. Sterling M. McMurrin, Salt Lake City: University of Utah Press, 1987, pp. 137–62

Richard Sennett, "The Age of Anxiety," *Guardian Saturday*, October 23, 2004, p. 34, available on-line at: *http://books.guardian.co.uk/print/0,3858,5044940-110738,00.html* (last accessed March 17, 2008)

Richard Sennett, *The Corrosion of Character: The Personal Consequences of Work in the New Capitalism*, New York: Norton, 1998

Omid A. Payrow Shabani, "Language Policy and Diverse Societies: Constitutional Patriotism and Minority Language Rights," *Constellations* 11, 2 (2004): 193–216

Ian Shapiro, *Democratic Justice*, New Haven: Yale University Press, 1999

Henry Shue, *Basic Rights*, Princeton: Princeton University Press, 1980

Peter Singer, *One World: The Ethics of Globalization*, second edition, New Haven: Yale University Press, 2004

Anne-Marie Slaughter, *A New World Order*, Princeton: Princeton University Press, 2005

Yasemin Nuhoglu Soysal, "Changing Parameters of Citizenship and Claims-Making: Organized Islam in European Public Spheres," *Theory and Society* 26 (1997): 509–27

Yasemin Nuhoglu Soysal, *Limits of Citizenship: Migrants and Postnational Membership in Europe*, Chicago: University of Chicago Press, 1995

Judith Stacey, "Sexism by a Subtler Name? Postindustrial Conditions and Postfeminist Consciousness in the Silicon Valley," *Socialist Review* 96 (1987): 7–28

Rudolf Stichweh, "The Genesis of a Global Public Sphere," *Development* 46, 1 (2003): 26–9

Joseph E. Stiglitz, *Globalization and Its Discontents*, New York: Norton, 2003

Ann Laura Stoler, *Race and the Education of Desire*, Chapel Hill, NC: Duke University Press, 1995

Servaes Storm and J. Mohan Rao, "Market-Led Globalization and World Democracy: Can the Twain Ever Meet?" *Development and Change* 35, 5 (2004): 567–81

Susan Strange, *The Retreat of the State: The Diffusion of Power in the World Economy*, Cambridge: Cambridge University Press, 1996

Wolfgang Streeck, "Public Power beyond the Nation-State: The Case of the European Community," in *States against Markets: The Limits of Globalization*, ed. Robert Boyer and Daniel Drache, New York: Routledge, 1996, pp. 299–316

Kok-Chor Tan, *Justice without Borders: Cosmopolitanism, Nationalism, and Patriotism*, Cambridge: Cambridge University Press, 2004

Charles Taylor, *Multiculturalism: Examining the Politics of Recognition*, ed. Amy Gutmann, Princeton: Princeton University Press, 1994

Khachig Tololyan, "Rethinking Diaspora(s): Stateless Power in the Transnational Moment, *Diaspora* 5, 1 (1996): 3–36

Alain Touraine, *Return of the Actor: Social Theory in Postindustrial Society*, Minneapolis: University of Minnesota Press, 1988

Philippe van Parijs, "The Ground Floor of the World: On the Socio-economic Consequences of Linguistic Globalization," *International Political Science Review* 21, 2 (2000): 217–33

Virginia Vargas, "Feminism, Globalization and the Global Justice and Solidarity Movement," *Cultural Studies* 17, 6 (2003): 905–20

Paul Voice, "Global Justice and the Challenge of Radical Pluralism," *Theoria: A Journal of Social & Political Theory* 114 (2004): 15–37

Ingrid Volkmer, "The Global Network Society and the Global Public Sphere," *Development* 46, 1 (2003): 9–16

Loïc Wacquant, "From Slavery to Mass Incarceration," *New Left Review* 13 (Jan.–Feb. 2002): 41–60

Michael Walzer, *Spheres of Justice: A Defense of Pluralism and Equality*, New York: Basic Books, 1984

Michael Warner, "The Mass Public and the Mass Subject," in *The Phantom Public Sphere*, ed. Bruce Robins, Minneapolis: University of Minnesota Press, pp. 234–56

Michael Warner, *Publics and Counterpublics*, New York: Zone Books, 2002

Leif Wenar, "Contractualism and Global Economic Justice," *Metaphilosophy* 32, 1/2 (2001): 79–94

Pnina Werbner, "Theorising Complex Diasporas: Purity and Hybridity in the South Asian Public Sphere in Britain," *Journal of Ethnic & Migration Studies* 30, 5 (2004): 895–911

Frederick Whelan, "Democratic Theory and the Boundary Problem," in *Nomos XXV: Liberal Democracy*, ed. J. Roland Pennock and John W. Chapman, New York and London: New York University Press, 1983, pp. 13–47

Christiane Wilke, "Habermas, the Alien, and the Escape to Cosmopolitanism," unpublished ms

Kenton T. Wilkinson, "Language Difference and Communication Policy in the Information Age," *Information Society* 20, 3 (2004): 217–29

Melissa Williams, *Voice, Trust, and Memory: Marginalized Groups and the Failings of Liberal Representation*, Princeton: Princeton University Press, 1998

Iris Marion Young, "Equality of Whom? Social Groups and Judgments of Injustice," *Journal of Political Philosophy* 9, 1 (2001): 1–18

Iris Marion Young, "Impartiality and the Civic Public: Some Implications of Feminist Critiques of Moral and Political Theory," in *Feminism as Critique*, ed. Seyla Benhabib and Drucilla Cornell, Minneapolis: University of Minnesota Press, 1987, pp. 56–76

Iris Marion Young, "Responsibility and Global Justice: A Social Connection Model," *Social Philosophy and Policy* 23, 1 (2006): 102–30

George Yudice, *The Expediency of Culture: Uses of Culture in the Global Era*, Durham, NC: Duke University Press, 2004

Nira Yuval-Davis, *Gender and Nation*, London: Sage Publications, 1997

Mark W. Zacher, "The Decaying Pillars of the Westphalian Temple," in *Governance without Government*, ed. James N. Rosenau and Ernst-Otto Czempiel, Cambridge: Cambridge University Press, 1992, pp. 58–101

Eli Zaretsky, Secrets of the Soul: *A Social and Cultural History of Psychoanalysis*, New York: Knopf, 2004

Index